Blues Legacy

D0879393

Discard

MUSIC IN AMERICAN LIFE

A list of books in the series appears at the end of this book.

Blues Legacy

Tradition and Innovation in Chicago

DAVID WHITEIS

Photographs by Peter M. Hurley

UNIVERSITY OF
ILLINOIS PRESS
Urbana, Chicago, and Springfield

Publication of this book was supported in part by a grant from the
Judith McCulloh Endowment for American Music.

1 2 3 4 5 C P 5 4 3 2 1
⊗ This book is printed on acid-free paper.

Library of Congress Cataloging-in-Publication Data
Names: Whiteis, David, author. | Hurley, Peter M. photographer.
Title: Blues legacy: tradition and innovation in Chicago / David
    Whiteis; photographs by Peter M. Hurley.
Description: Urbana : University of Illinois Press, [2019] | Series:
    Music in American life | Includes bibliographical references and
    index.
Identifiers: LCCN 2019021413 (print) | LCCN 2019022118 (ebook) |
    ISBN 9780252042881 (cloth : alk. paper) | ISBN 9780252084706
    (pbk. : alk. paper)
Subjects: LCSH: Blues (Music—Illinois—Chicago—History and
    criticism. | Blues musicians—Illinois—Chicago—Biography. |
    Blues musicians—Illinois—Chicago—Portraits.
Classification: LCC ML3521 .W46 2019 (print) | LCC ML3521 (ebook) |
    DDC 781.64309773/11—dc23
LC record available at https://lccn.loc.gov/2019021413
LC ebook record available at https://lccn.loc.gov/2019022118

Ebook ISBN: 978-0-252-05174-6

won't you celebrate with me
what i have shaped into
a kind of life? i had no model.
born in babylon
both nonwhite and woman
what did i see to be except myself?
i made it up
here on this bridge between
starshine and clay,
my one hand holding tight
my other hand; come celebrate
with me that everyday
something has tried to kill me
and has failed

—Lucille Clifton

Contents

Acknowledgments

First, I would like to thank Laurie Matheson, Julie Laut, and their colleagues and staff at University of Illinois Press for their support and encouragement throughout this project. The readers whom Ms. Matheson assigned to critique my manuscript were prescient and unsparing; their suggestions served to improve both the book's focus and its content. Brett Bonner, editor of *Living Blues* magazine, has been an invaluable fount of information and encouragement, as well as writing opportunities, for many years. I also thank Scott Barretta, former editor of *Living Blues*, for initiating the contact with University of Illinois Press that resulted in my first book, *Chicago Blues: Portraits and Stories*, and helped facilitate what has been a rewarding and productive collegial relationship. *Living Blues* cofounder Jim O'Neal, as well as Chicago-based blues mavens Bill Dahl, Michael Frank (Earwig Records), Bruce Iglauer (Alligator Records), Bob Pruter, Dick Shurman, and Steve Wagner (Delmark Records) have shared their knowledge and enthusiasm with me over the years; I hope that their expertise, wit, and tireless advocacy for the music have rubbed off and made me a better and more knowledgeable writer.

My deepest thanks also go out to each and every one of the artists, songwriters, industry representatives, and label executives who consented to speak with me: your openness has reflected a trust and confidence that I cherish with grateful humility. I thank Peter Hurley, whose photographs grace these pages and help make the music and its people come alive. We struck gold this time! Thanks as well to ace photographers Martin Feldmann, Gene Tomko, and Jack and Linda Vartoogian for their contributions to this project. I thank Pamela Price Williams for her assistance in setting up the interview with her husband, Lil' Ed; I thank Jacklyn Cotton for helping to facilitate my initial interview with James Cotton, and with providing valuable clarifications and additional information; I also thank Lisa Becker for helping to fill in some valuable biographical details about John Primer's early life, and I thank Renee Greenman Harrington Clearwater and Lynn Orman Weiss for facilitating my interview with Eddy Clearwater and assisting me on important historical and discographical information. John Hahn has been of inestimable assistance in providing access to Shemekia Copeland and helping to convey my follow-up queries to her.

Others whose expertise, friendship, support, and encouragement through the years have inspired me and helped me bring projects such as this to fruition include: Dee Alexander, Cicero Blake, Robert Bowman, John Brisbin, Brother Jacob, Jeneene Brown-Mosley, Barbara Campbell, the late Eddie C. Campbell, Larry Chambers, Quinton Claunch, the late Otis Clay, Nadine Cohodas, C. C. Copeland, Tommy Couch Jr, Steve Cushing, Daddy B. Nice (Bruno Nicewanger), Tony Dale, Ann Davis, the late Stan "Sarge" Davis, Dylann DeAnna ("Blues Critic"), Scott Dirks, the late Marie Dixon, Barry Dolins, Bill Fitzgerald, Jim Fraher, Michael Frank, Paul Garon, Robert Gordon, the late Susan Greenberg, Leola Grey, the late Ray Grey, Peter Guralnick, Queen Ann Hines, Dave Hoekstra, Larry Hoffman, Big Walter Horton, Abby Hotchkiss, Illinois Slim (Tom Morris), Bruce James, Jazzii A., the late Bob Jones, Star Johnson, Bettye Kelly, Sharon Lewis, Rick Lucas, Bob Koester, Sue Koester, the late Denise LaSalle, Sharon Lewis, Marc Lipkin, Mama Rosa, Howard Mandel, Tony Mangiullo, Barbra Marks, Charles Mitchell, Janice Monti, Philip Montoro and the editorial staff at the *Chicago Reader*, Mr. A., Mr. Lee (Lee Kirksy), Ms. Jody (Vertie Joann Delapaz), Ms. Nickki (Nicole Whitlock), Salim Muwakkil, Justin O'Brien, Bettie Payton-White, Judy Peiser and the Center for Southern Folklore, Sterling Plumpp, Sandra Pointer-Jones, Marc PoKempner, Jillina Arrigo Pope, Bobby Rush, Delores Scott, Pervis Spann, Peaches Staten, Sunnyland Slim, Edna Taylor, Brenda Taylor, Neil Tesser, Joyce "Cookie" Threatt, Twist Turner, the late Amy Van Singel, Steve Wagner, John Ward, Dick Waterman, Lynn Orman Weiss, Junior Wells, the late Artie "Blues Boy" White, Bettie White, Flora White, Kirk Whiting, Felix Wohrstein, Lynn Wohrstein, James E. Wolfe, Bridgette Wolfe-Edwards, the late Carl Wright—and once again, the artists and everyone else who took time out of their lives to talk to me and put up with my pestering questions over the course of interviews and follow-ups for this book.

As always, I have endeavored to be true to both the spirit and the letter of accuracy; all quotes are from my personal interviews, or else gleaned from works by established authorities and reliable sources (please check citations and Works Cited for details). I have cross-checked historical facts among multiple sources whenever possible. Unless they are part of direct quotes, all opinions—critical, social, and otherwise—are my own. I take full responsibility for them, as well as for any unintended errors of fact.

Blues Legacy

Introduction

"Little baby's gonna grow, I gotta tell her
what she needs to know . . ."

This book examines contemporary Chicago blues as representing a cultural continuum passed down through generations, from the music's roots in the South through the post–World War II era into the present day. Considered in this historical context, Chicago blues may be seen as both a soundtrack to, and a commentary on, the social upheavals—displacement, relocation, resettlement— that accompanied the African American Great Migration of the 20th Century. As people adapted to the demands of living in a new civic and social environment, freer in many ways than the South had been but which also presented new dangers, new challenges, new forms of racial and economic disenfranchisement, and new threats to both individual and cultural survival, the music changed and adapted, as well. And, of course, larger-scale changes in American popular culture, which became more media-driven and more youth- and consumer-oriented as the decades wore on, had a significant impact on music of all genres, including blues. Like most professional musicians, blues artists had always performed and recorded with popular tastes in mind; as those tastes became, paradoxically, both more flexible (in terms of welcoming new sounds that challenged established notions of cultural, aesthetic, and even moral, acceptability) and more rigidly defined (in terms of market-driven segmentation by age, geographic region, and other demographic variables), establishing a style that was both identifiable and universal enough to appeal to a mass audience became increasingly problematic.

The lives and work of the musicians profiled here illustrate these concerns. Some older-generation artists, such as James Cotton, continued to hew closely to the influence of their early mentors and role models, even as they updated their sound for younger audiences by hiring sidemen who could help them adapt to more contemporary material and ideas. In other instances, however, we can see more significant stylistic changes over time—and, contrary to stereotype, not all of these followed an easily definable, or even predictable, line from "rural" to "urban," or from "simplistic" to "sophisticated." Being inculcated into the blues legacy has long involved absorbing influences from records and commercial radio—that is, "pop" rather than "folk" culture—at least as much as it has meant sitting at the feet of elders and learning directly from them.[1]

Eddie Shaw, for instance, played R&B and jump-blues in Greenville, Mississippi; after moving to Chicago, he had to adapt to a rawer, ostensibly more "down-home" musical context to play in the bands of artists like Muddy Waters and Howlin' Wolf. Jimmy Johnson, a savvy R&B/soul man in his younger days, took on a blues-oriented sound to appeal to young white audiences when he began playing on Chicago's North Side blues circuit in the 1970s, but even then

Buddy Guy at his club, Buddy Guy's Legends, Chicago, 2018.

he continued to incorporate pop and progressive jazz elements in his music; his brother Syl, on the other hand, progressed from straightforward Chicago blues into increasingly aggressive soul and funk over the course of his career. Jimmy Burns, influenced by bluesmen like Lightnin' Hopkins and John Lee Hooker as a youth, nonetheless got his professional start in doo-wop; from there he moved into folk music, soul, and, finally, back to 12-bar blues over the course of his career.

Among younger musicians as well, honoring the tradition is inseparable from remaining contemporary, although the way this balance is maintained differs widely from artist to artist. Self-professed boundary-pushers like Sugar Blue and both Lonnie and Ronnie Baker Brooks exemplify a determination to resist "moldy-fig" purism while remaining true to roots. Others, though—especially some of the scions of musical families, such as Tim Taylor, the late Eddie Taylor Jr., the sons of Muddy Waters, and drummer Kenny Smith—have dedicated themselves to keeping earlier styles alive with an earnestness that sometimes seems to border on the obsessive. Still others, like Shemekia Copeland, Lil' Ed, Deitra Farr, and—at least to a certain extent—both John Primer and Larry Taylor, are as adamant about embracing change as they are earnest in their dedication to remaining rooted in the traditions that originally impelled them into music. (In some cases, bearing the weight of history can be both a blessing and a curse: Floyd Taylor, who looked and sounded uncannily like his father, soul legend Johnnie Taylor, revered his musical inheritance yet chafed under its burden. In his case, legacy became a lodestone.) Then there are figures like Nellie "Tiger" Travis, an erstwhile pop/soul stylist who came into the blues relatively late in life but has since embraced it as a marker of heritage and pride, even as she has continued to expand her scope and become a leading exponent of the postmodernist hybrid known variously as *soul-blues* and *southern soul*.

Part of the paradox evident here is the result of the tension between the globalist (and ever-shifting) definition of the "blues" aesthetic among most African American artists and listeners on the one hand, and the reductionist obsession with categorization and classification among (mostly white) critics, theorists, and industry bean-counters on the other—a fixation that has often resulted in attempts to force bluesmen and women into stylistic boxes not of their own making ("Who the *hell* are you to define my blues?" as Chicago vocalist Sharon Lewis has expressed it[2]). The truth, though, is that from the beginning, blues artists have prided themselves on the range and scope of their musicianship, and they have strived to make a living by garnering as wide and lucrative a listening

audience as possible (however much this might have been downplayed by various romanticists over the years). For a rural bluesman like Robert Johnson, this
meant including pop standards, country songs, novelties, and even polkas in his
repertoire; for a young Muddy Waters performing for plantation audiences in the
1940s, it meant tackling fare like "Chattanooga Choo-Choo" and "Red Sails in
the Sunset."[3]

Later, during the postwar Chicago blues era, as Buddy Guy has remembered,
"You had to do that jukebox in all the small blues clubs; if you couldn't play the
Top Ten records on that jukebox, you wasn't gonna get another play for that three
or four dollars a night."[4] In other words, blues artists who modernize their sound
and incorporate ideas borrowed from pop music and elsewhere are carrying on
the legacy of their forebears at least as much as—if not more than—those who
insist on maintaining "authenticity" by replicating their predecessors' styles
note-for-note.

The ironies cut even more deeply when we look at the changes in style and
nomenclature that have affected the blues overall in recent decades, and the ways
in which ethnicity and social class—the old bugaboos, still prevalent and still
disruptive—continue to both inform and complicate their impact on the music.
Artists who still work primarily on the African American club and concert circuit—in many ways, the truest carriers of the legacy if we consider performing
in venues, and for audiences, that represent the music's cultural roots to be an
important facet of this inheritance—specialize, to a significant extent, in modern soul-blues/southern-soul (which is still usually called "blues" by most of its
mainstream African American fans). Drawn from influences including postwar
urban blues; sixties-era deep soul and the funk and postfunk that evolved from
it; recent and contemporary R&B, and, increasingly, neosoul, rap, and hip-hop,
it's a sound that many of the same white aficionados who grumble at the rock,
jazz-fusion, and pop flavorings favored by iconoclasts like Sugar Blue and the
Brooks brothers decry even more forcefully. For their own part, at least some in
the southern soul/soul-blues community regard the tastes of white purists with
a disdain bordering on contempt. As one singer told me: "Black folk don't want
no one-man band sittin' up there playing one guitar and singin' them ol' songs
with some coveralls on, with suspenders hanging down his back and a straw hat
on—they'd run his ass out of that place!"[5]

This, of course, re-illuminates another issue to which I've already made reference: the contradiction of being carriers of a torch that, to a significant extent, has
been passed on to listeners—and, increasingly, musicians—with little connection

to the cultural and historical contexts without which the music loses much of its essential significance and meaning.[6] Most of the artists profiled here (and certainly the most commercially successful ones) record for labels that market primarily to white listeners; many front predominantly white bands; they work for mostly white audiences in clubs and at festivals that often book predominantly white lineups (it's long been a running joke that if you see a black face in a blues club or at a blues festival, it's probably a musician—but these days, even that isn't necessarily the case).[7] This becomes especially problematic for those who profess a dedication to "keeping the blues alive," as the saying goes, not only as music but as *black* music, relevant to contemporary, as well as historical, African American life and culture.

Despite the cultural specificity of blues expression, though, the blues, like any viable art form, also addresses universal human concerns—love, loss, yearning (carnal, spiritual/existential), the victories and tragedies of everyday life—and

Jamiah Rogers, Broad Street Blues Festival, Griffith, Indiana, 2017.

it's this dual quality of specificity and universality that helps explain why this music, as Sugar Blue says, has "grown and changed the musical understanding and mores of people around the world." Virtually every artist I spoke with expressed, in one form or another, the old dictum that "everybody gets the blues," meaning that almost anyone should be able understand the music and its message, if given the chance. At the same time, although there is no single consensus about whether the potential dilution of the music's ethnic identity represents a crisis—and, if so, what can or should be done about it—the acknowledgment that this identity is an inextricable component of its core meaning is also virtually unanimous.

In this spirit, then, this book focuses on the blues as a living component of a diasporan culture, dynamic and evolving, rooted in the twentieth-century African American experience but with a universality that speaks to diverse audiences and listeners. The first section, "Bequeathers," profiles selected older artists whose careers extend back to personal relationships with the progenitors of the style that has become known—and venerated—as postwar Chicago blues. We then progress to "Inheritors"—younger musicians, some of them direct familial descendants of earlier-generation trailblazers, all of whom absorbed those influences as they modernized the legacy to remake the music in their own image. Adjacent to the chapter-length profiles will be briefer synopses of selected artists whom I have identified as being significant in this historical continuum. The "Council of Elders" consists of Chicagoans, most of them still active, whose careers extend back to the 1950s/'60s postwar era; the "Heirs Apparent" are younger artists carrying on the tradition. I have tried to cast as wide a stylistic net as possible to show the variety and creativity that continues to inform this ever-evolving musical style.

As always in such projects, there is a certain arbitrariness involved in the selection. The reader should not equate inclusion in one or another of these sections with some kind of personal imprimatur. Rather, these profiles and synopses should be approached in the same spirit as one might think of a "sampler" CD: a taste, hopefully a tantalizing one, of the pleasures awaiting anyone exploring Chicago blues, as well as an affirmation of how rich this history is and how deep the lode of talent, in a genre which is too often consigned to "museum piece" status or patronized as a quaint tourist attraction (not unlike so-called "Dixieland" jazz in New Orleans). My intention is to present the music—and its practitioners—in the context of the history that gave rise to it, as well as the ongoing social and cultural reality of which both the music and the artists remain an integral part.

PART I

Bequeathers

"The World Lost a Wonderful Bluesman, and His Spirit's Still in the Air . . ."

I never intended this section to be a valedictory. At the beginning of this project, all the artists profiled here were alive and working. I had completed our interviews and was looking forward to the pleasure of eventually sharing the book with them. Now, of course, that opportunity is gone, and, more importantly, irreplaceable musical voices—James Cotton's, Eddie Shaw's, and Eddy Clearwater's—have been stilled. Nonetheless, as Chicago-based jazz vocalist Dee Alexander has pointed out, when artists make the transition from Elders to Ancestors, they don't really depart; their spirits live on in the gifts they've left behind. And as long as we continue to speak their names, their spirits also live within us. For this reason, I have made the decision to honor, and to help keep alive, the spirits of these ancestors by including their profiles in this book.

James Cotton

"The Blues Is Part of Me"

Harmonica master James Cotton's career spans the trajectory of postwar blues history. Schooled by the fabled Sonny Boy Williamson (Rice Miller) when he was a young boy, he later worked with Howlin' Wolf in Memphis and recorded for Sun Records. In 1954, he came north to Chicago to join Muddy Waters's band, and he stayed with Muddy for twelve years. He finally broke out as a frontline artist in 1966, just as the blues "revival" among young white aficionados was kicking into high gear. His bands have historically been versatile and soulful, capable of segueing effortlessly among down-home blues, funk, jazz-flavored innovation, and rock & roll—meaning that for all his reputation as a roots man, Cotton has always been fully contemporary, ready and able to incorporate multiple styles and influences into a sound that nonetheless harks back to the most venerated blues heritage.

He was born on July 1, 1935, and raised on the Bonnie Blue Plantation (named for an early Confederate flag and marching song), near the unincorporated hamlet of Clayton, Mississippi, about six miles south of Tunica. "We were sharecroppers," he recalls. "Plowed mules, shucked corn, picked cotton—anything you could do on a farm." Usually, there was musical accompaniment: "While doing that, people strike up a song, sing a song and make their day go a little bit better."[1]

James's parents, Mose and Hattie Cotton, were church people (Mose was a preacher as well as a farmer), and religious music was a staple in the family's life. Other sounds, though, also resonated through the quiet Delta countryside. "I used to hear 'em singing in church on Sunday morning," he remembered. "And about a mile from my house, the train whistle used to blow." Hattie Cotton played the harmonica a little bit, and she showed her son how to imitate the train sounds on it. One Christmas, "my mother made Santa Claus give me a harmonica. Out of nine kids, I learned how to do that."

"We used to have this old battery radio that my two older sisters put in their room," he said in a 1975 interview. "One day, I just happened to be plucking around in there, and I run across station KFFA, Helena, Arkansas, and I heard Sonny Boy Williamson—Rice Miller—play the harp. . . . I was seven years old then."[2]

More than seventy years later, he still remembered the thrill: "'Oooh! Listen at that! I never heard anything like that!' He's blowin' the harp, goin' off the air – 'Tune in tomorrow at 12:00 for Sonny Boy and his King Biscuit Boys'—so every time I got a chance, from then on, I would go and listen to the radio, keep it down low . . . Fifteen minutes [every day]."

No blues were allowed in the Cotton household, which is why James had to keep the radio "down low" when Sonny Boy was on. He'd sometimes sneak out into the fields to practice the songs he heard ("If my mother had knowed what I would do with that harp, she never would've bought it for me—never!").[3] But he had an uncle, Wiley Green, who was more permissive than his parents.

"Wiley was a 'day hand,'" he explained. "He was the plantation mechanic—fixed tractors and so on. He never chopped cotton and never picked it. He would haul it to the gin. He went out and got one of these windup Victorias [sic: Victrolas]. I could play records, [and] I could play harmonica at his house. I stayed with him more than I stayed home."

Through the years, there have been conflicting accounts of how young James eventually left that home to join Sonny Boy Williamson. The most dramatic version, in which a wide-eyed runaway charms the crusty harp man into taking him in as a kind of surrogate son, may appeal to our sense of blues romanticism, but the truth is somewhat more prosaic. "My father died when I was seven years old," James related years later. "My mother, my youngest sister—Lou Willie— and I were the only ones left in the family home. The three of us made two crops together, and then my mother died when I was nine years old. After my mother died, I had no parents, just Uncle Wiley":

> The boss put me on a little small tractor, making three dollars a day, getting paid every two weeks. This particular Saturday, we had got paid. At the commissary, the place we got paid off at, a guy walked up. He heard me play a little bit, said "Why don't you play some blues on that harmonica?" [I] pulled off my cap, he put fifty

cents in there. I started playing when I seen that! Then people, coming up there and getting paid off, I'm sitting there playing, they put quarters, nickles, dimes, all kind of stuff in there.

By the time my uncle got paid and come out there, I had made more money playing the harp than we made for two weeks driving the tractor. We just made thirty six dollars for working two weeks; I had forty six in my cap. [He] come out and looked at my cap full of change. He turned around and looked at me, he said, "This is no place for you." So he taken me to Helena to [meet] Sonny Boy.

[Wiley] told me to tell Sonny Boy I was lost and I didn't have no family. We found the radio station; they come out wearing white overalls, black shirts, and chauffeur caps: Sonny Boy; [guitarists] Robert Jr. Lockwood [and] Joe Willie Wilkins; [drummer] Peck Curtis; and a guy called Dudlow [pianist Robert Taylor], we called him Five-by-Five. I'd never seen none of 'em before. I said, "Where's Sonny Boy?" Everybody pointed at each other, said, "He's Sonny Boy." "No, I'm Sonny Boy." So they gave me the runaround like that.

It wasn't until the following day, when James returned to KFFA to try again, that he summoned his nascent flair for showmanship and finally met his idol: "I pulled out my harp, and I played the theme song for Sonny Boy's radio show: 'Good evening everybody, tell me how you do. We're the King Biscuit Boys, we come out to welcome you.' I played it note-for-note. He looked at me, said, 'Hey, man, I'm Sonny Boy. Come on over here and talk to me.'"

I'd been listening to him for two years. When I played for him, he said, "I don't know where you come from, but you been listening to me for a long time." That cat couldn't figure me out, man. I knew all his tunes. . . . He took me in on the condition that he was gonna help find my people; he didn't have time for no kid. But I was kind of a hip cat; I knew what to do. Like they never did have to tell me to do shit. I'd get up and try to help make the beds—stuff like that. And I was always asking questions, you know? He took a liking to me right away. . . . I stayed in his house and played with him for six years.[4]

Never less than resourceful, the eager youth managed to keep his gig even when he couldn't get in the door. "When I started playing with Sonny Boy, by me being a kid, some of the places wouldn't let me come in. So [fellow harpist] Forrest City Joe [Pugh] would show up, and we'd sit on the front of the car, sit there and play. The people'd come to see Sonny Boy, and they wouldn't make it in—we stopped 'em right there at the front door. We'd have as much money as [the band]."

Williamson also entertained at parties in people's homes, where his young apprentice had less trouble getting in. "They'd take out a bed or something . . .

James Cotton, SPACE,
Evanston, Illinois, 2016.

cook some fish and corn, drink some whiskey and have a party that night and
put the bed back later and go to sleep. So I started playin' the house parties."

"I wanted to be just like Sonny Boy," he added. "I just watched. If he played it
tonight, I played it tomorrow. . . . I watched every move he made, every word he
said."[5]

One night, after a show at a West Memphis juke called the Bebop Hall, Sonny
Boy bought a half-pint of whiskey, told James to take a drink with him ("wasn't
no bar, Sonny Boy went up to the guy who sold the whiskey and bought a half
pint and brought it back") and announced, "Well, I'm fixin' to leave the band." At
fifteen, with only a few years' experience under his belt, James Cotton suddenly
found himself the leader of one of the region's most prestigious blues bands.

By his own admission, he wasn't close to being ready for it. "Me being young,"
he said, "the band just kind of went to my head. . . . When Sonny Boy stepped
down, he gave the chicks a better chance to look at me; I never had that before, and

it really screwed up my mind. I started getting drunk, half showing up, everything I thought a star was supposed to do. . . . Those guys had been playing as long as I was old, and every time they tried to tell me, they just couldn't tell me nothing. So they finally just left, finally just cut me loose . . . because I was *crazy*. I don't blame them."[6]

On his own again, he went back to supporting himself with day jobs ("I drove truck, short-order cook, ice man, hauled concrete, I did all that"), but he never gave up on music, even if he was still too young to participate in it as much as he wanted. He gravitated to Memphis, the urban epicenter of the Mid-South and a longtime blues stronghold. "I worked in [Handy] park [on Beale Street] at the shoe-shine box. But every time I'd get a chance I used to slip in [a club]. I used to get on my knees and crawl through the door right through people's legs into 500 Beale Street, the Hippodrome, Rachel's Hotel on 11th Street. I saw Ruth Brown and Elvis Presley before he was Elvis Presley."[7]

"I knowed B.B. [King] before I knowed anybody," he added later. "B.B. was playing on Beale Street; I was shining shoes out in the park. So I'd just walk on down the street and listen to B.B., sitting there playing. And then he got on WDIA, and I kept the radio on out there."

He also scuffled as a musician, and by the early '50s, he'd begun to make his mark as an up-and-comer on the Memphis/West Memphis circuit. Howlin' Wolf, then in his own early ascendancy, took him on, which led to his first recording opportunity: On April 17, 1952, he accompanied Wolf on a session at the Sun studio that resulted in Wolf's "Saddle My Pony" (released on Chess, No. 1515) and "Dorothy Mae" (unissued at the time, but included on several Wolf compilations). Strangely, on Take 2 of "Dorothy Mae," someone who sounds a lot like James can be heard shouting "Blow, Wolf! Blow, Wolf!" but it's clear that Wolf is not playing harp.

Some accounts also place James at the October 7, 1952, Howlin' Wolf session at which Wolf recorded "Oh, Red" / "My Last Affair" (Chess 1528), but there's no audible harp on "Oh, Red," although it's possible that he could have been riffing along with the rough-hewn horn section. The harp solo on "My Last Affair" actually sounds like Wolf, but at this late date it's difficult to know for sure. Meanwhile, James also worked with drummer/vocalist Willie Nix, and in October he returned to Sun to play harp on Nix's "Seems like a Million Years" / "Baker Shop Boogie" (Sun 179).

James's first opportunity to record under his own name came about as the result of a lost gig. Willie Nix, a heavy drinker, "got in trouble" at an engagement and was fired. Realizing the precariousness of his situation as Nix's harp man, James went to KWEM in West Memphis and hustled his way onto his own radio show. This was probably also when he formed his first working band, James Cotton and the Rhythm Playmates, with guitarist Pat Hare and drummer John Bowers. His KWEM show, meanwhile, led to a call from someone at Sun Records (most likely Marion Keisker, Sam Phillips's partner and office manager), inviting him in to do some recording. On December 7, 1953, he went to Sun and recorded "My Baby" and "Straighten Up Baby," released in April of the following year (Sun 199). On these sides, somewhat belying his juke-joint apprenticeship with Sonny Boy, he did his best to approximate the style of a crooning pop singer as two tenor saxophones, along with pianist Billy Love and guitarist Pat Hare, riffed behind him. Moreover, he didn't play harp—perhaps the attempt to emulate a jazz or jump-blues feel made that instrument seem anachronistic.

For his next Sun session, "I came up with a song that I wrote, 'Cotton Crop Blues.' So we did this song, and my drummer, John Bower, didn't show up. That's the reason why there's no harmonica—I played the drums on that and sung the song. The man [Phillips] had a bass drum there, and a foot pedal. So I got that. And I got a box, put it on a chair; [they] gave me two drumsticks, that's what I played with. Cardboard box, and a little cymbal about like that [the size of a pie plate]."

"Cotton Crop Blues," recorded on May 14, 1954, and released on July 1 that same year (Sun 206), epitomizes the downhome/big-city dialectic that was coming to characterize what would eventually be dubbed the "postwar" blues sound. James's lyrics, which echoed Roosevelt Sykes's earlier "Cotton Seed Blues," portrayed a sharecropper struggling to wrest a living from the bossman and the uncompromising Delta earth; Pat Hare's barbed-wire-and-gunpowder fretboard explosions, meanwhile, prophesied the raw urban intensity that would soon characterize both the music and the lives of his generation of Southern bluesmen as they moved North. The flip, "Hold Me in Your Arms," was obviously based on Jr. Parker's "Mystery Train" and its B-side, "Love My Baby" (which had been issued the previous year). Apparently, Bowers made it to the studio in time to play drums on "Hold Me"; there's some powerful percussion work going on behind James's vocals.

As James recalls those early sessions, vignettes from his days on the Memphis/West Memphis circuit come rushing back with cinematic vividness:

You ever hear of Joe Hill Louis? "The Be-Bop Boy"! He played the guitar, harmonica, and drums—one-man band. He was supposed to open the show for me. He had drums set up everywhere—wouldn't be no room for me to get on stage. He said,

"Every damn thing up there, I'm gonna play it." He had a stick between his fingers, guitar, harp around his neck, and two bass drums. I said, "I'm gonna watch this!"

First time Koko [Taylor] sang, she was on my stage. [Her husband] Pops Taylor used to drive cab in Memphis, and I worked about twenty miles out of Memphis, when I had my first little trio, in Bridgewater, Tennessee. I played there every Monday and Thursday night, and I didn't have a car. Had to get a cab driver to drive me down there. [One] Monday night, he had Koko with him. That's how I met Koko. Junior Parker and I had a "Harmonica Battle." The rule was that whoever won got a chicken sandwich; the loser got a hot dog. I ate chicken that night.

Finally, in 1954, still working day jobs to help pay the rent, he met the man who'd change his life yet again and set him on the path that would eventually bring him to fame:

I was hauling cement, putting a dog track in, in West Memphis, Arkansas. I got off, stopped at the liquor store, bought a half pint, knocked the dust out of my throat. I was playing at the Dinette Lounge [in West Memphis]. . . . Muddy Waters was there to meet me before my set started. Somebody told him who I was, you know. He said, "How you doing?" I said, "I'm doing all right." He said, "I'm Muddy Waters." I didn't believe him [at first]—I said, "and I'm Jesus Christ!"

They were on a tour through the South; [harpist] Junior [Wells] had went back to Chicago. He said, "Meet me in Memphis, eight o'clock tomorrow night; I'm playing at the Hippodrome, 500 Beale Street." When I got there, [guitarist] Jimmy Rogers was there, [pianist] Otis Spann was there, Elgin Edmonton [*sic*: drummer Elgin Evans, née Elga Edmonds] was there, and [saxophonist] Bob Hadley. Jimmy Rogers said, "Showtime!" He was the band leader. I ain't seen Muddy Waters yet, right? So after a while, Jimmy walked up to the mic and said, "Here's the man you all been waiting for. Here's Muddy Waters." The minute he opened his mouth—I knew all his records—I said, "Well, I gotta play this." So I fell in line, started to playing it the best I knowed how. After the set, he said, "We're leaving tomorrow, going to Chicago . . . if you want to go." I said, "Yeah, I want to go." That Sunday morning, we drove to Chicago.

Once there, James found himself in dauntingly fast company. "Little Walter and Junior Wells and all of 'em was in Chicago," he remembers, "and Muddy started telling me, 'I want my music played just like you hear on that record.' That was [mostly] Walter. And I said, 'What am I gonna do now?' I got pretty close to it, [but] I finally told him, 'Man, I'll never be Little Walter, but I can play your music.' So he eased up on me a little bit, let me do something of what I know to do."

Nonetheless, Muddy didn't use him in the studio for quite some time, relying mostly on Walter instead. Finally, in 1956, he came in to share the duties with

Walter on "All Aboard," which ended up being the "B" side of the epochal "Forty Days and Forty Nights," recorded at the same session. (James's train-whistle effects on "All Aboard" probably evoked a lot of childhood memories for him.) But it wasn't until 1960, he says, after he appeared on one of the most famous shows Muddy ever played, that he really felt at home in the band. "We went to Newport, Rhode Island, to the Jazz Festival. We did 'I Got My Mojo Working.' That's when he turned me loose." A famous film clip, available on Youtube, shows Muddy and James, locked in an embrace, jitterbugging together as the song reaches its climax.

Despite the occasional tension or stylistic disagreements that may have arisen, James's twelve-year tenure with Muddy Waters remains one of his most cherished memories. "I love Muddy. He was a good man—once you play his music right. And once he knowed what you was doing, playing his music, he was a great guy to work for. I loved every minute of it. I had three guys that I watched, and I think Muddy was the strongest one. Sonny Boy, Howlin' Wolf—Muddy was more together than those guys. I watched him for twelve years and noticed everything he did."

In 1966, during a West Coast tour with Muddy (now performing largely for white audiences), James met pianist Alberto Gianquinto at a club in San Francisco. "I started talking [with Gianquinto] about [putting together] a band; I told him about the people I could get around Chicago. I said, 'I can get [drummer] Sam Lay, [guitarist] Luther Tucker, and [bassist] Bobby Anderson.' And then this guy, Gordon Kennerly, he said that he wanted to be the manager. So we come back to Chicago. Later this [same] week, about one o'clock Tuesday night, the phone rang. I answered it. 'Hey, this is Albert. I'm in Peoria, Illinois.' He hitchhiked across! And the next day, I get a call from the manager; he's in St. Louis."

James gave Muddy his notice (Muddy recruited George "Harmonica" Smith to take his place) and embarked on a fresh musical journey: leading an integrated band on the newly integrated Chicago blues circuit. Harpist Paul Butterfield and guitarist Elvin Bishop, who'd been hanging out in various South Side clubs, had already told him about Big John's, a hipster stronghold on North Wells, where Butterfield had the regular gig. In classic head-cutting style, the new James Cotton band showed up there one night and ended up taking the job.

"We played one tune," he recollected with a satisfied chuckle. "One tune! The guy come up and say, 'What you doing this weekend?' I said, 'Nothing.' He said, 'You want a job?' I took the job so fast, I forgot to get the manager paid! First black bandleader over there [the North Side]. I'm [also] the first one carried whites to the South Side."

It was a little risky in those days for white boys to hang out in the 'hood, but James was resolute: "'He ain't gonna mess with you—he gotta see me.' I had my pistol in my back pocket at that time; they gotta give me respect." (Violence haunted the blues world in those days. In 1961, a mentally disturbed man accosted James while he was standing at a bus stop and shot him; he took five bullets, at least one to the head. The shooter might have been the same man who had threatened to kill Muddy's entire band the year before.)

Once ensconced at Big John's, James decided to share the good times with his erstwhile mentor. "I went by [Muddy's] house, said, 'Hey, you can come to the North Side; get you a job over there.' I talked to him three years, trying to get him to go to the North Side. He finally told me he'd go. Walked through the door, Bob Wettlaufer was managing Big John's. I said, 'Bob, this is Muddy; let's call up Muddy.' Just like that. He ended up staying there for six weeks."

Meanwhile, James Cotton's own world kept expanding. Although Kennerly remained his manager until the early '90s ("I owe Gordon the recognition he deserves. He remains to this day a cherished friend"), he also got bookings through Albert Grossman, whose clients through the years included Bob Dylan, The Band, Janis Joplin, and other rock heavyweights. As James remembers it, Janis Joplin first encountered him when Grossman booked him and his band to open for her at a show in Long Island.

"I looked back, Janis was standing there, peeping out from behind the curtain. That Monday morning, she was in the office, asking Albert, 'Where you get that band from?' So we toured with Janis for a good long while. Me and her was drinking buddies—Southern Comfort. Kept me drunk! The Southern Comfort company, the people who make it, they had a case in her dressing room every night."

Through the next several decades and into the next millennium, James toured almost constantly. His bands were among the tightest on the circuit, and his stage show, at least in the early years, was one of the most exhilarating in all of blues. Drenched in sweat, blowing his harp in a turbocharged updating of what he'd absorbed from Sonny Boy Williamson, he'd somersault across the bandstand, jump up and down, pop his eyes and mug like an old-time Beale Street showman, and in general rev up the audience to near-insanity, all the while playing with such ferocity that he'd sometimes suck reeds right out of his instrument. If he lacked some of his mentor's timbral and rhythmic subtlety, the excitement he generated outstripped anything Sonny Boy had ever envisioned.

His recordings, meanwhile, gave him the opportunity to show more versatility. In 1964, while he was still Muddy Waters's primary harp man, he and Muddy's pianist Otis Spann recorded a duet session for the Prestige label, released the following year as *The Blues Never Die!* Their interplay, jubilant and meditative in turn, exemplified the quick-minded improvisational acumen, as well as the emotional resonance, that lay at the heart of both men's blues craftsmanship. But his career as a frontline recording artist really kicked into gear over the next few years with LPs on Verve and Vanguard, and it continued virtually undiminished for the next five decades, with critically acclaimed albums on such labels as Capitol, Alligator (his 1986 Alligator LP, *James Cotton and His Big Band—Live from Chicago! Mr. Superharp Himself!* garnered him the first of his eventual ten Grammy nominations), Blind Pig, Antone's, and Telarc, among others.

At times he was backed by horns, without a harmonica, crooning in a manner reminiscent of Bobby "Blue" Bland—something of a culmination of what he had tried to achieve on those long-ago first sessions at Sun. (According to James, this was no accident—in fact, it might even have been genetic. "Well, I guess I got to tell you," he said with an impish grin. "Me and Bobby Bland supposed to have the same father.") Some outings, like 1975's *High Energy* (Buddah), attempted, with varying degrees of success, to graft him onto a more commercially oriented funk background. At various points, he also took on pop ballads (Todd Rundgren's "Goodbye My Lady"); Bobby Rush's "funk-folk" ("Chicken Heads"); remakes of jump-blues classics (most notably his motormouth assault on Louis Jordan's "Caledonia," from 1976's *Live & On the Move* on Buddah); and smooth-blues standards such as Percy Mayfield's "River's Invitation" and Little Willie John's "Fever."

But throughout most of his post-Muddy recording career, and certainly in performance, he was showcased primarily as a hard-charging, leather-lunged harp man. He not only toured the roadhouse/club/festival circuits with what sometimes seemed like near-obsessional dedication; he appeared on stage, either as an opening act or a special guest soloist, alongside rock powerhouses ranging from Steve Miller and Santana to the Grateful Dead. His reunion with Muddy Waters on Muddy's career-rejuvenating '70s-era LPs, featuring the blistering guitar of producer Johnny Winter along with Muddy's indelible slidework, was both a reaffirmation of a fabled blues brotherhood and a tantalizing taste of what those iconic Waters bands must have sounded like in Chicago's urban jukes during the waning glory days of the postwar era.

James Cotton with bassist
Noel Neal (son of Louisiana
harpist Raful Neal Sr.), SPACE,
Evanston, Illinois, 2016.

For a long time, it seemed as if James Cotton was an indestructible force of nature, but in 1993, his musical activities came to a temporary and frightening halt when he was diagnosed with throat cancer and had to undergo surgery. His voice, already raw, faded into a whisper, and for a while the future looked grim. But James soldiered on: "I didn't hide it. The people—I let them know what happened to me. Tell 'em I'm glad to still be there with 'em. They accept me as I am."

Over the next few years, despite his diminishing vocal prowess, James enjoyed some of his most satisfying moments as a recording artist. In 1996, he joined forces with guitarist Joe Louis Walker, pianist David Maxwell, and esteemed jazz bassist Charlie Haden on *Deep In the Blues* (Verve/Gitanes), a low-key but impeccably realized outing that garnered that year's Grammy for "Best Traditional Blues

Album." The last recording on which he sang was 2000's *Fire Down Under the Hill* (Telarc), which also included a couple of tracks featuring Darrell Nulisch, who subsequently took over as James's primary voice man, both on stage and in the studio. But his harp prowess remained undiminished, and if his latter-day bands didn't always rise to the heights of some of his earlier ensembles (his sidemen/soloists through the years included such legendary figures as Luther Tucker and Matt "Guitar" Murphy), they were still tight and versatile, capable of both goading and following him in any direction he might choose to go. A star-studded 2010 tribute at New York's Lincoln Center served as both a career capstone and a reaffirmation of the status he had enjoyed among his fellow musicians and his fans for decades.

In 2013, James returned to Alligator and released *Cotton Mouth Man*. Most of the songs were originals, and despite the presence of guest stars like Gregg Allman, Joe Bonamassa, Delbert McClinton, Ruthie Foster, Warren Haynes, and Keb' Mo' (as well as James's old standby, Nulisch), a strong autobiographical theme wove through the set. (On "Midnight Train," he revisited the train-whistle and chugging locomotive harmonica effects he'd first learned on the plantation.) The centerpiece was the acoustic "Bonnie Blue," another autobiographical tale, which James himself delivered in a hoarse rasp, and which featured his Sonny Boy–influenced harp work at its most raw and unadorned.

At least in public, James has never been given to introspection or melancholy—he's always been a good-timer, and there are plenty of stories from the early days of younger traveling companions reduced to near-catatonic exhaustion in their attempts to keep up with his partying habits—but in private conversation he reveals a more reflective side, even as he refuses to succumb to sentimentality or nostalgia. He honors the memories of the musicians he's known and worked with ("I think about 'em all the time. I've had so many good musicians . . . the top musicians around Chicago"), but if *Cotton Mouth Man*, with its array of rock and blues-rock celebrities filling out the bill, sounded like a declaration of intent from an unbowed veteran roots man determined to stay on the blues highway for as long as possible, that's probably because it was. "I don't even think about retiring," he insisted not long after the CD's release. "What [else] I'm gonna do?"

Focused, as he's been for most of his life, on accentuating the positive, James has continued to proclaim his sense of mission as a torch-bearer ("I'm trying to keep the blues alive"), but unlike some, he refuses to criticize artists who may take the music in unexpected, and perhaps less "authentic," directions. "I don't down no music," he has asserted, "because I'm a musician myself. I like [soul-blues], but I just don't play it. I like it because it's keeping the music going. I like a lot of jazz, too, but I just don't play it."

He's likewise sanguine about the changes he'd seen in blues demographics over the years. "My first gig [as a band leader] was a white audience," he notes. "I've always played white audiences. My main work has been in the white field." Any mixed feelings about this? "Don't make no difference to me, if they done me good, what the color of the skin is—they're with me."

Asked to name his favorite harp player, he responds with alacrity (and a disarming smile): "Me!" But he quickly adds other names. "Kim Wilson, Charlie Musselwhite, Sugar Blue . . . Billy Branch; me and Junior [Wells] taught Billy Branch. I got this little grandson, my musical grandson. He's twelve years old. His name is Josh King, and he can play the harp. He can sing, too. He's a little white kid, and he sits on my knee."

After all these years, it's clear that James still sees himself as both inheritor and benefactor—a living conduit of a legacy both timeless and evolving. "As long as I stay around," he concludes, "I think [the blues] is going to stay around—'cause I'm gonna keep playing 'em. The blues is part of me. I could do something else if I tried, but the blues is me. I'm all right with the blues, and they're all right with me."

Coda: "One More Mile to Go"

By the time *Cotton Mouth Man* was released, James Cotton had begun to curtail his performing schedule. Over the next few years, his public appearances became even rarer, as he relaxed in quiet semiretirement in his adopted hometown of Austin, Texas. His death on March 16, 2017, although not entirely unexpected, was still a shock, and it brought a torrent of tributes and remembrances from musicians, friends, and colleagues from both the blues and rock worlds. Meanwhile, those of us who revere the living tradition he represented felt more of a chill than ever, realizing how precarious the roster of veterans representing that tradition has become.

But it would be wrong to end on such a note. The blues, in James Cotton's hands, was a music of celebration, a font of energy and an upward-arcing impetus toward joy, prophesying a world of both struggle and victory, in which the best is always yet to come. That's the spirit in which he made his music, it's the spirit with which he lived, and it's the spirit in which he will be remembered.

Eddie Shaw

"Been Through a Lot—Trying to Keep the Tradition Alive"

I t's a chilly, late-autumn night in Chicago. Even the usually frenetic North Side club stroll feels eerily desolate, as if the streets themselves are battening down in anticipation of winter. But inside B.L.U.E.S. on Halsted, one of the city's premier blues tourist destinations, the atmosphere is charged. Eddie Shaw, the legendary tenor saxophonist who had been Howlin' Wolf's band leader and musical director for many years, is making a rare local appearance tonight with his band, the Wolf Gang. During his forty years at the helm since Wolf's death in 1976, he's led various incarnations of the Gang around the country and the world (early lineups included other former Wolf sidemen, but Eddie is now the sole remaining alum), cultivating a sound that evokes Wolf's trademark intensity leavened and deepened by a jubilant, forward-driving musical thrust that critics have variously praised and panned as either a creative updating or a history-defiling dilution of the gold-standard original. These days, though, as a "living legend" and elder statesman, Eddie Shaw himself is virtually beyond criticism. Health problems have curtailed his live appearances recently, so a night like this is even more special than it might have been a few years ago—a chance to see up close, in a cozy club setting, one of the last living links to the glory days of postwar Chicago blues.

The audience sees the horn before they see the man—it waits for him, propped up in its homemade cast-iron stand, in front of the chair he'll sit in throughout the evening. The Wolf Gang, under the leadership of guitarist Eddie "Vaan" Shaw Jr., who wields a triple-neck Fender and plays in an aggressive, arpeggio-laden style, churn out a couple of stage-warming numbers that also feature alto saxophonist Mike Peavy and keyboardist Ron Scott. Finally, Eddie himself, gaunt and slow-moving but dapper in captain's hat, sports shirt, and slacks, eases himself onto the stage and into his chair.

Vaan fires off a series of crunching blues-rock chords as the band locks into a Chicago shuffle, goosed by Peavy's deep-pocket riffing—the modernist/traditionalist dialectic that characterizes their sound these days making itself immediately apparent. Eddie bends forward to his horn, cups his lips around the mouthpiece, and the room explodes into ecstasy as he boots out a series of caustic yakety-yak phrases that evoke the anarchic spirit of a vintage bar-walking sax honker, all grit and spittle but girded by the rhythmic and improvisational bedrock he has cultivated throughout his sixty-plus–year career.

Eddie's sax blowing, his squalling harmonica breaks, and his deep-chested baritone vocals sound virtually undiminished, belying his somewhat frail appearance—although he never lifts his horn from its stand, and soon, as he will do repeatedly throughout the evening, he leans back to rest, allowing Peavy to take over for a solo or two. Vaan's own solos, predictably, take things into a dizzying postmodernist stratosphere—if every note tells a story, Vann's stories cascade down in meteor showers. But despite Vaan's relentless modernism, an overall mood of rootsy celebration has been established, and it will prevail throughout the night. The set leans heavily on blues chestnuts from the oeuvres of such fabled figures as Sonny Boy Williamson, Elmore James, Muddy Waters, and—of course—the Mighty Wolf himself. Toward the end, in a rare onstage moment of introspection, Eddie quiets the band down and takes a few minutes to ruminate on his long tenure as a musician. "For sixty-five years, I've been trying to keep the blues tradition alive," he attests, adding that he attributes his track record to hard work, determination—and, he concludes, "the biggest thing of all: You gotta love people."

· · ·

Nelson Street winds into Greenville, Mississippi, from the fields abutting an elongated backflow of the Mississippi River known as Lake Ferguson; it runs east through town for about twenty blocks before it meets Railroad Ave. and juts sharply south as Eureka St. In its heyday, Nelson was a cultural and social epicenter, one of the nexuses of the old Chitlin' Circuit—the loosely amalgamated network of jukes, show lounges, theaters, and nightclubs, based primarily in the South and Southwest but extending to Indianapolis, Detroit, Chicago, and other northern outposts, along which African American blues, jazz, and R&B artists plied their trade on grueling tours of back-to-back one-nighters during the mid–twentieth century.

In the late '40s, when a young Eddie Shaw moved to Greenville with his family, Nelson Street was at its latter-day peak. "The prime location!" Eddie exults, still savoring the memory. "Joints back to back; back-to-back restaurants. Something like Beale Street."

Not yet in his teens, he was no doubt primed for some excitement. He'd been born on a Stringtown, Mississippi, plantation in 1937; he then moved to Rosedale, the town Robert Johnson had immortalized in "Traveling Riverside Blues," where he attended school for a few years. He soon moved again, though, this time to

Eddie Shaw, New Orleans Jazz
& Heritage Festival, 2005.
Photo © Gene Tomko.

Greenville, where his mother had secured a job running an ice cream parlor. He was in sixth or seventh grade, as he remembers it, when he began playing in the school band under the directorship of Winchester "Little Wynn" Davis, one of Greenville's most esteemed educators and community leaders.

"I loved Mr. Wynn," Eddie affirms, remembering that when he joined the Coleman High Marching Band under Davis's tutelage, the entire outfit consisted of about fifteen members ("We were marching down the street in different parades, we didn't have uniforms—black pants and white shirts"). By the time he left, it had swelled to nearly a hundred. His first instrument was the trombone, but he soon moved on to the saxophone, his original first choice, and became proficient.

"I always wanted to play the sax," he attests, attributing his enthusiasm to the myriad influences and inspirations he absorbed while growing up. Contrary to stereotype, Delta communities like Greenville often nurtured music of considerable polish and sophistication—a far cry from the atavistic "juke joint blues" too often still solely associated with the region:

> Man, we had some helluva sax players in Greenville, man. Me and Oliver Sain kind of grew up together, went to school, we did a lot of things together. Willie Dotson, Otis Green, C. W. Tate—all these saxophone players in Greenville could play, man.[1] And we had the Gardner brothers—[trumpeter] Burgess Gardner, played with Count Basie—him and his older brother Beverly, who turned out to be the band director at Coleman High after they got rid of Mr. Winchester Davis.
>
> Ike [Turner] was two years older than me [actually six years], and he was the program director at WROX in Clarksdale. That's where I met Ike. I was with a band [led by] Charley Booker, makin' our first record—something like "Leland Smokin' and Greenville Burnin' Down."[2] We had an old car, man, didn't have no heat or nothing in it. Four guys—Imagine!—four guys sittin' on the front seat with a blanket all the way across us, halfway sittin' on one another's lap. That's the only way we could keep warm.

Ironically, perhaps, Charley Booker was the kind of elemental guitarist/vocalist whose style was rapidly being replaced by the more forward-looking, jazz/R&B-influenced blues and jump blues that Eddie and most of his running buddies were delving into. As Eddie remembers it, his own first working ensemble was assembled, or at least selected, by Winchester Davis himself, who was also a bandleader in his own right: "He picked out five or six guys that could play. We played blues, a little rock & roll—all the club gigs. On a Friday and Saturday, you'd make six, eight dollars a night; that's enough to last me all of next week."

It was a long-standing Southern tradition for black show bands to entertain for white functions; the groups Eddie worked with, well-appointed and in command of a wide repertoire, adapted easily to assignments like this. One band he played in, in fact, dubbed themselves the Green Tops in homage to the region's best-known black society band, the Red Tops out of Vicksburg, Mississippi. "I knew the Red Tops, all them guys," he affirms. "I had one white club I played, the guy liked me; I didn't have no automobile, [so] he let me use his Pontiac station wagon. He said, 'Keep it at your house—pick up your musicians and bring 'em to work.'"

As Eddie developed, he also freelanced, eventually working with Little Milton, Ike Turner, and anyone else who was looking for a good horn accompaniment. He and Oliver Sain often worked as a team on these gigs. That, in fact, was how Eddie landed the job that would change his life. It was a year or two after he graduated from high school; he was attending Mississippi Vocational College (now Mississippi Valley State) in Itta Bena when Muddy Waters came through town. Muddy, of course, is known as the man who helped codify the classic guitars/keyboard/ harmonica/bass/drums postwar blues lineup, but he also used horn players at times, and on this particular evening he was looking for a sax man, or maybe two.

"He said, 'You guys can play good, man. I'm going on a ten-day tour—Arkansas, Louisiana, Texas, and back to Mississippi—and I'd like for you guys to come along.' Oliver couldn't go because his mom was sick, but I hung on. I had dropped out of school because I didn't have any more money and I couldn't pay for tuition. For ten, maybe twelve days I was with Muddy, and when I got back, he thanked me, gave me a few dollars, and said, 'If you want to come to Chicago, I'll make room for you.'"

Eddie stayed around Greenville a while longer, holding down day jobs. But he soon decided it was time to move on. "I called Muddy," he recollects, "and he said, 'Can you be here by next Tuesday? I got an opening for you.' I came to Chicago, and we started working that Tuesday at a club near 64th and Cottage Grove."[3]

Muddy had already recorded some of his biggest hits by that time, and although his performing career still consisted primarily of gigs in modest venues in Chicago and on the road, a job with him was among the most prestigious in all of blues. Eddie, though, was never starstruck. The work was steady, the pay was probably as generous as a sideman could expect, but he found himself getting restless—the big-city blues up north turned out to be frustratingly pedestrian next to what he'd been playing back home.

"In Greenville," he has remembered, "every band had two or three horns. We were playin' the charts. And you get to Chicago, man . . . the bands with the big names, and they got *one* horn. Four pieces, one horn, and it was unbelievable. You start thinkin', man, all these years you been writing' and arrangin', tryin' to get your act together, and you get to Chicago and those guys were playin' the blues and . . . didn't need nothin' but just 'get up there and blow, baby,' you know what I mean. So after a while I got tired of Chicago."[4]

He went back home, but he still kept his options open. He'd developed a reputation as a dependable sideman; over the course of the next few years, as he remembers it, he'd return from Greenville every few months to pick up gigs with some of Chicago's premier blues bandleaders—Otis Rush, Magic Sam, Freddie King—and he eventually decided to come back full-time and rejoin Muddy himself. Again, though, things didn't work as he'd hoped. On a good night, Muddy's band was as tight and exciting as any in blues. But not every night was a good one; Eddie, an abstemious man who prided himself on his professionalism, began to resent the way some of his bandmates carried themselves:

> I was with Muddy, but everybody in the band drink a lot, getting so high sometimes— I ain't into that shit, I never drank or smoked—so we're playing at a place called Mel's Hideaway, 1400 Roosevelt Road. Muddy would never do the first set. Before Muddy got there—I was kind of hot-tempered—I jumped up and quit, packed up my horn, go about six blocks to where Wolf was playing, at a place called the Key Largo [at Roosevelt and Damen].
>
> So he said, "You wanna sit in, man?" I said, "Yeah, I'll sit in." So I got my horn— this was Wolf's second set—I played, so Wolf said, "Hey, ain't you down there with Muddy?" I said, "Man, I just quit—too much shit goin' on down there." "You want a job?" I said, "Yeah, I want a job! I'll be here tomorrow night." He said, "No, if you want to work, you gon' start tonight."

Thus began one of the most fabled musical partnerships in Chicago blues.[5] Even then, though, Eddie continued to work with other bandleaders when the opportunity arose, sometimes for extended periods, which probably accounts for the confusion that has arisen over the years as to exactly when he became Wolf's full-time horn man and musical director. ("I stayed with Wolf for a long time," he told writer Bill Dahl, adding that "I was in and out of that band for a while, but for the last five years, I was back permanent with him."[6]) In fact, it's unclear at this late date whether many of his recollections of working with Otis Rush, Freddie King, and others stem from when he was commuting between Greenville and Chicago, the years after he first joined Wolf but kept freelancing, or both.[7]

Wolf could be a daunting figure; between his public persona as a feral force of nature and the stories that circulated about his strictness as a bandleader, some musicians were actually afraid to work for him. (Many who did, however, affirmed that his reputation for fierceness was overblown—if a man did his job, played the music right, and didn't act the fool, he'd get no trouble from the Wolf.) Nevertheless, he and Eddie shared some core values, especially where professionalism was concerned. After his experience with Muddy Waters's crew, Eddie found it a relief to work for a man who prohibited onstage drunkenness, demanded at least a modicum of decorum from his musicians when they were in public, and ran his band like a business. (With the assistance of his wife, Lillie, Wolf arranged to provide his men with unemployment insurance and social security, which some continued to collect years after his death.[8])

Having apparently made peace with the role horn men played in Chicago's blues bands, Eddie finally found both personal and professional satisfaction in the city. In 1965, he recorded his first sides with Wolf at Chess—"Tell Me What I've Done" / "Ooh Baby"; "I Walked from Dallas" / "Don't Laugh at Me"—followed up the next year with "New Crawlin' King Snake" / "My Mind Is Ramblin'," and both "Poor Wind That Never Change" and "Commit a Crime," the latter two unissued at the time but eventually included in compilations. In 1967, he recorded with Wolf again, resulting in two released sides, "Pop It to Me" and "I Had a Dream."

By this time, Wolf was performing regularly for white audiences at festivals and in clubs (he'd been booked on his first European tour in 1964, and in 1965 he'd made his now-legendary appearance with the Rolling Stones on the TV show *Shindig*). Some of these new fans were collectors who combed record stores for blues 45s; increasingly, however, LPs were the hipsters' stock in trade, and labels like Chess were putting artists like Muddy, Wolf, John Lee Hooker, and Sonny Boy Williamson on albums—some with titles like *The Real Folk Blues* or *Folk Festival of the Blues*—designed to penetrate this new market. At the same time, though, blues artists in Chicago continued to record singles, ostensibly aimed at the dwindling African American blues audience, often saddled with self-conscious attempts to sound contemporary—virtually the opposite of the "folk" pitch being made to whites. (Within a year or two, Chess would reverse course somewhat and begin imposing pseudo-psychedelic studio effects on artists like Wolf and Muddy in an effort to update their sound for the white counterculture.)

The sides Wolf cut with Eddie on sax give a hint of these burgeoning cultural and stylistic tensions. "Poor Wind," with its faux-Dixieland clarinet warbles, comes off as little more than a novelty throwaway; "My Mind Is Ramblin'," an update of Wolf's earlier "Mr. Highway Man" theme, is structured around a tepid-sounding reprise of his trademark "Killing Floor" riff. "I Had a Dream" conveys an amiably rough juke-joint exuberance, but "Pop It to Me" sounds like a ham-handed attempt to transform the Wolf into a purveyor of teen-dance fluff. Some of the others, though, especially the harrowing "Commit a Crime"—one of the most brutal slices of raw paranoia ever committed to wax—showed that Wolf still had it in him to convey blues of unrivaled intensity and emotional force.

Over the next several years, Eddie would also participate in sessions alongside some of Chicago's finest bluesmen—well-known figures like Jimmy Dawkins[9]; local celebrities such as guitarist Milton Houston and bassman Willie Kent.[10] His first opportunity to record under his own name, in fact, resulted from one of these outside sessions. On February 6, 1966, he was scheduled for a session with Magic Sam at MBS Studios in Chicago; he later remembered that the project was initially under the aegis of the Delmark label, which played a major role in introducing Chicago blues artists to the new white audience in those years. Sam was late, so the producer decided to record Eddie as leader on a few songs. When Sam finally arrived, he good-naturedly agreed to back Eddie up.

The result was the 45 "Riding High" / "Blues for the West Side," which was released on the Colt label as by "Eddie Shaw & Band." The sides, both instrumentals, are elemental R&B/rock & roll—"Riding High," an up-tempo jump-boogie on which Sam and Eddie trade bluesy solos; and "Blues for the West Side," an after-hours ballad that features Eddie's sax work, alternately moody and fervid. After Eddie finished recording his own numbers,[11] Magic Sam cut several tracks with Eddie playing behind him as originally planned. These have since been released on Delmark anthologies; "Blues for the West Side" and "Lookin' Good," another joint Eddie Shaw/Magic Sam outing, were also included on Eddie's *King of the Road* LP on Rooster Blues in 1985.

In 1968, again with Eddie on hand, Sam recorded what became *Black Magic* (Delmark), now considered a classic of mid-'60s Chicago blues. Sam was a forward-looking young bluesman who included elements of soul, R&B, and rock & roll in his sound; the ease with which Eddie can be heard working alongside him reflects some of the versatility he'd prided himself on since his early days in Greenville.[12]

Howlin' Wolf suffered a heart attack in 1969 after returning from a European tour; a few weeks later, in Toronto, he was hospitalized again and was diagnosed with early-stage kidney disease. In 1971, after another heart attack, he began taking dialysis. It was during this time that Eddie became Wolf's full-time bandleader and musical director, pacing his shows for him, trying to keep him from overexerting himself on stage, and making sure he took his medication and adhered to his dialysis schedule. Lillie Burnett, Wolf's wife, played a major role in these efforts. "I'd go out to the [Hines] VA hospital in Maywood [Illinois]," Eddie remembers "and shave him. The government had a dialysis machine put in his house, in the basement. So I went with Lillie out there, to learn how to operate it, clean it. Everybody else had to go to these different places to get dialyzed, but he could get dialyzed [at home] because she knew how to run that machine. So sometimes, if we're out of town, he'd fly home and she'd put him on the machine and send him back out."

Photos from these years show Eddie tending to Wolf on stage with an almost paternal tenderness—quite a contrast to the roughshod machismo stereotypically associated with bluesmen. But there were still plenty of good times to be had on the road, and occasionally they could even widen a man's musical horizons. "Wolf and I would have a bet on," he remembers:

> Sometimes we'd drive through a town, "Hey, man—I bet you twenty dollars we ain't gonna see no black folks." "Hey man—next twenty miles, I bet we ain't gonna see no El Dorado Cadillacs." So this was about 1973 or so. We's coming out of Boston; we loaded up, coming home, put a [tape] on, 'Sittin' on Top of the World' [probably the version Wolf had released on Chess in 1958]. So Wolf said, "Hey, motherfucker, I'm gon' bet you. I bet you can't play 'Sittin' on Top of the World' [on harp] by the time we get in Chicago." He told me, "You can't play no harmonica." And I had never tried to play it. But—"Twenty dollar bet?" "That's it!"
>
> So we hit the turnpike, come on through New York—Rochester; Buffalo; Cleveland, Ohio—and when we got to Chicago, I was playing 'Sittin' on Top of the World' just as good as he was. "Man, you playin' that motherfucker mighty good, man." I said, "Hey, man, give me my twenty dollars." He said, "You ain't playing like I want you to play it"—I play the harmonica left-handed, upside-down, but I could still listen to the notes that he was hitting, in the key he was in—"but here's the goddam twenty dollars." That's how that got started.

It was at about this time that Eddie acquired the club in Chicago that eventually became nearly as closely associated with his name as his saxophone and his Wolfian legacy. Some years earlier, he'd bought into a club on West Madison—the 4300 block, as he remembers it; the 4400 block, according to Alligator Records president Bruce Iglauer,[13]—and rechristened it Eddie's Place. The business did okay for a while, but when he was on the road he had to entrust it to someone else, and he found it almost impossible to keep track of things—specifically, the liquor supply and the money in the till—when he wasn't around. Within a few years, he gave it up.[14]

But later on, when a lounge at 1815 Roosevelt Road became available, he decided to take the chance again.[15] This place had a history that extended back to the height of the postwar blues era, as well as what was arguably the seminal moment of Eddie's own career. When he acquired it, it was called the Alex Club, in honor of its erstwhile proprietor, Alex Evans, and his nephew, Alex Moody. But the business had originally been located a few blocks east at 1400 Roosevelt, where it had been known at different times as the Tay May Club and Mel's Hideaway—the very spot where Eddie had been playing on that fateful night when he left Muddy Waters's band to join Wolf (and also the source of the name of Freddie King's guitar-jam classic). It eventually passed into the hands of Alex Evans (or, according to some accounts, Alex Moody), who moved the enterprise to 1815 Roosevelt.[16]

After acquiring the club, Eddie immediately began booking frontline talent—Freddie King, Jimmy Reed, and Mighty Joe Young are only a few of the esteemed figures who performed there. As white aficionados began to venture more frequently to Chicago's South and West Sides to hear the blues, the 1815 Club became something of a tourist mecca, but it never lost its unpretentious neighborhood feel.

The 1815 also became Wolf's unofficial home base when he was in Chicago. "Wolf had just got out of the hospital in Toronto," Eddie explains, "so when we was comin' on back home, he said, 'Goddam it, if you're gonna open a place, I'm gonna play in it. I'm gonna call the rules. If you gonna run a club, I'm gonna play there.' I said, 'I didn't ask you to play there, man.' He said, 'I don't care what you asked me, I'm gonna play there.' So I always had two bands. I had Howlin' Wolf and Mighty Joe Young, Freddie King, Luther Allison, or somebody else, every Friday, Saturday. A lot of people [even] thought it was Wolf's club."

Eddie's last recording with Wolf was *The Back Door Wolf* in 1973, which also turned out to be the big man's final studio album. (The title tune, an instrumental cowritten by Eddie and producer Ralph Bass, featured Eddie's grits-and-testosterone sax squalls along with a somewhat incongruous harpsichord accompaniment from keyboardist Detroit Junior.) Wolf was getting very weak by then, finding it increasingly difficult to sustain himself on tour. As his health deteriorated, Eddie's role became more dominant:

> Wolf said, "Now you go get the money; pay everybody off, pay me off. Keep the rest of the money until you get home, and Lillie will straighten up with you."
>
> So I given Wolf, like, two hundred dollars a week out of that money, and I carried all the little proceeds and receipts and everything, after I paid the band, home to Lillie. And then we'd sit at the kitchen table and work all that other stuff out.

Wolf stayed in the VA [hospital] for a long time . . . so we started Eddie Shaw and the Wolf Gang. We played at the VA for all the veterans—they got an entertainment room out there—and he said, "I know that's my band! I hear Eddie Shaw playing!" So I said, "Wolf, I'm gonna still play." He said, "Go 'head on, keep them motherfuckers working, man, 'til I get out." So I had a few jobs. Sometimes I had to pay [only] twenty five dollars a night on the road, but I kept it going on, man—called it Eddie Shaw and the Wolf Gang. That started when he was still alive. And that went on, man, until now.

Howlin' Wolf died on January 10, 1976, two months after his heroic and now legendary final performance at the Chicago Amphitheater. The publicity surrounding his death turned out to be a boon to the 1815 Club—it reignited popular interest in Chicago as the "home of the blues," and it spurred more white blues lovers to make the trip to West Side for a taste of the real thing (in the Immortal Wolf's own sanctuary, no less). But for Eddie Shaw, still working to keep the Wolf Gang together, the problem of trying to run a club while having to be on the road remained vexing. In about 1980, he rented it out to new proprietors, who changed the name to the Brown Sugar; in 1989 he took it back (it became the New 1815 Club), this time with his cousin Leroy Edwards as his partner. But the two couldn't agree on how to run the business, and by the mid-'90s it was shuttered for good. The building found new life as a church for a few years, but when the University of Illinois Medical Center expanded and transformed most of the surrounding community into the Illinois Medical District (complete with high-rent condominiums and student housing), it was demolished.

Meanwhile, Eddie realized that in order to remain viable, he and the band would have to get some recordings out. Lillie Burnett, as eager as he to keep the legacy alive, agreed, and she provided the financial backing. *Have Blues Will Travel*, billed as by Eddie Shaw and the Wolf Gang, was released on the Simmons label, owned by harpist Little Mack Simmons, in 1977 (it was later reissued on Rooster Blues). The band—guitarist Hubert Sumlin, keyboardist Detroit Junior (Emery Williams), bassist Lafayette "Shorty" Gilbert, and drummer Chico Chism, along with Eddie himself—was the last one Wolf had fronted.

Significantly, none of the tracks on the album were well-known Wolf standards—only "Back Door Wolf" was closely associated with him, and it had never been a major hit—and all were attributed to Eddie as writer (although at least one, a cover of Don Gibson's country classic, "I Can't Stop Loving You," which Eddie had sometimes played on Wolf's shows, was obviously mis-credited). There was little evidence, in fact, that Eddie or anyone else was self-consciously trying to

Eddie Shaw, Chicago Blues
Festival tribute to Otis Rush,
2016.

re-create Wolf's sound (Sumlin's personalized fretboard style notwithstand-
ing). From the beginning, he refused to present himself as nostalgia or merely a
tribute act—a stance he has maintained, over the course of multiple albums and
countless club and festival appearances, both in the United States and overseas,
for over four decades. (Eddie and the Wolf Gang also contributed a few tracks to
the Alligator anthology, *Living Chicago Blues, Vol. 1*, released in 1978).

Blues fans, though, can be a contrary breed. For all their dedicated musicianship and the quality of their live shows, the Wolf Gang have been criticized over
the years for not sounding Wolfian enough, for their good-timey sound, and
for their tendency to avoid the dark emotionality that some romanticists still
consider the essence of blues "authenticity." As the personnel has changed, the
carping has increased. Ever since Vaan Shaw took over lead guitar duties for
Sumlin in the '80s, he's been variously praised and scathed for his hyperkinetic

fretboard approach. Some, including his father, consider his contributions to be a timely and savvy updating of traditional themes ("I appreciate that because that gives the band a little more leeway in there"), but hard-core Wolf adherents (and blues purists in general) have often viewed them as nothing less than apostasy.

And, in fact, it's undeniable that not all the band's recordings capture them at their best. Eddie's voice is a powerful instrument, deep-chested and resonant, but if it's not mic'd properly in the studio, his singing can sound labored. His horn work is jubilant and dexterous, and his harmonica playing is serviceable, but over the long haul they both can get repetitive, especially in the sedate confines of a listener's living room. Nonetheless, their best recorded work provides a more than satisfying taste of what they've sounded like at their high points.[17] Meanwhile, their dynamism as a live act is undiminished, and it remains their strongest asset.

For his part, Eddie looks back on his life and career with a mixture of hard-earned pride and philosophical resignation. His children have turned out well; Vaan, of course, is both the Wolf Gang's bandleader and an acknowledged front-line performer in his own right; another son, Stan Shaw, is an accomplished actor with extensive stage, screen, and TV credits.[18] Although Eddie is reluctant to commit himself to defining the significance of his own career—braggadocio doesn't wear well on him, but neither does false modesty—he takes satisfaction in knowing that he's recognized alongside such figures as Muddy Waters, Magic Sam, Freddie King, Otis Rush, and Wolf himself as a participant in the forging of one of popular music's most beloved and influential genres.

He also continues to speak of Wolf with a love bordering on reverence; in some of his songs—"Blues Men of Yesterday" on *King of the Road*; "Ode to Howlin' Wolf," from 1999's *Too Many Highways* (on the Austrian Wolf label)—he pays direct tribute to the great man's memory. Through the years, as his own recorded catalogue and performing career have expanded, he has settled into his role as torch-bearer by showcasing Wolf's material both on record and on stage, and he has participated in numerous tributes and remembrances. He still emphasizes, though, that what he's carrying on is much more than one man's legacy. "I've been through a lot, man," he attests, "trying to keep the tradition alive in Chicago."

At the same time, he's less than sanguine about that tradition's future, especially as pertaining to its identity as living African American culture:

Ain't no young boys playing any blues in Chicago, I mean young black kids playing. See, a lot of the guys playing the blues now ain't playing the blues, you know what

I'm saying? They run a lot of changes; I can't even imagine what they're playing. But now, the white boys is learning good. I ain't puttin' 'em down, 'cause them muthas can play, some of 'em, you understand? They learned! They wasn't stealing, they was learning, okay? And the one that's going to stop playing is the black guy. It's a thing where we ain't living up to what we're supposed to do. You know, we wanna play the hip-hop, we wanna make them records about "yo' mammy," "motherfucker," and all that ol' kinda shit and get rich—when they're twenty-five years old, they're millionaires.

At this late date, Eddie doesn't delude himself into believing that a blues-man—especially a veteran like himself—will ever reap that kind of recognition or reward. But true to the sustaining spirit of the music, he sees a kind of victory—or at least redemption—in remaining steadfast in the cause. "The blues, man," he reflects—no doubt remembering funerals he's attended where collections had to be taken up to inter the body, and fund-raising efforts he's participated in to purchase headstones for "living legends" who died broke—"You get seventy, seventy-five, eighty years old, somebody have to bury you."

"But," he concludes, "You kept the tradition going on."

Vaan Shaw: Ass Whoopin' on the Trail of Tears

When Eddie "Vaan" Shaw Jr. stepped in to replace Hubert Sumlin as guitarist in his father's band in the 1980s, a lot of longtime listeners were appalled. Vaan's style seemed at least as indebted to blues-rock as it was to the postwar tradition, and when he tore into a screaming multinote barrage in the middle of one of the band's deep-pocket shuffles, reactions sometimes echoed those of the British purists who'd recoiled from Muddy Waters's electrified sound in 1958—once again, white avatars of "authenticity" were demanding that a black bluesman play music that they, not he, considered representative and true.

The irony ran deep. Vaan, in fact, had grown up steeped in the very tradition his naysayers accused him of defiling—a "tradition" that had always embraced change and innovation, at least before the retro-folk crowd got hold of it and decided to make it into a museum piece. His early mentors included Magic Sam (whose meld of blues, soul, and rock & roll would be considered "fusion" today) and Sumlin himself, an improviser of unpredictable genius whose surrealism-tinged flights of fancy presaged the psychedelic explorations of Hendrix and his legion of acolytes. By the time Vaan was in his early teens, he was a professional musician; he honed his chops in his father's 1815 Club, among other venues,

Vaan Shaw, "Eddie Shaw
Tribute: Brass in the Blues,"
Logan Center, University of
Chicago, 2018.

backing up such storied figures as Eddie Taylor, Freddie King, Otis Rush, and
Hound Dog Taylor—and, of course, Howlin' Wolf himself, when Wolf was in
town.

After Vaan joined the Wolf Gang, he remained their de facto musical director
until the end, wielding his trademark triple-neck Fender both on stage and in
the studio, refusing to temper his modernism even as he continued to profess his
allegiance to the living blues tradition. His own discography includes several outings on the Austrian Wolf label, as well as his self-released *Ass Whoopin!!* in 2001,
and it's on these that he reveals his gifts most fully. His voice at times sounds
like an approximation of his father's, although he can also ascend into a taut,
vibrato-toughened tenor. His fretwork, meanwhile, even on tributes to forbears,
such as his remake of Eddie Sr.'s "Blues-Men of Yesterday" (from 1994's *The Trail*

of Tears), remains the kind of thing that can make purists cringe, but beneath the freneticism lies a rich lode of musicianship, a Coltrane-like "sheets of sound" technique in which the soloist creates entire scalar improvisations within each chord.

Vaan's lyrics can cut just as deeply as his leads. The acoustic "Bull Shit Blues," from 2005's *Give Me Time*, tones down the aural intensity but ramps up the ferocity as Vaan vents frustrations both quotidian ("Everybody tells me, bullshit makes the world go 'round") and existential ("What's the point of livin', when all you gonna do is die"). A slash of tormented blues existentialism, to be sure, but also, no doubt, Vaan's riposte to the critics who've dogged him throughout most of his career—a meld of outrage, anguish, and wounded militance that cuts to the very heart of blues expression.

$$\bullet \quad \bullet \quad \bullet$$

Coda: "Can't Stop Now"

This book would never have been written if it hadn't been for Eddie Shaw.

One night in 1978, while I was living in Boston, I decided to go across the bridge to Cambridge where Eddie Shaw and the Wolf Gang were playing at a club called the Speakeasy. I'd read about them, I'd probably heard a few tracks from the Alligator *Living Chicago Blues* anthology or *Have Blues Will Travel* (their only recordings up to that point), and of course I knew that Eddie had been Howlin' Wolf's sax man, but I'd never seen them in person. Hubert Sumlin was still the guitarist; Shorty Gilbert was on bass. I can't say for sure, but I'm guessing Detroit Junior was playing keyboards and the drummer was Chico Chism. The band probably played an introductory number or two; then the man himself took the stage and blew down firestorms that sounded as if they'd been ignited in the Mississippi Delta and spread northward on the winds of history and fate.

You can probably predict what happened—it galvanized me. Before I left that night, I'd made the decision: I had go to where this music came from. I went home and wrote a letter of application to a community organization I knew in Chicago; a few weeks later, they called and told me I had the job. Over the course of about three caffeine-crazed days I shut down my entire life, packed my worldly possessions into a sputtering 1975 Datsun B-210 hatchback, and limped out to Chicago—it was January, and I arrived the first day the city was open after the legendary Blizzard of '78. A week or two later, having lucked into an apartment, I made my initial pilgrimage to Theresa's Lounge at 48th and Indiana; not long after that, I found my way to Eddie's 1815 Club. He wasn't there that night, but a stalwart crew of West Siders, none of whom I knew yet, were holding down the fort.

That was the beginning, and it only got better from there. Through the years, the opportunity to immerse myself in this music, and to become accepted and embraced as "honorary family" by the blues community—and then to be able to give a little something back through my writing—has been the deepest and most profound blessing of my life. In a very real sense, I owe it all to Eddie Shaw. When he passed away on January 29, 2018, the world lost a legendary bluesman. I lost a touchstone—a man without whose influence my life would have been different in ways I can't even begin to imagine, but infinitely poorer.

I told this story at Eddie's funeral, and I tell it again here. All I can add now is, "Thank you"—and, as our old compatriot Big Walter Horton would have put it—"I mean it from my heart."

Jimmy Johnson

"I Give It My Best—That's the Way It Should Be"

"Watch yourself, Dave. Don't start no shit—you're in the ghetto!"

Jimmy Johnson's eyes glint with steel, but he's grinning and his voice lilts merrily as he extends his hand and ushers me into the front room of his modest one-family home on a tree-lined block in suburban Harvey, Illinois.

Jimmy's everyday demeanor reflects his musical persona—playful, even lighthearted, but toughened with irony-honed combativeness. His high tenor voice is one of the most recognizable in blues. Whether he's singing or talking, it seems to exemplify the ambiguities that define him: Sinewy yet sweet, almost seductively smooth, it textures even the rawest emotions with layers of complexity—joy girded with harshness; sorrow redeemed by hope; anger softened by love. His guitar work is similarly multifaceted—charged with classic Windy City aggression yet fleet and dexterous, bespeaking a lightness of spirit even as he hones its intensity, as if he's firing notes straight into his listener's heart.

That voice and guitar sound are considered something of a miracle among blues lovers, emanating as they do from a man born over ninety years ago in Holly Springs, Mississippi, a man whose career spans nearly seventy years and has taken him from hardscrabble urban jukes to nightclubs, concert halls, and festivals around the world, whose stylistic influences range from gospel, doo-wop, and deep soul through country music and jazz, as well as the venerable Delta-Memphis-Chicago blues lineage. Like most of his contemporaries, he reflects on his life in music, the contributions he's made, and the modest rewards those contributions have earned him, with both hard-earned pride and hard-eyed realism. He's an affable man, always ready with a helping hand for a promising newcomer or warm greeting for a longtime buddy, but it doesn't take much for the toughness to show itself. "I draw a line," he affirms. "I take shit; when I get enough, I got enough, and that's when I draw the line. Then, it's like—what's that word they use? It's on!"

It can be a precarious balance to maintain, but it's a survival tool he acquired out of necessity as a young boy growing up with his brothers Syl and Mac on the family farm outside Holly Springs. "We weren't sharecroppers," Jimmy explains. "We rented the land. I had to go to the field and plow that mule, all by myself—eight years old! Can you imagine that? You're a baby! I had to go to the field and plow. My grandfather taught me. I don't know where my daddy would be; he wouldn't be around. And [when] he would come around—I don't know if I had love for my father or not, 'cause he was very mean. He wasn't what you'd call abusive, but he was mean. And I wasn't happy when I saw him."

Nonetheless, Samuel Thompson[1] had qualities his son could admire: "My daddy, he was a 33rd [Degree] Mason. And he didn't take no shit from nobody. Things he would probably do, [another black man] would get beat up or killed about it. Like if the white man would tell him, 'Now you do this,' he'd say, 'No, I'm not doing it like this. I'm doing it this [other] way.' He would [just] say, 'Yes, Mister Johnny, I'm doing it this way.' 'Okay, Sam.'"

Sam's wife, Erlie, meanwhile, instructed her sons in the darker rules of the crushing, often deadly, Jim Crow survival game—sometimes, you had to go along to get along ("She would just say, 'Well, that's just the way it is.'"). It didn't take long for that to become untenable. As Jimmy remembers, "I just said to myself, I got to get out of this place. There has got to be a better place somewhere in this world."

Sam Thompson played guitar and harmonica, and occasionally he could be talked into making a little music around the house, often with one of Jimmy's uncles accompanying him on the fiddle. Jimmy's own initiation into music came the usual way for a country boy—"Ever since I was around ten years old, I was singin' in church"[2]—and he also found inspiration at school, where he's sneak into the gym during lunch breaks and work out on a piano that was stored there. Inspired by his schoolmate Matt Murphy, who was destined to become one of the most esteemed fretmen in blues, he also began noodling around on the guitar.

When he was sixteen, Jimmy decided to make good on his determination to leave. His first port of call was Memphis, where he worked for a time as a bellhop at the Peabody Hotel. But his primary focus, he says, was finding a way to escape the South entirely—"I had to get away from Jim Crow."

The opportunity came when Jimmy was nineteen. His uncle, the Rev. W. G. Smith, came to Memphis from Chicago to visit; when he went back north, Jimmy went with him. He landed a job as a welder in a sheet metal plant, and he also hooked up with "some other boys from Mississippi" in a gospel group called the United Five. A little later, he began singing with the Golden Jubilaires, who worked out of his uncle's church and whose ranks also included future soul legend Otis Clay.

Jimmy would sometimes slip into that church, which was downstairs from where they lived, and tickle out a few songs on the keyboard. What he really wanted, though, was a guitar, even though his uncle was horrified at the idea.[3] He finally purchased one from Billy Boy Arnold, best known as Bo Diddley's original harp player but also an accomplished guitarist. Jimmy's musical role models, he

Jimmy Johnson, Chicago Blues Festival tribute to Otis Rush, 2016.

remembers, were diverse—everyone from jazz masters Grant Green and Kenny Burrell through Chicago bluesmen like Otis Rush and Magic Sam, who were then in the process of developing the intense, R&B-toughened style that would eventually be dubbed the "West Side" sound by latter-day blues critics.

He began looking around for opportunities to play, but it wasn't easy to get a toehold on the cutthroat Chicago scene. A few people were welcoming: Jimmy remembers Freddie King, for instance, as a generous man who'd allow him on stage even when "I played very bad, you know? But he still would let me come up and mess up."[4] At least once, King's sidemen, bassist Big Mojo Elem and drummer T. J. McNulty, actually walked off in disgust, but King simply picked up Elem's bass and accompanied the newcomer as he struggled through a song or two.

On July 4, 1959, Jimmy played his first actual gig, as a sideman, in a club on the corner of 39th St. and Indiana Ave, but apparently he still wasn't ready—he was fired after a single night. As if that wasn't bad enough, the man who'd been hired to replace him then asked to borrow his amplifier! Such humiliations were part of the dues, though, and Jimmy toughed them out. He began latching onto other sideman jobs on the South Side circuit, and he also took guitar lessons from Reginald Boyd, a highly respected guitarist and teacher. A little later, when he'd gotten his own chops more in order, he went on the road with Earl Hooker, a masterful guitar player but a less than reliable band leader—at one point, during a sojourn through Missouri, Hooker left town while Jimmy was still asleep in the motel, and Jimmy had to pick cotton for a few days to earn carfare back home.

As Jimmy remembers it, he quit his day job as a combination Class A welder not long after he began gigging around town. He formed his own band about a year and a half after that.[5] Then as now, club audiences demanded entertainers with diverse, crowd-pleasing repertoires; with his longtime admiration for jazz and pop artists, Jimmy found it easy to accommodate them, covering hits by popular R&B and soul artists of the day. Jimmy has said that he was also the first leader on the local circuit to include two horns in his band.[6]

For a long time, in fact, Jimmy wasn't considered a "blues" man at all—even less so when he ventured out to perform in the better-paying white clubs on the North Side and in the suburbs. "I wasn't playing blues," he affirms. "You had [to] learn how to play some of that white-boy music. We learned 'Hang On Sloopy,' a whole lotta stuff you had to play. We were playing Top 40. Back then, I don't think you could've got away with playing blues; they wouldn't have hired me to play blues."

It took a different kind of resolve, though, to negotiate the racial minefields that were still strewn across the landscape, even in an allegedly desegregated northern city like Chicago. Maybe a grown man didn't have to address a sixteen-year-old white boy as "Mister" anymore, as Jimmy had in Mississippi, but in other ways freedom—or at least equality—could seem as remote as ever:

> Here's what used to happen. Me, Chuck Smith, Singing Sam [Chatmon], [and] Matt Murphy was with one of the groups called the Sparks; it was a bunch of us playing in the white clubs. When you get this gig, they would tell you, "You can't socialize." You stayed in the dressing room. You accept it or you don't accept it." They had some in [suburban] Calumet City they told me about, where you played behind a curtain.[7]

By about 1967, Jimmy had decided that being a bandleader was more trouble than it was worth. For one thing, the racial tensions in some of the white clubs had begun to roil to the surface in ways that recalled the bad old days down South. Musicians, tired of the humiliation, began to push back against the rules prohibiting them from socializing, and it didn't take long for things to turn ugly:

> These cats started talking with these white women and dancing with 'em. Singing Sam, he got beat up, and I remember another one got beat up. And I remember one cat got killed. They wiped 'em out of the clubs. You couldn't play in 'em no more. Now all we got is these little black clubs. And [then] you got these big spinners, start spinning records, they don't need a band no more. So that's what killed us. Now there was no place to play.

Jimmy had established a reputation as a versatile guitarist, though, and he had little trouble landing gigs accompanying vocalists, both in town and on the road. He remembers working with Tyrone Davis, Otis Clay, Ruby Andrews, Walter Jackson, Denise LaSalle, Bobby Rush, and Cicero Blake, among others. He might still sing a few songs over the course of a show, but his primary job now was to make the star sound good—a task at which he excelled.

Nonetheless, he harbored dreams of becoming a recording artist himself. His first opportunity had arisen back in 1960, when Chicago-based drummer Jump Jackson, who was working with Willie Dixon to organize the American Folk Blues Festival tours for German promoters Fritz Rau and Horst Lippman, compiled an audition tape of ten Chicago blues artists and sent it to Europe. One of the tracks was "Long About Midnight," credited to "Jimmy Thompson." As it happened, Jimmy didn't participate on those now-legendary tours, which helped fuel the '60s-era blues "revival,"[8] but he was assured that the recordings would be released as an anthology and that he'd get paid. That never happened either, although copies of the tape have circulated among collectors over the years.

In about 1968, he recorded his first 45 under his own name[9] on the Stuff label out of Chicago, a two-sided instrumental titled "Get It" / "Work Your Thing," credited to Jimmie [*sic*] Johnson & the Lucky Hearts; Jimmy's string-bending leads showed the influence of his erstwhile patron, Freddie King. He also cut at least one more Stuff 45, another two-sider, "Let's Get a Line (Pts. 1 and 2)," patterned after the style of James Brown. But it was quickly snatched up by a different label, retitled "(Funky) Four Corners," and credited to JerryO, a Chicago-based vocalist (née Jerry Murray) who'd had a few hits as half of the duo Tom and Jerrio[10] (with Robert "Tommy Dark" Tharp). JerryO's Archie Bell–like spoken imprecations, as well as backing vocals intoning the new title, were laid over the original instrumental track for the new version. A close listen to the original release suggests that JerryO might have contributed the spoken lead vocals to that one, too.

Jimmy also lost control of his next recording, the soul-boogaloo "Sock It to Me (Pts. 1 and 2)." In 1968, when "Sock It to Me "was released, he was working with a show band called the Deacons; among the artists they backed up was Jimmy's brother Syl, who by that time had scored several chart hits, including the similarly titled "Come On Sock It to Me" in 1967. Syl released the new "Sock It to Me" on his Shama label, but he credited it to the Deacons instead of Jimmy himself, a slight that stung even harder when the record reached No. 24 on the R&B charts. ("One thing I never did was hold a grudge," Jimmy says today, although he admits that things were pretty tense between him and Syl for a while.[11] For that matter, when the earlier JerryO record came out, he says, he "carried my .38 for many days, looking for [the producer]" before he finally cooled down. He ran into JerryO himself years later, and they were able to laugh about it by then.)

Meanwhile, Jimmy maintained his career as a first-call sideman. It was a tough way to make a living, though—even when he hit the road with a name act, the pay was usually meager and the accommodations often less than that. On one tour, he recalls, "I got in the [hotel] bed, and I felt something crawling, and I looked—man, there's bedbugs. So I got up, I put my clothes on, and I walked around in the town half of the night." Meanwhile, as deep soul morphed into funk and eventually disco, opportunities closer to home shrank as well. "That's when soul music was goin' really to the dogs [even in black clubs]," he has said. "It used to be where you could play that kind of music and make money. But that faded away."[12]

It all became too much for Jimmy, a family man who'd never really felt comfortable with the so-called "blues life" in the first place ("It was very hard for me to deal with drunks, and I'm the only one in the band that's sober, and they're drunk, and I just had to drink to deal with 'em. I had to do that, and I only did that about a year or two. I haven't touched no drink since then"). He'd gotten married back in 1954; he met his wife, Sherry Ewing, "in a club," as he remembers. "She was seventeen; she and her sister came in. She had on a blue dress. She looked older than seventeen. When I looked at her, she was the prettiest thing I'd ever saw. She liked me, and we liked each other."

It was a brash move, to say the least, to get involved with a white woman in those days, but Jimmy says the couple never looked back after they realized they were in love: "Some of her people was real cool, some wasn't," he said. "We didn't worry about it." That doesn't mean, though, that it was easy: "We got it from both black and white. We always carried guns; I did and she did, too, because we knew we was going to have a problem.

"So we had three little children, and man, I gotta take care of my little children; I can't mess with this music. I had been on the road with quite a few people, but it was getting to be too hard. They didn't half pay you. [So I] put my guitar in the closet."

Jimmy made a living for a few years as a cab driver, gigging now and then when the opportunity and the money were right, but it wasn't until the mid-'70s that he got back into music on anything approaching a full-time basis. By this time, the white blues "revival" was in full swing. "This is when I had my mind directed toward the blues," Jimmy has said, adding that "I already knew how to play [blues], it was just a matter of getting the feel of it."[13] On some occasions, this meant digging into earlier styles he hadn't played for years, if ever—he remembers dates with acoustic guitarist/mandolinist Johnny Young and the elemental West Side drummer/singer "Winehead" Willie Williams—but if that's what the new fans wanted, that's what he'd give them. The irony was inescapable: Jimmy Johnson, whose earlier gigs in white clubs had required that he stay as far from blues as possible, had made a living in black venues playing, not blues, but what was then known as R&B or soul. Now, a new white audience was about to embrace him as "authentic" for playing music he hadn't played for black folks in decades, if ever (and which a lot of younger black listeners would now probably have derided as passé).

This new circuit wasn't quite the postracial promised land some of its more idealistic habitués imagined, either:

> Now [one well-known North Side club owner], he didn't like black people, period. Probably still don't. I would go by there on a Saturday night, and he'd have an all-white band up there, half of 'em didn't really play that well, and he'd have ten people. One weekend he decided to hire Otis Rush. He picked the top dog! And the place was just sold out for the whole three nights, or whatever it was.
>
> After that, if you go in [his] place with a white musician in your band, he didn't like it: "Oh, no, Jimmy—no, no, no, no. Gotta have all black musicians." Oh, well. That's just the way life is. The dollar! The dollar will override that prejudice.

Jimmy began working steadily again, often alongside Jimmy Dawkins, a forceful guitarist with an intense, brooding onstage presence and a lyric sensibility to match, and Otis Rush himself, another of the architects of the emotionally fervid "West Side" sound (Jimmy appears on Rush's highly acclaimed *So Many Roads*, recorded live in Tokyo in 1975 and released on Delmark three years later).

Despite this spate of activity, and despite his willingness to modify his sound to fit the demands of these newly minted aficionados bent on "keeping the blues alive" as they saw fit, Jimmy says that labels catering to this audience were leery of him, at least at first. Even when he covered blues standards, he brought fresh harmonic and chordal ideas to them ("I'd learned some theory [from Reginald Boyd]," he asserts, "and you listen to a lot of my records, you hear me play a chord in there—no other blues player will play it. Because they don't really understand it. But I know it's gonna fit, and it works"). His vocals—emotive, yet leavened with an almost milky sweetness—were a blend of rawness and urbanity; his lyrics reflected a keen-minded modernist sensibility, both in his own compositions and his reworkings of others' hits. When he sang "Tobacco Road," for instance, he'd emphasize the song's timeliness by inserting a reference to a notorious Chicago housing project.

In other words, Jimmy avoided cliché. Even at its most direct, his music demanded full listener engagement—no "blooze-and-boogie" boilerplate for him, no stereotypical "cryin'-in-my-whiskey" bathos. As a result, he maintains, labels like Delmark and Alligator initially found him "too sophisticated. They didn't want my music; they said I wasn't playing no blues. [I told them], 'Man, don't you know I know how to play blues?' But anyway—so much for that."

If he was getting resistance at home, though, others were listening and liking what they heard. In 1975, the French MCM label came to Chicago and initiated a series of live recordings at Ma Bea's, a neighborhood club on West Madison Street. (The postwar style, although it hadn't been a major force in mainstream black music for decades, retained a small but enthusiastic fan base, consisting mostly of older working-class people with strong Southern roots, on the South and West Sides.) The result was the label's *Direct from Chicago* series, which included *Ma Bea's Rock*, cofeaturing Jimmy and guitarist/vocalist Luther "Guitar Jr." Johnson (no relation—best known for his '70s-era tenure with Muddy Waters), accompanied by Dawkins and his band. Another album cut at Ma Bea's, Dawkins's *I Want to Know*, features Jimmy on second guitar, as does Dawkins's *Blisterstring*, released on Delmark in 1976.

A few years after *Ma Bea's Rock*, MCM returned to the West Side and recorded a full Jimmy Johnson album, *Tobacco Road*, this time with Jimmy fronting his own working band, at a roughshod juke on Pulaski Road called the Golden Slipper. None of the MCM disks lived up to Jimmy's standards ("a lot of people don't like good quality"[14]), but they helped further his reputation and his career. He toured Europe in 1978 and again the following year; meanwhile, back home, some of the label owners who'd doubted him in the past finally began to show an interest ("After I did this thing on the French label, and they kept watching me . . . they said, 'Yeah, he'll play the blues'"[15]). In 1978 he made his first appearance on Alligator, contributing four tracks to the anthology *Living Chicago Blues, Vol. 1*. From there he went to Delmark, where he released *Johnson's Whacks* (1979) and *North/South* (1982). *Heap See*, which he recorded in 1983 for the French Blue Phoenix label, was reissued on Alligator in 1985 as *Bar Room Preacher*.

With the marketing power of labels like Delmark and Alligator behind him, along with enthusiastic press notices and a burgeoning touring schedule, the '80s were a fertile period as Jimmy cultivated his reputation and his success as both a recording artist and a charismatic, musically challenging, live performer. Then, early in the morning on Friday, December 2, 1988, it all came crashing down.

Jimmy was driving. They were heading north on U.S. Highway 65, coming out of Indianapolis on their way to Ypsilanti, Michigan. A few miles south of Lowell, Indiana ("at the 238 mile marker," Jimmy remembers), he lost control of the van; it veered off the road and crashed. Bassist Larry Exum and keyboardist James St. John (née Bryant) were killed; Jimmy himself suffered what were described as "minor internal injuries and burns on his hands."[16] The other musicians, guitarist Larry Burton and drummer Fred Grady, escaped serious injury.

"I had drove all [the previous] day," Jimmy remembers, "played that night, and got back in the car."

> We should've gotten a room, stayed that night and got up that next morning and went to Ypsilanti. But I'm gonna drive all the way, 'cause I had been doing it, oh, man, for many years. And it caught up to me. That was one of the mistakes I made. I didn't have to do that, but I didn't want to pay for that hotel in Indianapolis. "No, we can make it. No, we can make it."
>
> It was about 2 or 2:30 at night; we probably had another five or six hours to drive. 'Cause I know how to stay awake driving—pat on my legs and sing—and I was patting on my leg and singing, and still dozed. I just dozed at the wrong time, going into a curve, and went straight off the road.

As he related this story, Jimmy's voice remained steady and his gaze never wavered. But the anguish remains fresh. "It was tough to live with," he said softly, "and it ain't easy yet."

> What's really tough—I had to quit trying to use it—is *If! If! If! If! If!* Them *ifs.* I was wishing I could move to an island where didn't nobody know me, 'cause what used to bother me most is when I'd see people, and they'd come up and [say], "Man, I heard about the accident, and I'm so sorry . . ." That's what used to bother me. It was something [I did] that was stupid; I was trying to forget it—you cannot forget it. You have to learn how to live with it. And it was hard for me to get that.

He says he considered getting out of music entirely, but then, "What else am I gonna do? Because I'd have to make a living, and I was—what? Fifty-some years old?[17] It's hard to go tryin' to find a job."

Over the next few years, Jimmy gradually regained his equilibrium, even as his recording activity slowed. He had two new releases in the '90s: *I'm a Jockey* (Verve) in 1994, and *Every Road Ends Somewhere* (Ruf) in 1999. More recently, the new millennium has seen a few reissues, including the original *Heap See* (Black & Blue) and *Ma Bea's Rock* (Storyville), the old MCM live recording. *Pepper's Hangout*, produced in 1977 by Ralph Bass (at a session vividly described by Peter Guralnick in *Lost Highway*[18]), which was originally released on Red Lightnin' in 1984 as part of that label's notorious *I Didn't Give a Damn if Whites Bought It!* series, appeared in 2000 on Delmark with several previously unreleased tracks added. The only fresh material has been *Two Johnsons Are Better than One* (Evidence), Jimmy's long-awaited collaboration with his brother Syl, issued on Evangeline in 2001 and on Evidence the following year.

Jimmy Johnson, Buddy Guy's
Legends, Chicago, 2017.

He also cut down his performance schedule as the road became more wearying
(and, no doubt, more haunted by ghosts and grief in the wake of the accident).
His patience, meanwhile, never exactly robust, became shorter. He'd always
maintained high standards—both musically and personally—and he expected
his sidemen to do the same. Inevitably, that led to conflict. "I don't do tours in
the United States no more," he asserts. "I quit in 2004."

It gets very hard, and dealing with musicians was very crazy. If I would've had some
really cool cats, like the cats I go to France and play with, I probably would still do it.
But man, them cats I used to deal with—God almighty! Smoked a lot of weed—all
them cats, they're like children. And a bunch of them cats was women-crazy. Man,
I didn't go to this gig to get no woman! And some of them places, you know who
we're playing for—Caucasian people. Some of them places, they don't want that.

And you go there, and you see a woman over there by herself, and you go over and hit on her, it's the bartender's wife or old lady. Man, they ain't gonna like that. Now I'm gonna get these calls from the agent, "Jimmy, you got to tell your musicians. . . ." I tell 'em: "You ain't in Chicago!" But I just finally got tired—I'm not doing it no more.

That's basically when I started doing solo; I do a lot of gigs solo. I hadn't touched the keyboard since back in high school, because back then you couldn't carry keyboards around. The first one I had was a Wurlitzer; I never liked the sound of the Fender Rhodes. And then they came out with the synthesizers—get a piano sound almost like a real piano, organ sound almost like a real organ—that's when I decided to take it on a gig.

When he's not playing a solo keyboard set or a duet with another guitarist, he often appears as a featured guest with Dave Specter's band. Specter is an accomplished Chicago-based fretman who often hires veteran vocalists and/or guitarists to join him on his shows. (A sample of his and Jimmy's work together can be found on the 2008 Delmark DVD *Dave Specter: Live in Chicago*, which also features vocalists Sharon Lewis and Tad Robinson.)

The shows with Specter, as well as Jimmy's duo appearances with guitarists such as Leo Charles and Giba Byblos, raise yet another issue that has concerned him for a long time—and it's an issue that seems to have little resolution, even for a man with Jimmy's pride and determination. He's seen the demographic changes that have altered the blues world since the 1960s, and while he respects any musician with taste and ability (Specter, Charles, and Byblos definitely count among that number), he also feels deeply that the increasing incursion of white artists into the blues—especially on well-paying festival gigs and at nationally recognized blues awards ceremonies—represents just the latest in the series of race-driven insults he's had to endure since his Southern childhood ("I probably wouldn't've lived if I'd stayed there; I might've taken a few with me, but I probably wouldn't have lived"), and which his people, of course, have been struggling against ever since they've been in America.

The Blues Music Awards in Memphis, formerly the W. C. Handy Awards,[19] are a case in point:

> You know who W. C. Handy was, right? So why did they include white boys in that? This is ours! And look at all the shit that we aren't included in.
>
> That's one of the reasons I didn't play the [Chicago Blues] Festival for a long time. They bring Stevie Ray Vaughan in—he's an upstart. They pay him $15,000—they was paying me $1,000. I don't think that's fair. They said, "A thousand dollars, take it or leave it." I said, "Well, I just left it."

When he really warms up to his topic, Jimmy won't even give whites credit for being savvy enough to pull off cultural appropriation. "They ain't took nothing from us," he avers, "'cause they can't handle it!"

> Look, only one out of all I ever heard came very close—Stevie Ray Vaughan. Other than that, they ain't took nothing, 'cause they can't sing it, and they can't play it. Not the way we play it. Totally, it's in another world. And they have tried to.
>
> Now I tell you what they did steal from us, was like, what we call rock & roll, what they categorized and called it rock & roll. When we used to do it, they called it rhythm & blues. But they called it rock & roll so they could say Elvis Presley was the king of rock & roll. And you probably know, when he first came out, you know what's that stuff he was doing? I never heard [the term] "rock & roll" until after Elvis; but I do know that the songs he was doing, a lot of white people didn't know where he got them songs from. He did "Mean Ol' Frisco," "That's All Right, Mama"—that's Arthur "Big Boy" Crudup—and [Big Mama Thornton's]"Hound Dog" . . . but you know, I daresay most of the white people didn't know where he got them songs from.[20]

Nonetheless, he refuses to let negativity consume him. As his collaborations with Specter demonstrate, as well as his duo appearances with guitarists such as Charles and Byblos, he has the seasoned musician's ability to look past superficial (and not-so-superficial) considerations when the music itself is at issue. He also still has plenty of new ideas—after all these years, it's almost impossible to stop them from coming—and he's more than willing to record again, but the conditions have to be right. *Two Johnsons Are Better than One*, despite the publicity it garnered, didn't turn out as he'd hoped. (He blames a contentious studio atmosphere that developed—both he and his brother are famously strong-willed.) Especially frustrating was "I Feel the Pain," a song he wrote about the Middle Passage and its murderous legacy, which is spellbinding in solo performance (he sang it for me, accompanying himself on keyboard, in his home studio when we spoke) but sounds labored, almost forced, on the recorded version.

Then there are the politics—personal and otherwise—of dealing with record labels. Jimmy holds a grudging respect for Alligator's Bruce Iglauer ("You know who really paid me? Bruce. I hurt his feelings so bad one time, I was sorry I said it. I apologized to him later. I said, 'Bruce, you know what? You're the only record company that paid me some of my money.' 'Oh no, Jimmy, I paid you all of your money.'"). Others, though, are a different story. In one case, a label purchased some of his earlier masters and reissued them without his permission or even his knowledge (he discovered the album by accident while browsing in a record store). Legally, they were within their rights—Jimmy didn't own the publishing—but it still rankled him. He confronted the owner, bristling with righteous fury:

> I asked him, "How you gonna put out a record and you didn't even ask me? You don't think I deserve no money? I don't have nothing coming? It's just free?"
>
> "Yeah, but you got your money up front."
>
> "That was a long time ago. I got a hundred dollars! Man, you could-a at least offered me something!"
>
> I looked at this little ol' cripple-ass man—oh, he's younger than me but he's a little old crippled man—I wanted to catch him up in the collar and knock the shit out of him. I looked at him, said, "Man, if I hit this little ol' man one time, he might die." So—"That's okay. 'S'all right. God bless you, man."
>
> That's probably why he's so messed up and sick. 'Cause he's a welch, and then he try to make like he's such an honest guy.

A similar resolve informs Jimmy's aesthetic vision. He's determined to remain true to his values, to create music that will satisfy him, within the constraints of a marketplace still defined, to a significant extent, by the tastes of retro-minded purists. "Sometimes," he concurs, "the diehards, they don't accept what you're doing. It's kind of hard for me to just write, like, a regular blues, because [then] I'm gonna play the same thing that's been played a thousand times."

Although he's obviously a man of great pride, Jimmy eschews any grandiose notions about "keeping the blues alive" or somehow being the last true blues-man standing. He does, though, derive special pleasure from admirers who tell him that after all these years, he still sounds as if he puts his entire heart into everything he does. "I do," he concurs. "I give it my best. That's the way it should be."

> Anytime you play whatever you are playing, somebody's gonna like it or somebody ain't gonna like it. So if you don't really think that's a good idea, what I'm doing, I don't mind if you say it. That don't bother me. You will see it's different—"Oh, I ain't never seen nobody do that before!" Well, I love being different. It's not like Johnny Lee Hooker, it's not like—those are some of my favorite people, Lightnin' Hopkins, Johnny Lee Hooker, Son House, Arthur "Big Boy" Crudup—but I probably couldn't play like them anyway, even if I tried. So I just got my way of doin' it.
>
> I'm like Ol' Blue Eyes—I'm doin' it my way.

Eddy Clearwater

"A Little Bit of Blues, A Little Bit of Rock and Roll"

When historians discuss the link between Chicago blues and the evolution of rock & roll, they usually focus on artists like Chuck Berry and Bo Diddley (and sometimes sidemen such as pianist Lafayette Leake, harmonica player Billy Boy Arnold, and guitarist Jody Williams). It's often forgotten, though, that others who had begun their careers as blues artists, and are still recognized as such, also adapted their styles to the youth-oriented sounds that began to revolutionize popular culture in the early- and mid-'50s.

One of the most significant of these is Eddy Clearwater, whose early singles in the 1950s and '60s updated the Chicago blues sound with rock & roll urgency and are now collectors' items. Since then he has continued to record, tour, and expand his international reputation as one of Chicago's most colorful and imaginative blues innovators. As evidenced by his most recent release, 2014's *Soul Funky*, on his own Cleartone imprint, Eddy's creativity and chops remain focused and powerful; although he has cut back on his touring schedule, he continues to perform when the occasion is right and he's able to give his best.

In recent years, he's also begun to receive at least some of the recognition due him. In 2001, the Memphis-based Blues Foundation named him Contemporary Blues Male Artist of the Year at their annual Blues Music Awards (then the W. C. Handy Awards); three years later, his album *Rock 'N' Roll City*, on the Rounder subsidiary Bullseye Blues (featuring the flamboyant garage/surf/roots-rock aggregation Los Straitjackets), garnered a Grammy nomination. In 2008, along with his cousin Carey Bell, Willie King, Jesse Fortune, and gospel singer Brother Joe May, he was honored with a historic Mississippi Blues Trail marker in Macon, Mississippi, celebrating the blues legacy of the state's Black Prairie region; more recently, in August 2015, the Jus' Blues Music Foundation presented him with their Lifetime Bluesman Award, named in honor of the late Little Milton, at their annual meeting in Tunica, Mississippi. The following year he was inducted into the Blues Hall of Fame in Memphis, in a ceremony held in conjunction with the 37th Blues Music Awards.

Eddy Clearwater was born Edward Harrington in Macon, Mississippi, in 1935, and in retrospect it seems as if he was destined to play "fusion" music almost from the beginning. As he related to *Living Blues* magazine's D. Thomas Moon in 1996, some of the earliest musical sounds he heard were the field hollers of farmworkers toiling in the cotton fields around Macon; he was also exposed to hymns, spirituals, and gospel music at a young age, both in church and on records. As he grew up, he listened to the radio and heard country artists such as Red Foley, Hank Williams, and Chet Atkins; he also played blues records by the likes of John Lee Hooker and Muddy Waters as well as more sophisticated stylists such as Louis Jordan and Charles Brown (with Johnny Moore on guitar). His uncle, the Rev. Houston H. Harrington, dreamed of owning a record label someday, and he had acquired a miniature disc-cutter ("You'd just put a disc on there and you brushed it, like making a demo or something") on which young Eddy made "little plastic vinyl discs for him." By his early teens, when Eddy and his family moved to Birmingham, Alabama, he had already acquired a guitar of his own. His earliest public performances consisted of playing for various gospel groups; his family disapproved of the blues (or "reels," as blues and other secular songs were called), especially if someone tried to play or listen to them on a Sunday.[1]

In 1950, in response to a letter from his uncle, who'd moved to Chicago several years earlier, Eddy Harrington migrated north. Again, he initiated his musical activities in gospel, but by 1953 or so he'd landed his first professional club gig in a band led by harpist Little Mack Simmons. Not long after that, he formed a trio called The Cutaways (named for his gold-colored cutaway Gibson ES-295 guitar). Finally, in 1958, he recorded his debut, "Boogie Woogie Baby" b/w "Hill Billy Blues" for his uncle's recently inaugurated label, Atomic-H. By this time, he'd abandoned his earlier stage moniker, "Guitar Eddy," in favor of the more colorful "Clear Waters," which he'd been given by drummer/booking agent Jump Jackson, who apparently felt that the pun on "Muddy Waters" would be a selling point.

Eddy has said that he was rocking the blues almost from the beginning, and his first two recorded outings certainly back up that claim. He cites proto-rockers like Fats Domino as early favorites, along with the country and gospel musicians he'd been listening to for years. In fact, it's likely that his sound actually became bluesier as he traversed the Chicago club circuit and came into contact with established figures like Howlin' Wolf, Muddy Waters, Earl Hooker, Jimmy Reed, and Elmore James. Nonetheless, it was younger bluesmen like Magic Sam, with their eyes and ears to the future, who really caught his attention. "[Magic Sam] had that touch," he remembers. "He would do stuff that had a tinge of rock & roll, country, and soul—'21 Days in Jail,' that was more like a rock & roll-ish type of thing, rockabilly. That's one of the things that drew me closer to Magic Sam, because he was doing the kind of stuff that I had in my head to do."

> My first encounter of Chuck Berry, I was driving down Michigan Avenue, now it's called King Drive [actually, Martin Luther King Jr. Drive used to be South Park Way], and had my little radio on. Al Benson was the disk jockey [on WGES]; all of a sudden, a record came on the radio: "Oh, baby doll, when bells ring out the summer breeze / oh baby doll, will it end for you and me / We'll sing our old Alma Mater / and think of things that used to be . . ." And I said, "Who is that?" 'Cause I liked the guitar sound, I liked what he was singing, his diction and the way his words coincided with his music. And then when the record finished, Al Benson said, "That's Chuck Berry," and I said, "Oh, I got to pay attention to that name."

Chuck Berry's "Oh Baby Doll" was a hit in 1957; his iconic "Maybellene" had debuted in 1955, two years earlier. It would appear, then, that Eddy, despite his professed enthusiasm for the popular music of the day, was a bit late to pick up on Berry. But once initiated, he was hooked. Both sides of his 1958 Atomic-H debut show the Berry influence, although Eddy has also said he had jump-blues stylists like Louis Jordan in mind when he wrote "Boogie Woogie Baby."

In 1960, still billed as "Clear Waters," he released "I Don't Know Why" b/w "A Minor Cha-Cha," again on Atomic-H. Stylistically, these sides were different from their predecessors. "I Don't Know Why" was a 6/8 ballad laced with strong country and doo-wop flavorings, uplifted by a churchy piano; the instrumental "A Minor Cha-Cha," meanwhile, was easily Eddy's bluesiest outing thus far. Its minor-key structure and rhumba rhythm, as well as Eddy's across-the-strings flatpick scrapes, showed the influence of Otis Rush, whose "All Your Love (I Miss Loving)" had been issued on Cobra the previous year. "I like the minor blues a lot," he affirms today. "I've always been a big fan of minor blues, mainly like Otis Rush. It's not that common; not that many guitarists—Jimmy [Johnson], he's a

Eddy Clearwater, Broad
Street Blues Festival,
Griffith, Indiana, 2017.

killer with that. I'm working on one now, called 'Signifying Blues.' It's minor-key, all the way."

His burgeoning local celebrity soon landed him a slot on the local TV show *Bandstand Matinee*, an American Bandstand spin-off that aired on WGN-TV. Performing opportunities expanded, as well. Eddy and his wife Earline co-owned a storefront business—he, as proprietor of Clearwater's Record Shop; she, as a beautician in the adjoining space—and their shop wasn't far from a South Side club called the L&D Lounge. Eddy had one of his steadiest early club gigs there, running from Fridays through Sundays.

His next recordings were the Berry-esque "Cool Water" and the ballad "Baby Please," both produced by Jump Jackson and released on Jackson's LaSalle imprint. (Two other LaSalle sides, "Ain't That a Shame" and "Dancin' Time," remained unissued until the Dutch Redita label put them out on an unauthorized compilation years later.) Perhaps the most interesting thing about these records is the backup band—a Hispanic group out of Texas called Mando and the Chili Peppers, led by bassist Armando (or possibly "Amando") Almendarez. Eddy met them through their saxophonist, Chuck Smith, who recommended him as a fill-in when Almendarez got sick and couldn't make the gig at a club called the Wagon Wheel. After Eddy went over well there, the band decided to keep him on; they were one of the few integrated acts ("a bunch of Mexicans and two blacks—Chuck Smith and myself," as Eddy later told Moon[2]) working at the time.

He also hooked up with vocalist Eddy Bell, a renegade from Chicago's thriving polka scene (his actual surname was Blazonczyk) who'd remade himself into a rocker and formed Eddy Bell & the Bel-Aires. Eddy joined the Bel-Aires for gigs in Chicago's western suburbs; that association led him to the Mercury label, where he played on Bell's singles, "Knock, Knock, Knock (Knocking on My Door)" and "Hi Yo Silver (The Masked Man)," as well as on an outing called "Johnny B. Goode in Hollywood" (released on producer Lenny LaCour's Lucky Four logo), which featured Eddy on yet another Berry-styled guitar solo. Meanwhile, his own output on Federal—"I Was Gone" b/w "Twist Like This" and "A Real Good Time" b/w "Hey Bernardine," both released under the name Eddie [*sic*] Clearwater—also remained strictly in the Berry mold. The Federal sides didn't make much commercial noise, though, and Eddy continued to support himself mostly by gigging around the Chicago area. He was already establishing a reputation as a showman, but to make those gigs even more exciting, Eddy Bell designed a leopard-skin Telecaster for him, which for a time was one of his most recognizable trademarks.

From today's perspective, it might be difficult to imagine how radical it was for an African American artist to be performing, in integrated bands, in predominantly white clubs in Chicago at that time:

> Before [other blues artists] started to venture out into the suburbs, the North Side of Chicago, suburbs like Stone Park, Melrose Park, and all the way out west—I was doing it. I would work five and six days a week, sometimes seven, with a Sunday matinee. They say, "He didn't play blues; he plays a rock & roll song like Chuck Berry and Fats Domino, little Richard stuff." So the club would book me because they knew I had that variety, what the kids wanted at that time, the white kids. As long as the kids come and see you, they would keep you booked there—two or three months at a time.

Eddy even told writer/historian Bill Dahl that he worked "a lot of hillbilly bars, playing country and rockabilly"[3]—virtually unheard-of then, and not very common now.

His showmanship was yet another asset. "I've always had that kind of an edge," he says, "to want to give an appearance, along with the music. I wanted to give the people some flash, to let 'em see there's more to the music than 'just' the music. You come to see an Eddy Clearwater show, you see not only the music, but a show." (When he finally got to share a bill with Chuck Berry in 1967 at a suburban club called the Manor Lounge, Chuck told him, "Oh, my God! I thought I was looking in the mirror!"[4])

One thing he did not attain during these years, though, was commercial success as a recording artist. Two sides he released on the Chicago-based U.S.A. label in the mid-'60s disappeared without a trace. In 1969 or so, his old cohort Eddy Bell released another Clearwater single, "Doin' the Model" (a James Brown–styled funk workout) b/w "I Don't Know Why" (a different song from his earlier Atomic-H release) on Bell's Versa imprint. Again, though, sales were meager. "Doin' the Model" was also issued on Atomic-H, which was still in operation.

Finally, in the mid-'70s, the blues "rediscovery" began to find its way to Eddy Clearwater's door. Keyboardist Bob Riedy, who'd helped spearhead Chicago's North Side blues boom by booking postwar blues artists to front his band in various clubs, included him on a couple of tracks on the Bob Riedy Blues Band's 1974 LP *Just Off Halsted*, released on Flying Fish. By this time, Eddy had also established his own Cleartone label, on which he issued two singles, "True Love" and "Lonely Nights," in 1975.

By this time, "rediscovered" American blues artists had become big business in Europe, and the French MCM label decided to make a sojourn to Chicago to record blues performances by local artists on their own turf, so to speak, in African American neighborhood clubs. One of these, titled *Black Night (Live)*, recorded at Ma Bea's Lounge on the West Side, featured Eddy; it was a raw, bluesy set, not necessarily representative of a typical Clearwater performance but apparently just what his new overseas admirers (and many like-minded Americans) wanted from an "authentic" Chicago bluesman. In 1978, promoter George Wein included Eddy on a blues package tour that included dates in France, England, Spain, Sweden, and Switzerland. The headliners were Buddy Guy and Junior Wells; the bill also included Jimmy Johnson, Hubert Sumlin, Dave Myers, and vocalist Andrew "Big Voice" Odom.

There were a few more sessions during those years—one recorded by Ralph Bass, eventually released on Red Lightnin' in 1984 as part of their *I Didn't Give a Damn if Whites Bought It* series (named for a quote attributed to Bass in the 1940s) and later reissued on Delmark; another recorded live at the Kingston Mines, a popular North Side blues club, which wasn't released at the time but has since appeared on several collectors' imprints. In 1978, Eddy expanded his activities into self-production with a series of sessions that resulted in an LP, originally intended for release on Cleartone, that eventually came out on the British Charly label as *Two Times Nine* (sometimes rendered as *2 x 9*). It's been reissued several times since then. Clearly aiming for his new audience, he included topical material ("The World Is in a Bad Situation;" the slow-grinding, minor-key "Came Up the Hard Way;" a remake of "Chicago Daily Blues" from the Ma Bea's recording), along with the Berry-infused title tune and the jauntily rocking "A Little Bit of Blues, A Little Bit of Rock and Roll"—a catchphrase he'd originally envisioned as the album title and which could serve as his manifesto.

His next recording opportunity arose from his longtime friendship with Jim O'Neal, cofounder (and, at the time, coeditor) of *Living Blues* magazine, who had recently launched his own Rooster Blues label. The two had known each other for at least a decade—O'Neal had written a cover story on Eddy for the magazine in 1972, and it was through O'Neal that Eddy rediscovered some long-lost relatives (and eventual musical compatriots):

> Jim O'Neal discovered the fact that [harmonica ace] Carey Bell and myself were cousins. He's the one that brought that fact to light, because I had never met Carey; we were from the same hometown—Macon, Mississippi. Jim always supported my ideas in music, and then when he started *Living Blues* magazine, he wrote a story about me, so that helped my career a whole lot; it helped me get out of just the Chicago area.
>
> I had been to Europe. I came back, and I had to work at the Kingston Mines [then on Lincoln Avenue] that night. Jim called me at home, he said, "I'd like come down to the club and talk to you tonight about making an album. Would you be interested?" I said, "Yeah!" When I came to work that night at the Mines, I drove up, and Jim O'Neal was standing in front of the club waiting for me to arrive. So I got out of the car, he talked to me, and we set up a date. That's when we did *The Chief* [in 1980].

The cover photo of *The Chief*—Rooster Blues' first release—portrayed Eddy astride a horse, hoisting his guitar and bedecked in the Native American headdress that had been his onstage trademark for several years by then. The story behind that headdress exemplifies both his showman's savvy and his generosity of spirit. "I was working at a club," he recalls. "The Trieste Lounge, in Westmont, right by where Muddy used to live. This lady, Pat Sweet, she was the head bartender. She invited the band and myself to a party one night after the club closed.

When we walked in the front door, in the vestibule in the den, she had this really pretty headdress hanging on the wall."

So I said, "That's a beautiful piece." She said, "Thank you." And I expressed, I said, "I'd like to have that to wear for my stage appearance; I'd like to buy it from you, if you wouldn't mind selling it to me." She said, "Well, I'm sorry, I can't sell it to you because it belonged to my deceased husband." And so I said, "Okay"—I accepted that.

But from time to time at the club, after that, I kept mentioning it. I said, "I really would like that piece for my stage appearance, because it's fantastic." So she said, "I'll tell you what. I won't sell it to you, but I'll give it to you as a good luck charm, providing you never part with it." So we shook hands. I said, "You have a deal." And as we speak, it's downstairs now, in my archives. I bought others that I wear on stage, but the one I got from her—I kept it.

Occasionally, he says, people, including some Native Americans, have questioned his use of the prop. "Well, I'm part Indian," he tells them, "so I'm not making a mockery of anything; it's part of my heritage [too]. My grandmother's [picture] on the wall right over there, she's part Cherokee, almost full-blood Cherokee. So I'm one of them, in a way of speaking."

The Chief, followed by a reissue of *Two Times Nine* on New Rose the following year, further enhanced his international reputation. In 1986, he recorded *Flim Doozie*, his follow-up to *The Chief* on Rooster Blues; *Real Good Time: Live!* appeared on Rooster Blues in 1990. Other labels—including Black and Blue, Evidence, Blind Pig, ROIR (a belated 1992 release of his late '70s Kingston Mines recording), Delmark, and others—also released material on him.

Eddy had always been an entrepreneur at heart—he'd co-owned a business with his first wife; he'd formed his own label; by the mid-'90s he was producing or coproducing a lot of his own material—and in 1999, he took it one step further. He and his wife Renee, whom he'd met in 1993 and married a few years later, purchased a building on Milwaukee Avenue in Chicago's Wicker Park neighborhood and opened a nightclub, Eddy Clearwater's Reservation Blues. A well-appointed establishment with French doors, brick walls, hardwood floors, and stained-glass artwork (much of it crafted by Renee's daughter, Heather Greenman), and with a menu that featured spicy Southwestern cuisine, it fit perfectly in the rapidly gentrifying community. Although Reservation Blues booked mostly local artists, occasionally an act from out of town, such as Johnny Rawls or Eddy's old friend Bobby Rush, also appeared there. Eventually, though, the dual responsibilities of running a nightclub and maintaining a musician's itinerary proved incompatible, and Eddy went back to being a full-time bluesman.

The Chief: Eddy Clearwater,
Broad Street Blues Festival,
Griffith, Indiana, 2017.

Finally, in 2008, he signed with a major blues label. "I had known [Alligator Records'] Bruce [Iglauer] for a long time," he relates. "I've always been very fond of Bruce, the work that he does; we just never got together for some reason. But after we did [the LP that became] *West Side Strut*—I produced it, myself and Ronnie Baker Brooks—I decided to take it to Bruce. He listened to it, and in a couple days he called back. He talked to Renee; he said, 'Renee, I got an album your husband did. It's a beautiful album; I'm going to put this out.' That's how I got a contract with Alligator."

His next release, 2014's *Soul Funky*, recorded live at a club called SPACE in the suburb of Evanston (owned by guitarist/bandleader Dave Specter), captured him in his latter-day glory as a house-rocking blues showman. Significantly, it also showcased his stylistic versatility and emotional depth—sides of him that occasionally get downplayed by critics. When the mood hit (as on "Lonesome Town" and "Came Up the Hard Way—Root to the Fruit"), he could dig into a chilling minor-key groove that evoked Otis Rush at his most emotionally wracked. The title tune carried echoes of late '60s rock (its intro sounds like a variation on Cream's "Sunshine of Your Love") as well as latter-era hard funk and soul-blues; "Find You a Job" wittily recalled Bo Diddley, "Too Old to Get Married" served as the obligatory Chuck Berry rocker, and there was plenty of straightforward Chicago blues along the way ("A Good Leavin' Alone," for instance, invoked Elmore James). For the most part, Eddy's leathery vocals remained uncompromisingly raw, yet an offering like "Please Accept My Love" showed that he could also still croon a ballad with the tenderness of a streetcorner doo-wopper. The overall impression one got from the album was that of an unbowed bluesman possessed by the spirit of a rock & roll tiger who refuses to be tamed.

And, in fact, that's not a false image. Eddy has high hopes for future projects (he says Iglauer has suggested embarking on another studio recording), and he's equally optimistic about the future of the music he's called his own for over half a century. "I think it's healthy," he asserts, "and I think it's going to escalate from the way it is now—with the Black audience, I hope, because this is our heritage. I hope the Black people give it more thought and say, 'Well, listen—this is our heritage and we're just pushing it out the door and letting someone else just take it over, and not supporting it.'" He cites Chicago guitarist/vocalist Toronzo Cannon, as well as Gary Clark Jr. ("He's doing a whole new type of a thing, but he's representing the blues; that's very important") and Shemekia Copeland ("very versatile—a lot of talent. She's one of the people I like a lot") among the leading lights of the younger blues generation.

Despite the vicissitudes of this "hard way to make an easy living" (the title of a song on his 1996 Bullseye Blues release, *Mean Case of the Blues*), Eddy also insists that even when things were at their leanest (he actually took a day job for a time in the early '70s, assembling guitars at the Harmony Guitar factory in Chicago), he never seriously considered giving up music, and he certainly doesn't want to stop now. "It's been some difficult times," he admits, "but I've always had enough courage to know, when there's a will, there's always a way. You have to be consistent—positive thinking, that's the key to it. You have to think positive, and you have to act on what you think—you can find a way to do it. And that's always been my ambition, to stay put and do what my true conviction is. That's what I put forth."

Coda: "I Wouldn't Lay My Guitar Down"

In his later years, Eddy Clearwater often claimed he wanted to curtail his performance schedule, but the trouper in him wouldn't let him carry that vow too far. When he passed away on June 1, 2018, just two weeks after what turned out to be his final performance, at Buddy Guy's Legends, he was already booked for five additional appearances over the next two months in locations ranging from Chicago to Texas, where he was scheduled to play back-to-back shows in Austin and Dallas that July. "There will never be anyone more humble and grateful for life, and his opportunity to play the blues for you, than Eddy Clearwater," publicist Lynn Orman-Weiss wrote on his website, an encomium that probably encapsulates as well as anything the joy, affirmation, and resolve he brought to his music and his life—both on stage and off—until the very end.

Eddy was laid to rest on June 5; his services were held at Chicago Jewish Funerals in Skokie, where he had lived with his wife Renee for over twenty years. (His love for his adopted hometown was such that he wrote a paean to it—"Skokie Is a First Class Town"—and he had been selected to be Grand Marshall for the village's 2018 Fourth of July parade.) Cantor Howard Friedland officiated at his funeral; speakers included Ronnie Baker Brooks, who also contributed several songs with the assembled band (featuring a guest appearance by Billy Branch on harmonica). All who spoke remembered the happiness and the love that had flowed so deeply through his heart, his life, and his home, as well as the richness of his musical legacy. His legendary headdress hung from a stand near the altar.

With Eddy Clearwater's departure, the roster of blues survivors from the postwar era continues to diminish, and the world becomes a quieter, less joyful place. "There's more to the music than 'just' the music," he once said—and now that he's gone, we realize yet again that we've lost so much more than "just" the music, as well.

Jimmy Burns

"There's Only One Type of Music—Good Music!"

The Shack Up Inn is located on the old Hopson Plantation, on Highway 49 just south of Clarksdale, Mississippi. One of the area's most hyped tourist attractions, it offers blues pilgrims the opportunity to spend the night in a genuine sharecropper's shack, upgraded with "indoor bathrooms, heat, air conditioning, [a] coffee maker with condiments, refrigerators and microwave in all the units" to ensure "comfort as well as authenticity." The shacks' "corrugated tin roofs and Mississippi cypress walls," we're assured, "will conjure visions of a bygone era."[1] Or, as the website *Hotel Scoop* puts it, "It's Cotton-Pickin' Fun at the Shack Up Inn."[2]

It would probably have come as a surprise to Albert and Eddie Mae Burns, who worked as sharecroppers on a plantation owned by the grandparents of Shack Up owner Bill Talbot in Dublin, Mississippi, that "cotton pickin'" was so much fun, let alone that their own modest dwelling might someday be marketed as a taste of "authenticity," available nightly for considerably more than what they might clear after an entire year's labor. Their youngest son would later recall the astonishment he felt as a boy, when he visited his sister in Clarksdale and saw running water and indoor plumbing for the first time in his life.

Nonetheless, the Burns family managed to extract some happiness out of their hardscrabble life. Albert was known around the area as a good musician, and he apparently passed that gift on to his children. His oldest son, Eddie, who played guitar and harp, moved to Detroit in the late '40s and formed a now-legendary partnership with John Lee Hooker. Another son, Willie Charles, played bass. Albert's granddaughter, Lee Vera, was a gifted singer who moved to Chicago with her mother Inez and eventually married guitarist Eddie Taylor; several of their children—as well as Larry, Vera's son from a previous relationship—have gone on to establish their own niche in the contemporary blues world. The baby of the Burns family, Jimmy, who was born on February 27, 1943—just a day before Vera—also ended up in Chicago, where he went on to forge a varied and long-running musical career, cutting a series of soul 45s that have become internationally sought collectors' items before eventually establishing himself as one of the city's most beloved blues elder statesmen.

Jimmy's own initiation into music happened at a young age. "My father played piano, guitar, and harmonica," he remembers. "Him and my mom say, 'Yeah, you remember this piece?'—they would call it a 'piece'—'This piece by Blind Lemon [Jefferson]?' Blind Lemon, Blind Boy Fuller, I used to hear him do Howlin' Wolf. I still remember some of the licks my dad played. I didn't know what he was playing, but if I heard it today—it's still in my head."

> He made a one-string on the wall. I found out later they called it a diddley-bow. That was probably some white folks' name for it. That's the first guitar I remember playing. The first time I played a real guitar was, probably, 1952 [or possibly '53] in Lyon, Mississippi. We had moved there from Dublin in '49; that's the longest we ever stayed on a place, was in Dublin. Then we moved up to Lyon, out there on Number Six Highway. A lady, Miss Anna, loaned my mother a guitar. It wasn't standard tuning; it was in open tuning. I didn't know what tuning it was; I didn't know nothing about the different tunings and all that. I thought it was right because I just picked it up and started playing it.

The first song Jimmy ever played, he recalls, was the gospel standard "You've Got to Move." Open-minded from the start, he followed that up with "Lucy Mae Blues," a stripped-down boogie romp that Texas-based Frankie Lee Sims released on the Specialty label in 1953. By then he was already enamored of the blues, with an apparent preference for Texans: Aside from Sims, his favorites included Lightnin' Hopkins ("I still love Lightnin'; if I want to play a guitar like anybody, it's Lightnin' Hopkins") and Smokey Hogg. But he also admired John Lee Hooker and Muddy Waters, and he insists to this day that he loves "that Delta stuff" more than anything else.

Jimmy's parents separated at about this time, leaving Eddie Mae to fend for herself and her children. A period of instability followed ("We moved to Shelby, stayed there a minute, then when we left Shelby we moved to Clarksdale [and] moved in with my grandmother and my grandfather"), and before long Eddie Mae decided to move to Chicago. Some of the family had already made the trip; Inez and Vera had gone north in the late '40s. "They'd come up," Jimmy explains, "get established, then send back and get the rest of 'em. Inez sent for my sister, Rosie, then my mom came up. I moved here in 1955."

By the time Jimmy arrived, twelve-year-old Lee Vera was already pregnant with Larry (she met Eddie Taylor two years later, when she was fourteen and he was thirty-four). Vera was carrying on a family tradition: her mother had been about twelve when she gave birth to her. For that matter, Jimmy's own mother, Eddie Mae, had married Albert when she was about fourteen and he was twenty-one. "This is in Mississippi," Jimmy explains. "Them old dudes with them young girls, it wasn't unusual. All my sisters were young mothers and got married young. Inez ended up marrying a man who was the same age as my mama, a year younger—ended up having about fifteen kids. Rosie was the only exception, my [youngest] sister. She's the only sister I have left. She'll be eighty-one this year [2018], and she don't look a day over sixty."

In Chicago, the Burns clan occupied several apartments at the Monterey Hotel on Oak Street, about two blocks east of the Cabrini-Green housing projects; in the summertime, Inez would set up a stand outside and sell tamales and home-made ice cream. It was a fortuitous location in other ways, too. Although often neglected by historians in favor of the city's South and West Side blues strong-holds, the Near North Side area around Cabrini was an incubator for some of Chicago's—and the country's—most important and influential black pop music during the 1950s and early '60s. Doo-wop groups such as the Von Gayles, the Serenades, the Players, and the Medallionaires (who would soon play a role in Jimmy's own story), along with future soul superstars like Major Lance, Jerry Butler, and Curtis Mayfield, grew up there. They'd go to nearby Seward Park fieldhouse or one of the neighborhood youth centers, commandeer a room, and practice their sweetly textured, church-honed harmonies, getting ready to face off on what the Magnificents' Johnny Keyes later remembered as "the legendary street corners," where they'd congregate in the evenings and go head-to-head (and voice-to-voice) in take-no-prisoners singing contests. You had to be on your game to even think about participating in one of these battles, and the young men honed their chops to a cutting edge.

"There was a guy that lived [at the Monterey] with his wife," recalls Jimmy. "His name was Zack Pierce, and he sang with a gospel group called the Dixieland Singers; they had recorded for Chess. So a couple of boys put together [another group], called it the Junior Dixieland Singers [later the Gay Lights], and me and my brother Doc joined 'em. I used to go over to Seward Park; you could get a room to practice, have a rehearsal. Woody [Woodtate Anderson] was the manager of the Medallionaires, he heard me singing, and he asked me to join. I replaced Willie Wright."

The Medallionaires were the kind of "one-hit wonder" who, by rights, should have been much more. (For that matter, their "hit" wasn't really a hit, and it didn't even showcase them to their best advantage.) Formed in 1958 by Wright, who had already made something of a local name for himself with the Quails (one of whose original members was a young Jerry Butler) and the Serenades, they specialized in "bell-tone" harmony: a singer would hit the keynote, another would blend in, and then another, until they achieved a full-bodied, bell-like resonance. The A-side of their first (and, as it turned out, only) release in 1958, "Magic Moonlight," included some sublime examples of this technique, further

Jimmy Burns, ca. late '70s, publicity photo, courtesy of James E. Wolfe.

enhanced by songwriter/lead vocalist Wright's better-than-average teen-dream lyrics ("Magic moonlight, hear my plea / Keep my baby in love with me"). Inexplicably, though, it was the flip, a labored-sounding paean to rock & roll entitled "Teenage Caravan," that local radio DJs picked up on for a while, but that one didn't go very far either. Frustrated, Wright quit the group, leaving the slot open for young Jimmy Burns.

Jimmy had at least one recording session as a member of the group, this one for the Allan label, but the record, "Two Months out of School," was never released; he remembers the year as 1959.[3] By that time, doo-wop was morphing into what would soon be called soul music (erstwhile Chicago doo-woppers like Mayfield, Butler, and Gene Chandler are among those who went on to fame as soul singers), and gigs were becoming almost as scarce as recording opportunities. Jimmy stuck it out for several more years, though, even though most of the gigs he remembers were freebies for promotional events, sometimes called "platter parties," hosted by local deejays. A label would send its artists into a major market like Chicago to lip-synch to their latest releases; a radio station or a DJ could promote the show, charge a cover, and keep the proceeds. It was basically payola by a different name.

"We were all doing those record hops together," Jimmy says. "You would go there with the DJs, you would lip-synch, you wouldn't actually sing. I did a lot of that. I remember doing shows with different people like Smokey Robinson and the Miracles, Solomon Burke, people like that; I remember doing something with the Five Stairsteps, Darrow Fletcher, Bobby Bland, Alvin Cash. We didn't get paid."

Contrary to myth, pop charts in the early '60s were relatively integrated (the R&B charts had been integrated for years), and Jimmy remembers shows featuring artists as diverse as Anita Bryant ("she had just won Miss Oklahoma and she recorded a tune, "Till There Was You'"), Brenda Lee, Clay Cole (a white pop-music TV show host out of New York who was probably serving as a guest MC), and Bobby Vee, along with R&B/soul mainstays such as Clarence "Frogman" Henry and the Marvelettes.

It was fun to perform alongside superstars like these, but fun didn't pay the rent, and Jimmy kept his eyes peeled for fresh opportunities. As it turned out, he didn't have to look very far.

Back in 1956, a pair of hipster entrepreneurs named Les Brown and Albert Grossman (the same Albert Grossman who'd go on to notoriety as the manager of Bob Dylan, Janis Joplin, The Band, and other '60s-era pop icons) had opened a folk music club called the Gate of Horn in the basement of the Rice Hotel at 755 North Dearborn, just a few blocks south of where Jimmy and his family were staying. During roughly this same time, Old Town, a somewhat amorphously defined enclave a few blocks west, was becoming a hipster mecca. Counterculturalists of all stripes began moving into the formerly working-class area, along with some of the city's first Puerto Rican immigrants, who likewise took advantage of the low rents resulting from "white flight" to the suburbs. Within a few years, Old Town was the Greenwich Village of Chicago—the city's Bohemian Ground Zero.

Some of the clubs and coffee houses that emerged, such as Big John's, Mother Blues, Poor Richard's, the Quiet Knight, and the Fickle Pickle, booked working Chicago blues artists, albeit presented in settings low-key and nonthreatening enough to appeal to the authenticity- seeking boho crowd. A few also brought in top-tier jazz—Miles Davis, Sonny Stitt—while others, like the Gate of Horn, the Earl of Old Town, and The Bear (in which Grossman also had an interest), tended more toward folk music (Steve Goodman, Joan Baez, Bob Gibson, Odetta, Josh White, et al.). Occasionally, a blues artist of grittier provenance, such as Memphis Slim or Big Bill Broonzy (who had transformed himself into a "folk" bluesman by then) might also hold forth.

Willie Wright had already made his entre into that scene, having remade himself as a folk singer after leaving the Medallionaires.[4] Jimmy, with his open-eared attitude toward music ("If it sounded good, I did it"), also found it easy to adapt. "I was doing all of that," he concurs. "Messing with the guitar. I don't know how well I was playing, but I was doing it. Gate of Horn, Fickle Pickle, people like Odetta, Josh White; Barbara Dane—she's a California girl—you had Willie Wright, Martin Yarbrough—I remember he used to be at the Gate of Horn, he used to do this tune, 'My Cuban Love Song.' I was doing stuff like Harry Belafonte, 'Jamaica Farewell.' I used to do that, and what I heard other people do."

It's ironic, to say the least, that artists like Jimmy and Willie Wright, who had already been performing and recording genuine urban folk music as doo-wop singers, had to hoist acoustic guitars and croon warhorses like "Jamaican Farewell" and "Wagon Wheels" to be considered "authentic" by white folkies, but Jimmy made the transition with equanimity. "I've always been a guy that did all types of music," he affirms. "That's when I discovered that there's a lot of similarity between blues and folk." He admits, though, that the experience was a bit daunting at first. "It was different to me," he says. "I had never seen nothing like that. A boy from Mississippi, in there with all them white folks? They liked us, and nothing ever happened, but it was—yeah, it was different."

He wasn't about to limit his options, in any case. In 1961 or so, he and the former Medallionaires landed a recording session with blues vocalist/guitarist Jimmy Lee Robinson. "We were hanging around with Eddy Clearwater at the time," he says. "Little neighborhood things, mainly for some Mexicans if I'm not mistaken,[5] and Jimmy Lee wanted us to do some background for him. That's us singing on 'Twist It Baby' [Bandera]. I think that might be Clearwater [on guitar]; I know it's Odie Payne on the drums."

He continued to perform doo-wop as opportunities arose, and he eventually also put together what he remembers as a "Top 40" band of his own ("I was doing whatever was hot—'Twist and Shout,' Solomon Burke"), often with his brother Will on bass. One particularly memorable gig was at the Devil's Rendezvous on Clybourn Avenue: "They had coffins and stuff in there. Yeah, it was odd." (The club was still active in the 1980s and early '90s as the New Fun Lounge, under the proprietorship of blues vocalist Willie Buck.) Then, in 1964, Jimmy initiated his own recording career with "Through All Your Faults" b/w "Forget It" on the U.S.A. label, the first of seven 45s he would release over the next decade or so (subsequent singles appeared on Erica, Tip Top, Minit, and Dispo), mostly in the lilting Chicago style that has since been dubbed "soft soul."

"I always loved [soul] music," Jimmy explains today. "And a boy introduced me to Charles Colbert [owner of the Tip Top label]; his boy, Charles Jr., was the first to be with Rufus.[6] I met them in '64."

> I had wrote these tunes, and I had this girl to help me. Usually at that time you had to have lead sheets to get copyrights, and I don't read music but she did, and she had to give me a hand. Look on those records, you'll see Margui, that was the name she used professionally, Margui. So I had those tunes, and Colbert decided he wanted to record 'em, so that's how that came about. He actually leased the record to U.S.A. I wasn't signed to U.S.A.; I was really signed to him, to Tip Top Records.

All the elements were there—the doo-wop–tinged melodiousness, the gritty romanticism he'd honed during his faux-Belafonte period, the emotional fervor of his blues and gospel roots, songwriting that balanced emotional depth with youthful yearning—but, although today they're praised as stellar examples of their genre, Jimmy's soul 45s pretty much sank without a trace when they were first released.

"You had a bunch of competition," he reflects. "I still remember, at the same time I had out 'Forget It,' the Four Tops had 'Baby I Need Your Loving.' I remember visiting radio stations, and I'd see a bunch of 45s in the back, on the floor, from major labels. Unless it takes off right away, ain't gonna do nothing."

> I had a record that was a hit in the U.K. and I didn't know it until twenty years later. This English DJ got a hold of me; it's going now for about four or five grand, collector's item. It's called "I Really Love You," on Erica [from 1965]. I never received a quarter from them. Those soul tunes—I never performed those tunes live. Once I left the studio, I never did 'em live. None of 'em! I would do shows and stuff, like on the South Side, and I was doing all the top soul tunes at the time or whatever I felt, but I never made no money off of those 45s. Not one quarter. Only time I got some money was when that DJ from the U.K. told me that "I Really Love You" had been a hit over there, twenty years earlier.

In 1965 or so, Jimmy encountered a flamboyant soul aggregation known as the Fantastic Epics, led by guitarist Martin Dumas and driven by the street-tough funk of drummer Lamont Turner. They accompanied him on "You're Gonna Miss Me When I'm Gone" b/w "It Used to Be" (Tip Top) in 1966. Jimmy delivered the vocals in a soaring baritone, sounding like a cross between Roy Hamilton and the Righteous Brothers' Bill Medley, as the Epics contributed an appropriately romance-sweetened backing. In person, though, the group was considerably more aggressive, as drummer Paul Coleman has remembered: "This was a hot smoking show band," Coleman told an interviewer in 2016. "I mean great singing, great musicianship and out of this world acrobatics, flips, flying though air, table walking, horns flaring, the whole nine yards."[7]

Jimmy stayed with the Epics for a year or two, although he says he mostly steered clear of the stunts. ("They did that. I never did do that. I was never a dancer until later.") They cultivated an avid following around the Chicago area ("we used to play, like, universities and stuff"), and they also had the opportunity to rub elbows, albeit briefly, with the blues and rock elite:

> We were playing up at Thumbs Up at Broadway and Surf [on the North Side]. I remember one time, Willie Dixon and them came by, with [harpist] Big Walter Horton. They called him Shaky Horton. This was like around 1965 or '66, somewhere in there. And the Yardbirds would come by there; they would sit in with us. That's how Jeff Beck came through there, with the Yardbirds. Last time I talked to Jeff, he remembered that. He drove the girls crazy! Had that long hair, good-looking guy, young at the time, and he was one of the first guys I remember seeing [who] had his guitar feed back. And it drove 'em crazy.
>
> At the Arie Crown Theater at the old McCormick Place, the one that burned down, they put together a show—the Buckinghams, the New Colony Six, and the Yardbirds. And we were on that show. And now that I think about it, we must have been the only black act! Funny, I never thought about that until now.

The Epics continued to gig around Chicago after Jimmy left, and they eventually evolved into the street-funk powerhouse Rasputin's Stash, whose '70s-era output on Cotillion, Gemigo, and Curtom is prized by collectors worldwide.[8]

Never less than adaptable, Jimmy next fronted a white Top 40 band called the Gas Company, even as he continued sporadically to record soul 45s (his last single was "Can't Get Over You" / "Where Does That Leave Me?" on Dispo, released in about 1971). It was frustrating, though, to grind it out in a musical "career" that showed few signs of growth ("A lotta stuff was happening—and then again, a whole lotta nothin'!") Finally, in the late '70s, he made the decision to refocus on the music that had originally inspired him. The impetus came from a group of young bluesmen who were then being touted as the music's future—hardly the "role models" one might expect for a thirty-five-year-old man entering his third decade as a professional entertainer. "I been in blues all my life," he asserts, "even if not predominantly."

> I was in it because I always liked Muddy Waters and that old Delta style, and when I heard, in 1978, when New Generation of the Blues got back from Germany—Willie Dixon, my nephew Larry, Johnny B. [Moore], James Kinds, Vernon and Joe Harrington, Lurrie [Bell], Billy Branch—I heard those guys playing the blues, I told my wife, I said, "I'm gonna put together a blues band." And that's when I did it. I started with a trio. I had several people in it. My brother Will, on bass; I was playing guitar; and my nephew Larry Taylor on drums. A boyfriend of my daughter's named Gary, he's dead now, also sometimes played drums. Lurrie and Billy were the ones who made me put the band together. When I heard them, I said, "I'm gonna put me a band together," 'cause I liked what they played.

Despite his professed love for the Delta-to-Chicago tradition, though, Jimmy says he "hated the electric guitar" then, and in fact his early trios were primarily acoustic. "I used to put a pickup on an acoustic," he explains, " 'cause I learned on the acoustic; I didn't want to switch." But he finally purchased an electric instrument—it's now on display in the Delta Blues Museum in Clarksdale, Mississippi—and he's been playing both ever since.

It still wasn't a lucrative way to make a living, but contrary to what some previous biographies have suggested, he insists that he never got out of music entirely, no matter how slow things got. "They say I took time off, "he avers, "but actually I didn't. I don't know where that came from. I was always doing something one way or another, [even if] I just had no record at the time. I was always, like, working in a club or something, doing the stuff."

Jimmy Burns at Buddy Guy's
Legends, Chicago, 2016.

His sideline as a restaurateur might have been one reason some people thought he'd quit music. In about 1989, Jimmy opened Uncle Mickey's Barbeque near the corner of Madison and Keeler; it later moved a few blocks west to Madison and Laramie, but it still featured his "personal recipe" barbeque sauce, and it became, as Jimmy says, "Chicago's best-kept secret"—known mostly to a tight circle of admirers who lauded it as one of the finest of its kind in a city that prides itself on its soul food and southern cooking. Uncle Mickey's lasted for about twelve years and took up a lot of Jimmy's time, but even then he continued to play music whenever the opportunity arose.

Jimmy says the music really began to pick up for him in the mid-'90s when he joined forces with guitarist Rockin' Johnny Burgin, an earnest young revivalist who'd memorized the licks of the postwar blues masters and was purveying his version of their classic sound in the band led by Howlin' Wolf imitator James "Tail Dragger" Jones at the 5105 Club on North Avenue. "I wanted to do Delta blues," he explains:

> I didn't want to do R&B, like Tyrone Davis; I wanted to do [Little] Walter, Muddy, all that stuff. And that's what I liked about Johnny's group. They played Delta blues, and they played it right. So that got my attention there. And then Johnny said, "Hey, man, we got this thing at Smoke Daddy [a barbeque restaurant in Wicker Park opened by erstwhile keyboardist Mark "Max" Brumbach in 1994]." We're the ones that put Smoke Daddy on the map. We were playing every Monday night. Johnny said, "We can give you twenty dollars a night, food and booze."
>
> I actually was not doing it for the money. At the time I had a day job. I was making nine hundred dollars a week; I worked as a carpenter. I just wanted somebody to play the music right, and they played it right. So that's what got my attention.
>
> You know [harmonica player] Scott Dirks? I think Scott might have told [Delmark label owner] Bob [Koester] about us, and Bob came down to Smoke Daddy. He heard me with Johnny and the boys—Mark Brumbach, [bassist] Sho Komiya, and at the time [drummer] Kelly Littleton, who's playing with Lil' Ed now—and next thing I know we're in the studio. Everything happened so fast, [but] I had a lot of material that I had been working on, so we had an instant CD, pretty much.

That disk, 1996's *Leaving Here Walking*, included an appropriately wide-ranging mix of material and influences. Delta standards like "Catfish Blues" and "Rollin' and Tumblin'"—both featuring Jimmy's acoustic guitar—shared the setlist with Elmore James's "Twelve Year Old Boy," an ironically jaunty take on Tommy McClennan's "Whiskey-Headed Woman," and John Lee "Sonny Boy" Williamson's "Shake Your Boogie" (with a rare harp solo from Jimmy himself), as well as an acoustic remake of Curtis Mayfield's "Gypsy Woman" (a wry nod to Jimmy's dual former incarnations as pop-folk troubadour and Chicago soul man). Also featured were several Burns originals, including "Better Know What You're Doing," which grafted a John Lee Hooker boogie onto a soaring, pop-rock bridge. It remains one of Jimmy's favorites. "We were gonna boogie," he declares, his satisfaction still palpable. "We were gonna rock. And we did rock. See, you can rock any music; all depends on which way, how you want to go. And I love the rock. I don't have anything against that at all. I don't want to be dead all night."

Leaving Here Walking garnered positive reviews and decent sales, and it also led to Jimmy's first sojourn out of the country. In 1997, a Delmark package tour—billed as the Chicago Blues Revue, featuring Jimmy, Byther Smith, harmonica player Golden Wheeler, and vocalist Karen Carroll, fronting a band that included bassist Willie "Vamp" Samuel and drummer Cleo "Baldhead Pete" Williams—traveled overseas. Their ports of call included France, Belgium, Germany, Switzerland, and Austria. Since then, Jimmy has performed outside the United Sates numerous times, he remains a favorite on Chicago's North Side, and he has continued to release albums at a steady, if leisurely, pace. *Night Time Again*, in 1999, included a remake of the long-lost "Two Months out of School," on which he multitracked his voice to re-create the sound of a glory-era doo-wop ensemble. Four years later, the somewhat deceptively titled *Back to the Delta* made its appearance; most of it, although rooted in the 12-bar tradition, was shot through with big-city aggressiveness, and even on the most downhome-themed offerings, such as "Stranded in Clarksdale" and the delicate, acoustic "All about My Woman," Jimmy's pop-leavened croon bespoke his urbanity.

A live recording, made at the club B.L.U.E.S. on North Halsted, followed in 2007; it captured both Jimmy and his sidemen at their loosest and most improvisationally daring, the occasional rough edges only adding to the sense of immediacy. Especially gratifying were second guitarist Anthony Palmer's solo on a torridly rocking "Better Know What You're Doing" and guest vocalist Jesse Fortune's housewrecking take on B. B. King's "Three O'Clock Blues." (Two years later, in August of 2009, Fortune would be stricken with a fatal heart attack in mid-performance on stage at Gene's Playmate Lounge on West Cermak.) Jimmy's most recent, 2015's *It Ain't Right*, is another characteristic mix of the old (the title tune, originally recorded by Little Walter in 1956; the Junior Wells standard "Messin' with the Kid"; and Jimmy Reed's "A String to Your Heart," among others), the new (a pair of originals from guitarist Billy Flynn), and the unexpected (another doo-wop throwback, the "5" Royales' "Crazy Crazy Crazy"; a raw, deep-blues reimagining of Bobby Rush's "Snaggletooth Mule"; and a rare gospel offering, "Wade in the Water").

At an age when many are looking back on their lives and careers with autumnal satisfaction, Jimmy remains resolutely focused on the future, still taking pride in the scope and breadth of his musical vision. In fact, he insists that the balance he attempts to maintain between the traditions he was raised with, the multiple offshoots and variations he's embraced over the course of his career, and the diverse audiences he's gained along the way—the doo-wop and soul lovers of Cabrini-Green; the Old Town folk purists; the funkified hipsters who boogied and partied to the Fantastic Epics; the white blues aficionados who comprise the bulk of his admirers today—represents the true future of the blues as it struggles to maintain its relevance in a media-driven, innovation-obsessed twenty-first-century culture. "Most of the guys," he maintains, "there's something I understood that they didn't understand."

And that is that you're playing blues, but you're playing for a predominantly white audience, and they didn't get the blues from Muddy Waters or Howlin' Wolf. They got it from people like Stevie Ray Vaughan and other people. And a lot of the Black musicians don't understand that. So when they go out there with that same music, they ain't going too far with it, in my opinion.

See, I know the history of Black music; one thing I learned, even with jazz, the Blacks have always had the music, but they never controlled the music. You have to understand that. And what's going on now is a reflection of that. Even at the awards; what they callin' blues a lot of times is not really blues. One thing I notice about white musicians, a lot of 'em, they get loudness mixed up for soul. They shove it down everybody's throat.

But I don't go off into that. My philosophy is this: There's only one type of music—good music. I don't give a fuck who's doing it; if it's good, it's good. We all know where the music came from. Elvis didn't do no more 'n what a lot of people did; he didn't steal it, he just recorded it, and a lot of people bought it. Just like when the Stones come out with our music.[9] When the white boys play a song they like, they cheer them on. They support 'em. So that's what's happening. That's the reality of the situation. You gravitate towards your own. I ain't mad at nobody; I'm happy that they let me get a piece of it. That's where my mind is at. So apparently, a lot of people, they don't know—they haven't studied the industry, they haven't studied the history.

We're a very fast-paced society, and we don't hang onto stuff. Not only music but anything. So understand who we are. But our music is the most popular music in the world. I hear this when I go overseas. And I'm happy that they love my music. So blues will always be there in one form or another. But it's not only "my" music now; the music belongs to the world. That's just like saying only white folks can play the Beatles. You know, you make something good, everybody want a piece of it. And why not? I love to see people playing music.

PART II

Council of Elders

Although the roster has thinned significantly in recent years, some veterans of Chicago blues' postwar era continue to ply their trade, most with undiminished enthusiasm and still-potent chops. This section provides a survey of artists whose careers date back to the years when the modern style was being forged.

Once again, I remind the reader not to consider inclusion in this listing, instead of the previous section, to suggest "second-tier" status or a less than significant role. For instance, I have chosen to include Buddy Guy, arguably the most prestigious and financially successful Chicago bluesman of his generation (if not of all time), in this section, simply because his life story is well known—he's told it numerous times and written at least two autobiographies—so it was my decision that a relatively brief synopsis of his life and career would suffice. Some other decisions, though, involved painful choices—it's always difficult to make the inevitable cuts, in terms of who gets selected for in-depth profiles, in a project like this. Some artists are working on their own memoirs and so didn't want to give away any "spoilers"; others declined to be interviewed or didn't want to participate without financial recompense—perfectly understandable, but not feasible, and, of course, not congruent with journalistic ethics.

In all but a few cases, the artists listed here continue to work in Chicago (and, sometimes, on the road) on a regular basis. The old admonitions still pertain: Support live music, and catch the greats while you still can.

Billy Boy Arnold

Billy Boy Arnold's career spans no fewer than three historical blues epochs. Mentored by harmonica master John Lee "Sonny Boy" Williamson, who helped define the prewar Chicago style, he began playing professionally just as Muddy Waters and his contemporaries were kicking off the postwar blues insurgency. He remained active during the years when that new sound was taking hold; then, in 1955, he participated in what was, for all intents and purposes, the birth of rock & roll—in fact, he's often credited with coining one of rock & roll's most iconic stage monikers.

Born in Chicago in 1935, William Arnold grew up idolizing John Lee Williamson and other midcentury bluesmen, many associated with Chicago's Bluebird label, who were forging an urbanized updating of the sparse, acoustic blues still prevalent in the South. Williamson, who had revolutionized the blues harmonica by transforming it into a lead instrument roughly analogous to what the saxophone had become in jazz, was one of the leading lights of this new sound. In 1948, young Billy Arnold got the chance to meet his idol for a memorable tutoring session, only a few weeks before the harp maestro was murdered while walking home from a gig. Inspired, Billy hit the local circuit, and in about 1953 he released his own debut, "I Ain't Got No Money" / "Hello Stranger," on the Cool label, which billed him alternately as "Billy 'Boy' Arnold" (on one side) and "Billy (boy) Arnold" (on the other), a name he adopted quickly and has used ever since. These were straightforward 12-bar blues outings with little foreshadowing of what would soon come.

In those days, a scuffling musician often divided his time between the clubs and the streets. Billy Boy hooked up with a bold young singer/guitarist named Ellas McDaniel, who was busking around the South and West Sides with guitarist Jody Williams and a washtub player named Roosevelt Jackson in a group called the Langley Avenue Jive Cats. In 1955, McDaniel and his men, now augmented by Jerome Green on maracas, auditioned a raunchy blues with a propulsive, off-center beat called "Hey Noxema" (aka "Uncle John") for several local labels before ending up at Chess. Under Leonard Chess's direction, they cleaned up the lyrics, and they also changed the song's title to the equally distinctive "Bo Diddley," which almost immediately became the singer's stage name. (According to some sources, including Billy Boy himself, he was the one who suggested the name to McDaniel.) The flipside, the anthemic "I'm a Man," featured Billy Boy's harmonica overlaid atop a lurching, testosterone-driven stop-time cadence.

Billy Boy Arnold, Chicago
Blues Hall of Fame Induction
Ceremony, Buddy Guy's
Legends, Chicago, 2016.

These young African American urbanites were thrusting their manhood and their aggressiveness directly into the face of Eisenhower-era America, and popular culture would never again be the same.

Billy Boy also appeared on Diddley's "She's Fine, She's Mine" later that same year, but by then he'd signed with Vee-Jay, for whom he released a series of singles between 1955 and 1957. These disks, along with the Diddley sides, are the basis of his latter-day renown among collectors, although—as was often the case—they achieved only moderate success, at best, when they were released.

Part of the reason may have been their similarity to others' better-known hits. Billy Boy's harp style, predictably, showed the John Lee Williamson influence, but it was also obvious he'd been listening to Little Walter, who had stepped into Williamson's shoes and revolutionized blues harp all over again in the years following Sonny Boy's death. His rhythms, meanwhile, were often noticeably Diddley-esque. "I Wish You Would," his 1955 Vee-Jay debut, sounded like a cross between

Walter's "Mellow Down Easy" (from 1954) and Bo's "Pretty Thing" (released the same year as "I Wish You Would," although it didn't debut on the charts until January of 1956). "Here's My Picture," in 1956, similarly spiked a rhumba-boogie with a deep-Diddley feel; the B-side, "You've Got Me Wrong," though, was a grinding 12-bar outing that sounded almost atavistic in comparison.

That same year, Billy Boy released "I Ain't Got You," arguably his most distinctive outing yet (despite its lyric reference to a "mojo"), and one of the sides that would propel him into latter-day rock & roll immortality when the Yardbirds resurrected it, along with "I Wish You Would," on their 1965 *For Your Love* LP. Its flipside, the Willie Mabon–like "Don't Stay Out All Night," was another 12-bar blues, this time intensified by some seething urban-juke interplay between Billy Boy and guitarist Jody Williams. Like other labels during that era, Vee-Jay was pairing pop-tinged, ostensibly youth-oriented "A" sides with standard-issue blues, an indication of the uneasy balance some were still trying to maintain between the music's past and a future that was still, and confusingly, coming into focus.

"My Heart Is Crying," released the following year, was a mid-tempo 12-bar shuffle, a little old-fashioned for the hard-rocking youth audience he'd been courting up to then (the flip, "Kissing at Midnight," was even more so). Its lack of self-consciousness, though, was refreshing, even if Billy's harp work now sounded as if he had the "other" Sonny Boy, Rice Miller, on his mind. His next release, "Rockin' Itis," returned him to the rhumba-blues groove he'd dug into on "I Wish You Would" and "Here's My Picture." The flip, "Prisoner's Plea," grafted a woeful tale of prison-farm suffering to a jaunty, vaguely Diddley-driven cadence—which may have seemed like a good idea at the time, but which in retrospect sounds like a rather desperate attempt to land a best-of-both-worlds Hail Mary pass. (To be fair, at least a few other younger bluesmen, such as Junior Wells, with his "Galloping Horses A Lazy Mule" in 1960, featuring the redoubtable Earl Hooker on guitar, were attempting similarly unlikely old-school/new-school melds, with similarly anomalous results. The world was changing, and at least in the blues, even the youngbloods were having a difficult time keeping up with it.)

"Rockin' Itis" / "Prisoner's Plea" was Billy Boy's final release on Vee-Jay. After that, although he recorded sporadically for various aficionados' labels and gigged on and off on Chicago's North Side, he found it difficult to sustain a full-time musical career. He supported himself with day jobs along with occasional sojourns to Europe, where he was still idolized as a blues master and one of rock

& roll's founding fathers. His *Checkin' It Out: The 1977 London Sessions*, released on Red Lightnin' in 1979, provides a glimpse of what he sounded like during this time, complete with a raucous take on the old "Dozens" theme "Dirty Mother-Fuyer" that was actually billed as "Dirty Mother Fucker" on the album jacket.

Finally, in 1993, he launched a stateside comeback with *Back Where I Belong* (Alligator). He has continued to record since then—his most recent release is 2014's *The Blues Soul of Billy Boy Arnold* (Stony Plain)—and he has remained inter-mittently active as a live performer. In 2012, he dug into his roots and released *Billy Boy Arnold Sings Big Bill Broonzy* on Electro-Fi, a tribute to another of his early role models. He also contributed his own "I Wish You Would" along with versions of Broonzy's "Night Watchman Blues," Tampa Red's "She's Love Crazy," Memphis Slim's eponymous "Memphis Slim U.S.A.," and Williamson's "My Little Machine" to the 2009 anthology *Chicago Blues: A Living History* on the Raisin' Music label.

Even though his '50s-era discography, on its own terms, might be considered modest, those early disks also provide a tantalizing freeze-frame glimpse of a musical style caught in the throes of radical, even cataclysmic, change. Today, in the wake of that change, Billy Boy Arnold is universally feted as a carrier of the living blues heritage who helped forge the transition between blues, R&B, and rock & roll.[1]

Buddy Guy

Buddy Guy is recognized internationally as a major stylistic innovator, a driv-ing force behind the mid/late-twentieth-century blues "revival" and its ongo-ing aftermath, and a musical role model for several generations of blues, rock, blues-rock, and pop stars and superstars.

Born George Guy in Lettsworth, Louisiana, in 1936, he derived his early inspi-ration from Eddie "Guitar Slim" Jones, whose galvanizing stage show and rau-cous, overamplified lead guitar style set the tone (literally and figuratively) for the path Buddy would eventually blaze for himself. After cutting his teeth in the Baton Rouge area and recording a few demos at local radio station WXOK, he moved to Chicago in 1957. Encouraged by Muddy Waters, he started gigging around the South Side, and in 1958, he began recording for Artistic, a subsid-iary of the Cobra label. His Artistic disks—"Sit and Cry (The Blues)" / "Try to Quit You Baby" and 1959's "You Sure Can't Do" / "This Is the End"—feature his soaring, emotion-choked voice at least as prominently as his guitar leads, which are crisp and precisely articulated (and, on "You Sure Can't Do," patterned very closely after his early idol Guitar Slim), but betray little hint of the pyrotechnic fury his playing would attain in later years.

By 1960 he was at Chess, where he worked as a house guitarist and also recorded sides of his own. It was at Chess that he waxed his sole chart hit, "Stone Crazy," which peaked at No. 12 in 1962. In fact, as formidable as his skills were— and for all of his latter-day status as a "living legend"—he wasn't really a major figure, even on the local circuit, for most of his early career. He didn't record a full-length album under his own name until 1967's *I Left My Blues in San Francisco*, a rather labored attempt by Chess to capitalize on the burgeoning white coun- terculture and its newfound enthusiasm for Chicago blues. By then, though, he'd already appeared on the Delmark album *Hoodoo Man* accompanying Junior Wells (and billed, somewhat disingenuously, as "Friendly Chap" to avoid conflicts with Chess, with whom he was still signed). This ended up being Buddy's big break as well as Junior's, but even then the break didn't happen overnight. The turning point was manager Dick Waterman's offer to team them as a touring act (until then, Lefty Dizz had been standing in as the "fake Buddy Guy" on Junior's shows). Emboldened by the reaction he got, Buddy finally took the plunge and quit his day job, making music his full-time occupation for the first time in his life.

Meanwhile, chafing under what he considered both artistic and financial con- straints at Chess, Buddy moved to the Vanguard label, where he released *A Man and the Blues* and the live *This Is Buddy Guy!* in 1968, and *Hold That Plane!* recorded the following year but not released until 1972. By this time, enough interest in him had been generated to motivate various labels (including Chess, who seem to have finally realized what they'd let get away) to begin putting out Buddy Guy compilations and retrospectives. He was also featured on collaborations with other artists (including his brother, guitarist Phil Guy), but he didn't release another full-length studio album under his own name until *The Blues Giant*, which came out on the French Isabel imprint in 1979 (it was reissued in 1981 as *Stone Crazy!* on Alligator).

It's notable, in fact, that for much of his latter-day career as an American blues "legend," Buddy Guy's releases have been primarily on overseas labels. It wasn't until 2012 that RCA issued *Live at Legends*, capturing him in performance at his Chicago club, and then followed it up the next year with *Rhythm & Blues*—his return to a major American label for the first time in forty years. By then he had already garnered numerous Grammys for his albums on the British Silvertone imprint, bringing to mind the late Denise LaSalle's observation about how, and where, the blues finds itself finally getting appreciated: "When they got down on blues in America, blues went to Europe and became the toast of the Euro-pean countries and all that stuff; yet when it comes back home, it's being kicked around."[2]

A lot of blues artists, of course, would love to get "kicked around" the way Buddy Guy has been, at least since his '70s-era "rediscovery." One of the most widely traveled and high-drawing bluesmen in history, he's been cited by vir-tually every blues-based rock star as a major inspiration, and he has appeared alongside many of them on various recording projects and in concert films and documentaries. Whether Jimi Hendrix adapted his guitar technique from Buddy or vice versa (or whether, as is more likely, each man forged his own approach independently and then discovered later on that they shared a similar muse), the style Buddy has codified over the years has come to exemplify blues guitar mastery—or, to its critics, blues guitar overkill—for generations of aspirants and acolytes. For his part, Buddy insists that he was playing that way all along, but because his early producers insisted on reining him in, most listeners never got the chance to hear what he could do until the post-'60s white blues-revivalist juggernaut finally allowed him to present himself to the world on his own terms.

Buddy has also made his mark as a businessman, promoting both the music and himself, and, in a very real sense, being one of the major forces in "keeping the blues alive" as a commercially viable consumer product. For years he was coproprietor, with L. C. Thurman, of the Checkerboard Lounge on Forty-Third Street, which became a major tourist attraction with its ghetto location and raw "urban-juke" atmosphere, even after Buddy had begun to make good money traveling the world as a latter-day blues superstar. He split with Thurman in the mid-1980s; in 1989 he opened Buddy Guy's Legends, first at 754 South Wabash and then a few doors north at 700—prime downtown locations, close to major hotels and businesses, ensuring a steady, well-paying audience of business trav-elers, international blues fans, and tourists. Although lately the club has become somewhat more conservative in its bookings—local and up-and-coming acts tend to grace the stage these days at least as frequently as nationally and inter-nationally known figures—for years it consistently brought to Chicago the most gifted and prestigious artists in blues, along with cameo appearances by the likes of Eric Clapton, Van Morrison, the Stones, David Bowie, ZZ Top, Gregg Allman, the Pointer Sisters, Sheila E, and the Black Crowes, among many others.

Along with his commitment to running his nightclub, Buddy has contin-ued to tour with apparently undiminished energy. His fretboard chops seem as potent as ever, and he also remains one of the blues' most expressive and eloquent vocalists—an aspect of his gifts (heard to its best advantage on the spellbinding *Blues Singer*, his Grammy-winning acoustic outing released on Silvertone in 2003) that has been somewhat overshadowed by the flamboyance of his stage act and the sometimes relentless volume and intensity of his guitar work. In 2015, *Born to Play Guitar* on RCA finally netted Buddy a Grammy for a U.S.-recorded studio release.

Willie Dixon, one of Buddy's mentors and compatriots at both Cobra and Chess, took the phrase "I Am the Blues" as his personal slogan. Today, in Chicago at least, despite the criticism that occasionally comes his way for what some see as opportunism in both business and music, Buddy Guy may also legitimately lay claim to that aphorism and its legacy.

Syl Johnson

Chicago soul patriarch Syl Johnson was born Sylvester Thompson in Holly Springs, Mississippi, in 1936. He picked up the guitar and harmonica early on; by the time he moved to Chicago in 1950, he'd become proficient at both. His brothers, Jimmy and Mac, were already living in the city, and Syl got together with Mac, a bass player, to form a trio with singer/guitarist Sam Maghett (soon to be known as Magic Sam). His first appearance in a recording studio was in 1957, when he contributed some old-school sounding blues fretwork to Billy Boy Arnold's "My Heart Is Crying" / "Kissing at Midnight." His activities around Chicago eventually brought Syl to the attention of King Records. (According to one version of the story, he was bringing a demo to Vee-Jay, who had already expressed an interest in him, when he entered King's nearby Chicago office on a whim. He played the demo for King A&R man Ralph Bass, who called his boss Syd Nathan in Cincinnati and signed Syl to a contract.)

He was billed as Syl "Johnson" on his first release, "Teardrops" / "They Who Love," and it was under that name that he released six singles on King's Federal subsidiary between 1959 and 1962. He's kept it ever since. Although schooled in the blues, Syl readily adapted to the burgeoning soul style, although many of his King sides hewed closer to a "soft soul" sound, similar to what was developing in Chicago, than the churchier, more fervid stylings of deep-soul pioneers like Little Willie John and Bobby "Blue" Bland.

Occasionally, though, his producers at King/Federal took some bolder chances: "I've Got to Find My Baby," from 1961, found Syl affecting a B.B. King–like wail and unfurling some string-bending guitar leads over Sonny Thompson's piano

Syl Johnson, Motor Row
Brewing, Chicago, 2016.

triplets; the following year's "Little Sally Walker" grafted a children's ring-game chant onto a "Twist"-propelled dance rhythm ("Look at little Sally, over in the corner / doin' the Watusi with little Jackie Horner"); Syl's fretwork on the 1962 blues ballad "I Wanna Know" echoed T-Bone Walker. His final Federal release, though, "I'm Looking for My Baby" / "Please, Please, Please," sounded almost like a toss-off, marred by an out-of-tune guitar and unimaginative studio work.

After leaving King/Federal, Syl continued to record for various small labels—TMP-Ting, Special Agent, Zachron, Cha, Tag Ltd.—but he didn't score his first chart hits until 1967, when he released "Come On Sock It To Me" and "Different Strokes" (kicked off by some hysterical, piccolo-register giggles from a nineteen-year-old Minnie Riperton) on his own Twilight imprint, which he soon rechris-tened Twinight (he's since returned to the original name). Syl's pugnacity virtu-ally exploded all over these sides, making the otherwise standard-issue party songs sound almost like revolutionary manifestos—appropriate to the tenor of the times, and a harbinger of what was to come.

"Dresses Too Short," in 1968, was a lascivious ode to the pleasures of girl-watching, but Syl's next two hits, "Is It Because I'm Black" (1969) and "Concrete Reservation" (1970), exemplified the increasingly political turn that mainstream soul and R&B were taking. "Is It Because I'm Black" toned down the funk, replacing Syl's trademark high-energy thrust with a haunting (and haunted) sparseness; his meditations seethed with outrage, his choked tenor ascents bespeaking both anguish and militance. "Concrete Reservation" was harder-edged, as Syl delivered his tale of dissolution, despair, and death over Latin-tinged funk percussion and a sweet-sour string backing that heightened both the pathos and the urgency. After that, though, he returned to more middle-of-the-road offerings: his final two Twinight hits were 1970's lushly romantic "One Way Ticket to Nowhere" and the following year's "Get Ready," a street-tough cover of the Temptations' 1966 smash.

In 1971, frustrated with the inability of the previous year's *Is It Because I'm Black* LP—a "concept album" now praised for having been courageously ahead of its time—to garner much commercial success, Syl signed with Hi. It was actually the consummation of a deal that had been in the works for some time: Hi Producer Willie Mitchell, who by then was also a vice president at the company, had discovered Syl several years earlier, and since then Syl had been dividing his time between Chicago and Memphis ("Dresses Too Short" was recorded at Royal Studios, Mitchell's home base, with the fabled Hi Rhythm Section stoking the fires). With Pappa Willie at the helm, Syl's sound was smoothed out somewhat, but his vocals remained rugged (although he could also pull off an admirable approximation of Al Green's silken croon, as on "Could I Be Falling in Love," a track from his 1974 *Diamond In the Rough* LP).

Syl scored ten hits on Hi between 1972 and 1976, the most successful being his 1975 cover of Green's "Take Me to the River." As was often the case at Hi, he seemed to sound more and more like Green the longer he stayed at the label, but—at least on his major hits—his own personality remained solidly to the fore. On 1975's "I Only Have Love," he turned in a rare southern-fried harmonica break; he also contributed some harp to "Take Me to the River" itself, adding another element of backwoods funkiness to a song already drenched in an intoxicating mixture of holy water and boogie juice. His last hit for Hi, 1976's " 'Bout to Make Me Leave Home," was as uncompromisingly streetsy as anything he ever did for the label, laced with strong echoes of Bobby Rush's patented "folk-funk" groove.

Although Syl never again broached topics as blatantly social as "Is It Because I'm Black" and "Concrete Reservation," his final chart hit, 1982's "Ms. Fine Brown Frame" (Boardwalk), a swaggering paean to Black feminine pulchritude, could also be interpreted as a declaration of racial pride, as it no doubt was at the time. In 1994, after more than a decade out of the limelight (some of that time was taken up tending to various business interests, most notably a regional fish restaurant franchise called Solomon's Fishery), he launched a comeback with *Back in the Game* (Delmark); he has since followed that up with several more studio outings (the most recent, released in 2013 on Twilight, cofeatured vocalist Melody Whittle along with Syl's daughter Syleena), an in-concert recording (*Live in Russia*, released in 2018 on the Spinnup label), and several anthologies, the most definitive of which, at least in terms of documenting his pre-Hi catalogue, is probably the 2010 box set *Complete Mythology* (Numero Group).

He returned to the studio in 2017 to produce his daughter's CD, *Rebirth of Soul*, which was released on Shanachie and included, among other highlights, a starkly urgent remake of "Is It Because I'm Black." Meanwhile, although he remains at heart an old-school funk and soul man with a powerful blues feel, his ongoing relevance to modern-day R&B is unquestionable—"Different Strokes" alone has been sampled over 295 times—representing yet another way in which Chicago's blues legacy continues to make itself felt.

Mary Lane

Vocalist Mary Lane was never a star, but her longevity and her gritty charisma as a live performer have earned her a niche on the contemporary Chicago scene. For decades, though, her entire catalogue consisted of a single 45, "You Don't Want My Loving No More" / "I Always Want You Near," which she recorded (as "Little Mary") in the mid-1960s for the obscure Friendly Five label, accompanied by her husband, guitarist Morris Pejoe (misspelled "Pejae" on the record).

Born in Clarendon, Arkansas, in 1935, she sang in local jukes during her teenage years, working on shows with visiting celebrities like James Cotton, Robert Nighthawk, and Howlin' Wolf. In 1957 she moved north and settled in the Chicago suburb of Waukegan, where she met and married Pejoe, who had already garnered modest success with releases on such labels as Abco, Vee-Jay, and the Chess subsidiary Checker. They moved to the city in 1961, and their popularity on the local circuit led to Mary's sole recording opportunity, probably in 1963 (some sources suggest 1966). "You Don't Want My Loving," basically a guitar

Mary Lane, Buddy Guy's
Legends, Chicago, 2017.

showcase for Pejoe, was a thinly disguised remake of Freddie King's "Hide Away" with vocals added; Mary's singing was somewhat thin but winningly aggressive. The flip, "Always Want You Near," seasoned with a braying horn section, sounded more original, as Mary summoned a timbre that resonated with spunky brio.

The couple separated sometime after that, but Mary continued on, scuffling in clubs whenever she could find a gig, which pretty much defined her career until the '90s, when she cut a handful of tracks for the Wolf label and then, in 1997, recorded her first (and thus far, only) full-length album, *Appointment with the Blues*, on the Chicago-based Noir imprint. She continues to appear at various venues around the city, and despite a somewhat dry timbre and limited range (her voice has thickened considerably since she waxed those sides back in the '60s), she's honed a sassy, bad-ass blueswoman persona that goes over well with the predominantly white audiences she usually performs for. As of this writing, in 2019, she is preparing to release a new CD, her long-awaited follow-up to *Appointment with the Blues*.

Sam Lay

Born in Birmingham, Alabama in 1935, drummer Sam Lay arrived in Chicago in 1959 and hooked up almost immediately with harmonica ace Little Walter, whose penchant for grafting urban blues to ideas borrowed from jazz saxophonists made him the perfect foil for Sam, who by then had perfected his complex, multitextured "double-shuffle"—a rhythmic impetus that could both push with deep-pocket drive and swing with urbane hipness. The following year, he jumped to Howlin' Wolf's band, which purveyed a sound as primal as Walter's had been forward-looking; he also continued to do session work for other artists at Chess Records (his Chess discography includes over 40 sides).

By the mid-'60s, the white blues "revival" was underway, and Chicago-based harpist Paul Butterfield recruited both Sam Lay and bassist Jerome Arnold to join his band. On Sunday, July 25, 1965, Lay and Arnold, along with Mike Bloomfield, Al Kooper, and Barry Goldberg, accompanied Bob Dylan on Dylan's apocalyptic "electric" set at the Newport Folk Festival. Sam also backed the Chambers Brothers on the first night of the festival, and he accompanied Lightnin' Hopkins during a daytime blues workshop (which, unlike the Dylan set, undoubtedly didn't rankle the purists at all).

He then went on to participate in Dylan's *Highway 61 Revisited* sessions (that's probably him on the title track, although his name was left off the credits), and he also appeared on the famous *Fathers and Sons* LP with Muddy Waters and Waters's longtime keyboardist Otis Spann along with Butterfield, Bloomfield, and bassist Donald "Duck" Dunn of Booker T. & the MGs, among others. He was a member of James Cotton's early bands, and he provided the rhythmic impetus behind the Siegel-Schwall Band, a mainstay on Chicago's '70s/ '80s-era North Side club circuit. Finally deciding to cast his lot as a leader, he later formed the Sam Lay Blues Revival, which at various times featured such veterans as Jimmy Rogers, Eddie Taylor, and harpist George "Wild Child" Butler.

Unlike many of his contemporaries, Sam Lay has received significant "mainstream" (that is, white establishment) recognition—in large part, no doubt, because of his association with white notables like Dylan and the Bloomfield/Butterfield axis. He's an inductee of the Blues Hall of Fame in Memphis, the Jazz

Hall of Fame in Los Angeles, and the Rock & Roll Hall of Fame in Cleveland. In recent years, as health problems have impaired his once-fiery drumming style, he has transformed himself into an acoustic guitarist, specializing in vintage Delta blues and postwar standards—retracing, in a way, the historical trajectory of both the music and his own lifelong contributions to it.

Holle Thee Maxwell

Holle Thee Maxwell's career began in the mid '60s, which technically makes her a member of the "younger" musical generation who came of age following the postwar blues boom. Nonetheless, Holle, now in her early seventies, is notable as one of the few still-active veterans of Chicago's glory days as a soul music powerhouse.

Born in 1945 (she claims the birth name "Holly Thee MarClaRoDe' Maxwell"), she was classically trained in piano and voice, and by her own admission it took her a while to cultivate a grittier vocal sound when she decided to become an R&B singer. One of her earliest public performances in the genre, in fact, was something of a disaster—the audience at Peyton Place, a South Side nightclub, responded to her attempt to sing the standard "Misty" by throwing things at her. According to her own recollection, she responded by sequestering herself with records by soul singers like Gladys Knight and Aretha Franklin. When she reappeared at Peyton Place a few months later, she stunned the crowd with her version of Aretha's "Respect."

Paradoxically, though, by that time she'd already been singing soul music for several years. She sang with a girl group, the Tourjourettes, while attending high school, and a year or two after that, in 1965, she was discovered by Chicago-based promoter and music producer Bill "Bunky" Sheppard, who produced her first singles for the Constellation label. "(Happiness Will Cost You) One Thin Dime" was a lilting, candy-coated confection—at times, the neophyte vocalist sounded a little uneasy with the cutesiness of the arrangement and the song's overall conceit—but the follow-up, "Only When You're Lonely," was more substantial, and Holly (as she was billed then) immersed herself in its feel of wounded romanticism. On these early outings, her producers seem to have been attempting to mold her into a copy of fellow Chicagoan Jan Bradley.

Although none of her releases charted nationally, Holly garnered a decent amount of local recognition, even before her moment of truth at Peyton Place compelled her to take the plunge and dedicate herself fully to a career in R&B.

Holle Thee Maxwell, Motor
Row Brewing, Chicago, 2017.

"Philly Barracuda," a more aggressive dance number released on Star in 1966, was ostensibly an answer to the Mar-Keys' "Philly Dog"—a lot less funky, it must be admitted, but shot through with good spirits. At one point, Holly performed it at a sock hop hosted by DJ Herb Kent at Crane High School, where she leapt onto a cafeteria table and demonstrated the dance herself. "Don't Say You Love Me until You Do," the follow-up, was compromised by a labored-sounding melody line, but it gave Holly the opportunity to strut her classically honed vocal chops—the little-girl mewl of her earlier outings now sounded surer and more full-bodied. Subsequent sides, such as 1969's "Never Love Again" (Smit-Whit) and "Suffer" (Curtom), benefited from more robust production, but although Holly's voice had matured—and despite her professed ambition to emulate soul divas like Gladys Knight and Aretha—she remained mostly rooted in the fluffy, teen-oriented Chicago sound.

When her solo career began to falter, though, she began to showcase more of the musical depth she'd claimed since the beginning. After moving to California, she worked and toured with artists as diverse as jazz organist Jimmy Smith—a show she did with Smith in South Africa inspired critic Roy Christie to laud her as "virtually a reincarnation of Billie [Holiday]"[3]—and Ike Turner, whom she befriended in the '70s and worked with, on and off, primarily in Europe, between 1978 and 1992. (Her memoir, *Freebase Ain't Free*, which she self-published in late 2018, offers a rare—and, she insists, accurate and unbiased—insider's account of life as Ike's confidante.) A solo stint in Europe in the mid-1990s furthered her overseas reputation, but she soon returned home, and she's been based mostly in Chicago ever since.

These days, billing herself as "The Original Black Blonde Bombshell," she's as known for the outlandishness of her garb and her stage act as she is for her still-considerable vocal prowess—the former warbler of teen-dream love songs is now capable of venturing into realms of nasty-gal funkiness that might make even Tina Turner blush—but even when she risks reducing herself to a novelty act, her emotional commitment and her charismatic rapport with her audience convey a seriousness of purpose that can't be denied.

Otis Rush

Otis Rush recorded some of the most harrowing, emotionally intense blues ever waxed during his tenure at Chicago's Cobra label between 1956–1958. Although he continued to perform and record, sometimes brilliantly, for many years after that, those early sides remain the cornerstone of his reputation.

Born near Philadelphia, Mississippi, in 1934, Otis moved to Chicago in 1948. At first, he considered himself primarily a harmonica player, but he honed his guitar chops, incorporating some of the progressive, jazz-influenced ideas he absorbed from the recordings of T-Bone Walker. By the mid-'50s, he was leading his own band (as "Little Otis"), and in 1956, Willie Dixon brought him to the West Side recording studio owned by Cobra's proprietor Eli Toscano. There, along with fellow young lions Buddy Guy and Magic Sam, he helped codify a high-energy sound that emphasized guitar virtuosity and emotional fervor, a sound that became known in subsequent years as the "West Side" style of Chicago blues—something of a misnomer, since the artists themselves performed all over town, and they didn't all live on the West Side.

"I Can't Quit You Baby," Otis's Cobra debut, made it to No. 6 on the R&B charts in 1956. Although he never charted again, the song was a harbinger of things to come: He delivered Willie Dixon's lyrics in a tremulous wail pitched between anguish and terror; his guitar work, though somewhat muted in the production, achieved a similar intensity. Subsequent outings, especially minor-key master-pieces like "My Love Will Never Die," "All Your Love (I Miss Loving)," and "Double Trouble," mined depths of emotional devastation that few blues artists, before or since, have dared explore. Those last two, released in 1959, were the product of Rush's final session at Cobra in 1958, when the house band was augmented by Ike Turner and members of his Kings of Rhythm (that's Turner's tremolo-enhanced guitar searing its way through "Double Trouble")—considered by some to be among the most incendiary studio encounters in the history of Chicago blues.

It's all the more remarkable when we realize that someone at Cobra—probably songwriter/producer Dixon, who considered himself a pop songsmith at least as much as a deep bluesman, regardless of the image he cultivated for himself later on—wanted to market Otis as a pop singer, and a rather tepid one at that. Some of Otis's blues sides on Cobra were paired with fare—"Jump Sister Bessie," which virtually wasted a stellar harmonica performance from Little Walter (b/w "Love That Woman"); "Sit Down Baby" (b/w "I Can't Quit You Baby"); "Violent Love" (b/w "My Love Will Never Die")—that was almost laughably mediocre, gimmicky, and devoid of substance either musical or emotional. Among the more notable exceptions are from that final, epic encounter with Ike Turner: "Keep On Loving Me Baby" (the flipside of "Double Trouble"), in which Otis inhabits the persona of a man wracked with an erotic hunger so intense it approaches existential catas-trophe, and the rocking jump-blues "My Baby's a Good 'Un" (paired with "All Your Love," and not to be confused with the similarly titled "She's a Good 'Un" from an earlier session). For a stellar example of how Otis could take posses-sion of a song and remake it in his own image, compare his waking-nightmare version of Dixon's "My Love Will Never Die" with the lugubrious 1952 original by Dixon's Big Three Trio.

Cobra folded in 1959 ("All Your Love [I Miss Loving]" / "My Baby's a Good 'Un" was the label's last release), but Otis carried on. His "So Many Roads, So Many Trains," released in 1960 on Chess, was a highlight of his post-Cobra work; his 1962 single on the Houston-based Duke label, "Homework" b/w "I Have to Laugh," though somewhat lacking in originality ("I Have to Laugh" is obviously based on Bobby "Blue" Bland's "I Pity the Fool," and "Homework" incongruously grafts Otis onto a teen-pop setting, although he manages to extract some genuine bluesiness from it), is a collectors' item today. But it wasn't until the mid-'60s that he was "rediscovered" and canonized by a new generation of aficionados. His output over the next several decades was uneven, and he also suffered some

Otis Rush at his Chicago
Blues Festival tribute, 2016.

personal setbacks, but at his best *(Right Place Wrong Time*, released in 1976; *Ain't Enough Comin' In*, from 1994; various live recordings made at festivals and clubs), he summoned enough of his genius to solidify and further his reputation, even among newcomers unfamiliar with his early work.

In 2003, Otis suffered a stroke, and he never again performed in public. A tribute at the 2016 Chicago Blues Festival, coordinated by Chicago-based producer and writer Dick Shurman, who was also a longtime friend, returned him to the stage for the final time—although obviously impaired, he was aglow as he basked in the adulation of the crowd at the Petrillo Music Shell; he even summoned the strength to put a microphone to his lips and rasp out a few jubilant shouts to his admirers.

Otis Rush died on September 29, 2018, having lived out his final years in quiet convalescence with his wife, Masaki. His musical legacy, though, remains a living presence; it's among the blues' most powerful and commanding, and it's felt anytime and anywhere the music is played.[4]

Byther Smith

At his best, Byther Smith is as powerful (and sometimes frightening) as anyone in Chicago blues. His guitar leads are honed to a rapier edge, and as a lyricist he can invoke intensities of torment and darkness that surpass even such legendary angst-masters as Robert Johnson.

Byther's biography could stand as a virtual template for the archetypical bluesman's life. He was born in Mississippi in 1932.[5] His mother died in childbirth; his father died about six months later; a few years after that, one of his sisters perished in a house fire. When he was fifteen, he left the Mississippi farm on which he'd been eking out a living as a sharecropper. Traveling west instead of north, he ended up in Prescott, Arizona, where he labored as a cattleman and played acoustic bass in a country band. This was also when he began to cultivate his interest in boxing—for a man who'd had to fight to survive virtually since the day he was born, earning a living through fisticuffs must have seemed like the most natural thing in the world.

In the mid-1950s, he moved to Chicago. There, under the tutelage of his cousin J.B. Lenoir, he took up the guitar and began to gig around the local clubs. He eventually had the opportunity to work with such notables as Otis Rush and Howlin' Wolf, and he recorded a few sides for small labels—the most readily available, "Money Tree," released on the Be Be imprint in about 1974, was based musically on B.B. King's "Why I Sing the Blues," although Byther's flint-rasp vocals ignited fresh sparks as he wailed out the song's tale of a free-spending, unloving woman. But it wasn't until the 1980s, when he began cutting LPs that sold primarily among white aficionados (his most recent, both from 2008, are *Got No Place to Go* [Fedora] and *Blues on the Moon—Live at the Natural Rhythm Social Club* [Delmark]), that he began to enjoy a reputation even mildly commensurate with his talents. And even then, neither his recording opportunities nor most of the gigs he was able to get came anywhere near reflecting the magnitude of his capabilities and his gifts.

Now in his late eighties, Smitty—as he is affectionately known—has mostly retired from performing, but his recorded canon, relatively sparse though it is, includes blues as raw and uncompromising as any that have ever emanated from Chicago.

PART III

Inheritors

"Great Black Music—Ancient to the Future" is the motto of Chicago's trailblazing free-jazz collective, the Association for the Advancement of Creative Musicians (AACM). The music made by these inheritors of the blues tradition also reflects that spirit.

From the traditionalism of the Morganfield brothers and most of the Taylor family though the synth-heavy, pop-tinged fusion of the "southern soul" or "soul blues" represented by Nellie "Tiger" Travis and the late Floyd Taylor, to the eclectic "Americana" stylistic meldings of Shemekia Copeland, all the way to the iconoclastic post-blues/rock modernism of figures like Sugar Blue and Ronnie Baker Brooks, these artists' music illustrates the diversity that characterizes the "Legacy" they have chosen to embrace and carry on. In some cases, the balancing act can seem precarious: Figures such as John Primer, Deitra Farr, Lil' Ed, and Shemekia Copeland herself, all to a greater or lesser degree, have worked to forge sounds grounded enough in tradition to pass the "authenticity" test while also staying relevant to changing social, cultural, and aesthetic values. An artist like Nellie Travis, meanwhile, strives to retain popularity among both her longtime white admirers, whose tastes run mostly toward traditional 12-bar Chicago blues and its heavier, rock-influenced progeny, and the predominantly African American "southern soul" or "soul-blues" audience she captured with her 2013 hit "Mr. Sexy Man."

Nonetheless, as diverse and even contradictory as their musical philoso-phies and aesthetics may sometimes seem, these inheritors of the legacy remain determined, each in his or her own way, to keep their music and their message both rooted and relevant. In fact, that's probably the most authentically "traditional" characteristic they all share. Roots thrive only when they nurture something alive and growing.

Lil' Ed

"It Lets Me Know Where I Came From"

You have to bring that music out through your body. Those lyrics have to come through your body, and [when you] play it on that guitar; that guitar has to say the same thing you're saying. All your love, all your hate, all your strength has got to come through your guitar. So the people can say, "Wow—I feel that." In order for them to feel it, it's got to come through you. There's some times when I've been singing, and that tear come out of my eye. 'Cause I'm feeling what I'm doing. I'm not just up there to show it; I'm up there to give it to you, to show you how I felt when it happened to me. The blues is saying, today might be bad, but tomorrow the grass is greener on the other side. That stuff back in the past, it's there, but I know now that tomorrow is another day.

That's why they call me a party band.

—Lil' Ed Williams

" **E**ven though my uncle's dead and gone, he's still teaching me through his music."

Lil' Ed Williams's high-octane blues showmanship—raucous slidework; stentorian deep-baritone vocals; a hyperkinetic stage routine that sometimes culminates in his leaping atop one of his sidemen's shoulders to be borne triumphantly off the stage—has earned him international blues stardom over the course of a thirty-plus–year career. By his own assertion, though, he has never strayed far from his roots. As he relaxes in the dining room of his home in the village of Riverwoods, Illinois, about thirty miles north of Chicago, his conversation returns often to those roots—specifically, his uncle and mentor, the late Chicago slide guitarist J.B. Hutto.

These days, Hutto is considered one of the giants of Chicago blues, but for much of his career he was little more than a local journeyman. He arrived in Chicago from Georgia in the late 1940s, just in time to catch the postwar urban blues boom in its first flowering. With his band, the Hawks (named for Chicago's vicious winter wind), he scuffled in neighborhood jukes and recorded a few sides for the Chance label in the mid-'50s. He then retired from music for almost a decade; when he returned, he found celebrity on the white blues "revival" circuit, where he became an international favorite before succumbing to cancer in 1983.[1]

Hutto's rough-hewn, declamatory style (one online critic praised his "wild and exuberant stage act . . . incomprehensible vocals and his focus on intensity rather than virtuosity"[2]) may have exemplified blues "authenticity" to his new fans, but for his young nephew, growing up on the West Side of Chicago in the mid-'60s, the man and his music were a hallmark of family, good times, and— eventually—inspiration. "It was at Lake and Paulina," he recalls. "My auntie and my grandmother raised me."

> I think I was six years old; we had a big back yard. We were close by the train tracks. Uncle J.B. used to come over there, and there was another building next to ours, they had a second floor, a big wide porch, and they'd send all the kids on the porch 'cause they didn't want us down there with them, 'cause they was drinking. And J.B. and them would be down there playing, and family would be down there—I had so many cousins, you know, they was just coming from everywhere—and the kids would just kind of hang on the porch and look down on 'em.
>
> If J.B. wasn't playing outside, he was playing in the house. He'd come in the house, bring his amp in. J.B. and them would be in the room, with my grandmother and them, doin' their little drinkin' thing, but the kids wasn't allowed in there. But we would come up to the room and peep in until they ran us out.
>
> What really caught my eye was the way the slide shimmered. 'Cause when we were coming up, we had forty-watt bulbs, and the [light] was always kinda diminished. I'd see that slide, and J.B. just shaking that slide, and it's shimmering from a distance, and I thought, "What is that?" And it sounded so good, too. And finally, Uncle J.B. seen me keep peepin' in on him, he told me to come in. He said, "Come in the room, set down right there; don't move."

Enthralled, Ed began paying more attention to the blues records his older relatives played at parties—Muddy Waters, John Lee Hooker, Howlin' Wolf—but despite his infatuation with J.B.'s slide, the instrument his uncle decided to teach him first was the drums. A little later, J.B. began instructing Ed's young brother Pookie [née James Young] on bass, and Ed watched carefully as Pookie learned how to play it. "This is a real good thing for me," he asserts today, "because now,

Lil' Ed, Rosa's Lounge, Chicago, 2018.

when I get ready to make my music, I can lay the bass line down. I can lay the drum line down. I already know about rhythm; I'm not worried about rhythm. And then I can lay my line down. So it gives the guys a better feel of what I want them to do for me."

The guitar, though, was what most captured Ed's imagination, and eventually J.B. mentored him on that, as well. One of the first things his uncle taught him was that his guitar sound, based on the style pioneered by Elmore James in the late '40s and early '50s, as rough and unhewn as it may have seemed, was crafted carefully, with strict attention to nuance and tone. "It's a lot that goes into it," Ed affirms, "a lot of fingerwork and tone issues." He explained:

Making your tone is the most important thing. J.B. had lot of different tones. One I like the best is the one he's got where his guitar sounds like it's like that [he holds his arms out wide]—put a little echo on it, and a little reverb—so I picked that up, and I took it and put a little distortion on it so it would growl a little bit.

I hear a lot of guitar players really want to try to sound like Elmore—anybody can slide when they learn it—but you have to feel like he felt and think like he thought in order to be able to recreate [his sound], and you got to know his touch. Because there's some things in there where he's plucking the string with his thumb and [also] sliding, and people actually think he's picking. But he's not—his thumb is what's making that really unique tone that he's got.

There weren't a lot of young folks on the West Side interested in the blues in those days. Ed, eager to hone his chops with a band, soon found himself working with musicians whose tastes were decidedly more contemporary—although, ironically, at least some of them would eventually become leading lights, along with Ed himself, on the city's blues scene. One, guitarist Rico McFarland, was "the only kid on the block that could play the Temptations and the Chi-Lites and all that stuff." Ed and Pookie would join McFarland and his brother Lumpy ("First time I had ever seen a cat with, like, a set of drums, like thirty-two-piece drums—and this cat could play every one of these drums"), and they'd work out on the soul hits of the day. The sessions, though, didn't always stay as focused as Rico might have wished:

> Rico would get me over his house so I could learn how to rhythm; he wanted me to rhythm to his songs. And I'd get up there and I'd be rhythming, and he'd run out of songs. So he had to go back to his paper, check what-all he had—"Why don't you play some 'til I get back?" Well, I look at Pookie—you know what I'm gonna play, right? Gon' play some blues. We start playing blues, Lumpy was all excited, he was drumming, and Rico would come back and look at me and shake his head, and tell me, "You fired! Get out of here!" "Man, you gon' fire me?" "Yeah, you fired—get outta here." And I start walkin' out the door, and he called me back, "Come on back! You know I gotta have a rhythm player." So he'd fire me and hire me.

By the mid-'70s, Ed and Pookie had decided to cast their lot fully with the blues. Their first band, Ed recalls was "just three pieces. We had a guy named George; he was our drummer, a little skinny guy. He had a bad heart. We'd do 'Mojo' [Muddy Waters's 'Got My Mojo Working'] fifty miles an hour—kick it off, and then we'd look back at him, and he's like he's gasping for air."

One of their first gigs was at Big Duke's Blue Flame Lounge on the corner of Madison and California; their pay for the night was six dollars, which they split equally (no bandleader's perks for Ed in those days). "They had all these weird people in there," Ed says, shuddering a little at the memory. "They had this guy called Popeye; he could pop his eyes out. I was playing, and every once in a while the people would go 'Aaaauurrggghh!' And I'm looking at Pookie, I'm thinking, what is going on? So I stepped up, and he turned around, and his eyeballs was sitting on his cheeks. That 'bout scared me half to death."

For the next decade or so, most of Ed's gigs were in roughshod West Side venues like Big Duke's—he remembers, among others, the Riviera at Lake and Kedzie (the old Silvio's Lounge, which had been one of Howlin' Wolf's strongholds); Waldo's near Lake and Pulaski; and the Delta Fish Market at Jackson and Kedzie ("Johnny Littlejohn was the man. . . . If you were on stage and Johnny Littlejohn pulled up, you had to get off"). Although, like most scuffling musicians, he nourished dreams of stardom, for the time being he had to be content with working his day job at the Red Carpet Car Wash in suburban Morton Grove, along with whatever low-paying gigs on evenings and weekends that he and Pookie could hustle up.

Meanwhile, Uncle J.B. was enjoying his latter-day career as a "rediscovered" bluesman. When he was in town, he'd invite Ed and Pookie to come see him in action, and at least once or twice they got to accompany him on the road. Along with the memories, Ed plumbed these experiences for lessons in stagecraft:

> J.B. used to take us to Wise Fools Pub [on North Lincoln Ave.] all the time. That was a little bitty stage they had there. He stepped off that stage one night, and he must've hit some water, 'cause his foots went up in the air, and he fell flat on his back. And me and Pookie reached down for him, and he shook his head no, and he laid there, played for about five minutes. And he got up, and he was all good. It was amazing—people were going nuts to see J.B. do some stuff like that.
>
> We played a club called Vegetable Buddies in South Bend, Indiana. They had this huge stage, and they had tree trunks for tables, kind of slanted, and J.B. jumped off the stage. We looked for him, and all of a sudden his head popped up, and he's walking these tree-trunk tables, and he got about halfway out, and he looked back at me and becked [beckoned] for me to come out. And I shook my head no, and he becked again, and I shook my head no, and he kinda gave me that look, "If you don't come out offa that stage, I'm gonna tan your 'hind."
>
> So I jump off the stage, and I squats, and my pants rips. So I just sprung right back up on stage backwards, and the people went crazy. And I don't know how I did it, but I know I would never even attempt to try to do that again.

In the mid-'80s, Chicago's Alligator label was recruiting a lineup for *The New Bluebloods*, an anthology that would feature some of the city's up-and-coming blues artists. Label president Bruce Iglauer had seen Ed once or twice at Big Duke's; his raw slidework and exuberant demeanor reminded Iglauer of Hound Dog Taylor, another Elmore James disciple, whose debut LP, *Hound Dog Taylor and the Houserockers*, had launched the label in 1971. Thinking he'd get a handful of songs for the anthology, he invited Ed and his band, which now included drummer Louis Henderson and guitarist Dave Weld ("J.B. had been coaching Dave to be my rhythm player"), along with Ed and Pookie, into the studio. What happened next has become Chicago blues legend:

> We was gonna go in and do two songs and call it a day. I was so amazed, 'cause I hadn't never seen that kind of—they had these nice amps sitting up, they had little baffles in front of you, and I'm thinkin', what are we doing here? And what really amazed me was the sound I was getting through the headphones, 'cause I had never used headphones before. So I had no idea—Bruce, like, "You gotta put these on." I'm like, "For really? I'm not gonna hear my band." He says, "Oh, yeah, you gonna hear 'em." So I got all this full feeling coming from these headphones. And I think half of the staff, this big glass—you could see Bruce, he wanted to make sure we could see him, and lotta the staff of Alligator was back there. And I started playing, 'cause I was so nervous, I was 'bout scared half to death, and I look at them, and they was smiling, and people were dancing behind the glass, and I thought, man, this is cool!
>
> We did thirty songs in three hours. They kept saying, "Play another! Play another!" So we just kept rolling, and I just played it like I was playing a show. 'Cause I didn't know no other way to play it. He came out, he says, "Guys, we did thirty songs already. Let's just make an album out of this." And I was like, "Okay!" That was a happy moment.

The album, *Roughhousin'* released in 1986, featured twelve tracks from the session, and it garnered accolades from blues and pop critics alike, almost all of whom raved about its spontaneity and its feel of raw, juke-joint abandon. Some were nonplussed, though, by Ed's autobiographical "Car Wash Blues" on which he proclaimed, with no apparent irony, "My boss, I tell everybody, he's a mean old Jew." A statement like that might not raise an eyebrow on Chicago's West Side, but Ed's new listenership wasn't so sanguine (Iglauer, for his part, blanched when he heard it, but he decided that realness, in this case, was the better part of valor).

Ed maintains he'd never really intended to sing that line—it just came out in the heat of the moment—and he was as nervous as anyone about how it might be taken, especially at work. "Right after we did that record," he remembers, "my boss at the car wash walks up and goes, 'When am I gonna get my copy?'"

> He had never heard me sing the "Car Wash Blues" and that freaked me out, 'cause I thought I was gonna get fired. And he played it, he was in his office playing it, and he comes out and he's got this big smile on his face, and I go, "Ah, man, I know I'm fired now!" And he walks up to me and he goes, "I love 'Car Wash Blues,' Lil' Ed.

And you said it just right. I'm a mean old Jew, and I want everybody to think that I'm a mean old Jew!"

As it turned out, Ed's boss wasn't so mean after all; he agreed to let Ed take time off to play the gigs that were already becoming plentiful in the wake of the album's success, and he eventually encouraged him to quit the job and go into music full-time; if it didn't work out, he could always come back to the car wash.

There was little danger of that, at least at first. *Genuine Houserockin' Music*, an Alligator anthology released the same year as *Roughhousin',* included "Older Woman," another track from that marathon first session; *The New Bluebloods* finally hit the streets in 1987, with Ed's "Young Thing" as one of the featured tracks. By this time, Lil' Ed and the Blues Imperials had become a full-blown phenomenon—their shows not only lived up to the promise implied by their recordings; they usually far surpassed it. But although their increasingly rigorous performance schedule honed their chops to a new sharpness, the band didn't manifest its true identity until a year or two later, after guitarist Mike Garrett and drummer Kelly Littleton had replaced Weld and Henderson. That's the lineup that exploded into full force on *Chicken, Gravy, & Biscuits*, the band's sophomore outing in 1989, and it's the lineup that has comprised Lil' Ed's Blues Imperials ever since—almost a quarter-century with the same personnel, an endurance record almost unheard of in blues.

Over the next few years they seemed unstoppable, releasing *What You See Is What You Get* in 1992 (once again to nearly universal acclaim); contributing four tracks to 1993's commemorative double CD, *The Alligator Records 20th Anniversary Tour*; and maintaining a touring schedule both exhilarating and exhausting, all the more so given Ed's high-energy performance style. His name had become virtually synonymous with the "Houserockin'" appellation Alligator had adopted as its catchphrase—a promise of a no-holds-barred, all-night blues party in the rough-and-ready Chicago tradition. Behind the scenes, though, darkness was gathering.

"Just messing around with the wrong people at the wrong time," Ed says today, refusing to make excuses for the descent into cocaine addiction that almost destroyed both his career and his life as the '90s wore on. "I was a fool. I indulged it because I was curious, and it took me into a whole different world. And things started getting a little rough; I was kinda missing a few gigs here and there, not thinking about what I was doing, and my life was—I was in misery. I thought that I was doing all right, but I wasn't doing all right. And I was having a bad love relationship at the time, too, so that didn't help matters." It took some tough love from his daughter for him to start turning things around:

> It had got so bad in my household 'til me and my old lady wasn't sleeping together any more. I was sleeping on the floor; she was sleeping in her room. I didn't want to leave my kids; I thought I was being there for them. But I wasn't there for them because I wasn't doing anything. I was getting high, paying the rent because I thought I had to, and just running the streets.
>
> So my daughter walked into the room one night, and I'm laying there, and man, I weighed ninety eight pounds. Ninety eight pounds! And my daughter looked at me, and she said, "Why are you here?" Just like that. I said, "What do you mean? What're you talking about, why I'm here? I'm here for y'all." "No," she said. "Why are you here? You ain't with Mom, 'cause Mom's doing her own thing. You're sleeping on the floor. Why are you here?" And I said, "Well, I'm here for y'all." She said, "No." Said, "We can manage. We'll manage if [you're] not here." She said, "I love you, but you don't have to be here, 'cause you're killing yourself."
>
> She was seventeen. And I looked at her, I looked in her eyes, and I looked at her, and I said to her, "What you say is true." I said, "But if I leave here, I won't be back for a long, long time." She said, "If that's what it takes to get you straightened out in your life, you need to go."

Some time earlier, at a gig, he'd met a woman named Pamela Price, a blues enthusiast who lived in suburban Mount Prospect, where she ran a daycare center out of her home. The two became close, although when she drove him home after a show he always insisted that she drop him off about a mile away from his house ("She didn't even know where I lived at, 'cause I wouldn't tell her"). Now, determined to flee the hell he'd created for himself, he bolted out of that house, eluded yet another relative who was also strung out and wanted to follow him into the night, and made it to a phone booth. He called Pam and asked her to come get him at the place where she usually dropped him off. As he remembers it, he then "took off running," and when he arrived at their meeting place—about two miles from where he'd made that desperate call—"Pam's car was coming up off the expressway. So I just went like that [he gestures], got in her car, she went back down to the expressway and took me to her house. Now this is my spiritual point of view; this is how I know God was in control. That's a blessing. And that's a miracle—the plan—that I was going to meet her right as I come over the expressway."

Life in Mount Prospect was a revelation ("I was in pain, I was in agony, I had a lot of hatred in my heart. But right then, I looked up in that sky, and I looked down and seen rabbits running 'cross the grass, and I looked up, and I seen the stars. I found a peace in my life right then"), but the climb back to sobriety was long, sometimes excruciating. He'd tried it a few times already—at one point, Bruce Iglauer himself had taken him in for a few weeks in a vain attempt to keep him off the streets and away from temptation—but this time he was determined. Among other things, his band had finally realized how dire his situation was, and they'd delivered their own ultimatum—they simply refused to play behind him anymore until he cleaned up. Iglauer, having seen Ed's problem up close, came to a similar conclusion: "Bruce said he wasn't going to send me on the road until I got myself together."

To make ends meet, Ed went back to his old job at the car wash for a while, but even with his tenure at Alligator on hold, he didn't abandon music entirely. He reunited with Dave Weld; the partnership didn't last, but the pair's 1996 CD on the Earwig label, *Keep On Walkin'*, represented a tantalizing stylistic widening for Ed, showcasing him in a variety of contexts that probably surprised a lot of his longtime fans. Several of the tracks were acoustic; one, "Too Late Baby," was a pop ballad complete with strings, which Ed delivered in a muscular baritone croon. In 1998, Earwig released *Who's Been Talking*, which paired Ed with bassist Willie Kent along with other Chicago veterans—guitarist Eddie C. Campbell, drummer Cleo "Baldhead Pete" Williams—on a set that sounds almost like a late-night jam session in an after-hours juke. Through it all, though, recovery remained his top priority. "I had been with Pam five years when I was truly clean," he remembers (they married in about 1998). "It took me ten minutes to get into that; it took me five years—no, actually, maybe seven—to get out of it. My daughter, I told her, I said I knew [I'd gotten clean]. It was awesome. She came to a show, where I was at. And she just stood up, and she had tears in her eyes, 'cause last time she seen me, I was in raggedy blue jeans. When she seen me again, I was clean-shaved, cut, and wearing a nice suit, and she was so happy. And we both cried together."

Get Wild!, Ed's 1999 release on Alligator, wasn't billed as a "comeback" CD, but that's essentially what it was. Reunited with the Imperials, who seemed not to have missed a beat during Ed's hiatus, he stormed through a predictably raucous set of boogie-shuffles and slide workouts, leavened by newfound (and hard-won) introspection and vulnerability. Contrary to his bacchanalian image, he'd always been an effective balladeer, but he'd seldom bared his soul the way he did here on "Change My Way of Living," a brooding, minor-key meditation that features Ed's leadwork at its most searing, over which he delivers his testimonial ("The Good

Lil' Ed (L) with Toronzo Cannon, benefit for 12-year-old Jameson Stokes, House of Blues, Chicago, 2018.

Lord sent me an angel, she helped me to see my way") in an emotion-choked rasp. "That's my heart," he concurs. "I play that song all the time."

> To sing that song, it took a lot out of me. Because I had to think about where I come from and where I was going, and where I had been, and that's the hard part. That's what it's about. Because it brings me back; it takes me back where I was, lets me know where I came from. Keeps me aware, keeps me on my toes. I had fell to the bottom, and I knew I had to do something about it. That's what we have to do. So people think, "Oh, man, he's having such a great time." But they don't know, some-time it's a lot of pain that goes through those guitar strings.

Nonetheless, Lil' Ed and the Blues Imperials never lost their primary focus; they're a "party band," unashamed, and that's what they're determined to remain; you won't find any blues Pagliacci laughing-to-keep-from-crying bathos on their shows or in their recordings. (Even when Ed performs "Change My Way of Living," he'll often temper the song's intensity with self-deprecating asides and playful signifying at his sidemen.) This, in fact, might be the rootsiest thing about them, even more than Ed's carefully crafted evocations of Uncle J.B.'s style. Blues, regardless of the stereotypes perpetuated by various romanticists through the years, has never been a pity-party; it has historically been a music that dares to stare down life, in all its brutality and horror, and then sing—or at least dance—in its face. That's its liberating power, that's its universal appeal, and that's what too many naysayers continue to miss when they criticize good-timers like Ed for not being "serious" enough, or for not conforming to the mythos of the tormented, self-lacerating bluesman.

Ed's hard-core admirers, of course, have no such problems. They've even organized themselves into an informal, widely dispersed fan club known as the Ed Heads; they show up at his gigs, sporting fezzes similar to the ones he's worn on stage for years (and not too different from some of J.B. Hutto's own headgear), ready to carry on all night with their hero. Ed even cut a song, "Ed Heads' Boogie" (from his appropriately titled 2002 CD, *Heads Up!*), in their honor. "Those are my fans, man," he says with a disarming tenderness. "Those are my Ed Heads, and I love 'em to death."

Meanwhile, he' looking forward to expanding his emotional palate even further. "My next CD, it's going to be interesting," he predicts. "'Cause right now, I'm into Frank Sinatra, [Perry] Como, I'm into these type of peoples."

> Patsy Cline, Willie Nelson and Ray Charles, Judy Garland—They sung meaningful stuff. A lot of that stuff was in movies, and it melted your heart. 'Cause she's crying, she's hurting, and you're listening to this—it was those lyrics, what was really making you cry. So can you imagine what's gonna come out of that for me?
>
> 'Cause I'm listening to this, and I'm thinking, these are great blues songs. And if you unscramble them, and put 'em right, you gonna have something there that's going to mean something to people. People hear the meaning in those lyrics. When we were young, we weren't looking for that. But as we get older, we can hear, you can hear things that speak to you. And that's what I'm into, now. I'm going to all these thrift stores, getting all these tapes, man, and I'm listening, and I can hear a song coming out of each one of these. There's a little more to Lil' Ed than you think, and they might find out on my next CD.

"Too Late Baby," from *Keep On Walkin'* in 1996, showed that Ed could comport himself with surprising grace as a pop balladeer, so the idea is probably not as outrageous as it may seem. There's little danger, though, that he will ultimately stray too far from the blues. Even as he extols the virtues of Sinatra, Willie Nelson, Judy Garland, and Patsy Cline, he makes it clear that he wants to adapt their aesthetics to his own, not vice versa ("I'm listening to this stuff, and I'm thinking, there's some great blues music in that").

But that can work only if there continues to be enough interest in the blues to keep the music itself viable. Ed is optimistic enough to believe the blues will endure, but he also believes it will endure largely as it has up until now—as a niche-market specialty, adjacent to, but not truly within, the pop-culture main-stream, however much that mainstream may borrow and appropriate its ideas. And whether because he's perfected the art of embracing paradox, or because he's learned not to demand more from life than it's capable of delivering, he seems sanguine about it:

> Blues will be here forever, because everybody have some blues. I think it's going to be at a certain level; I don't think it's gonna get any higher. Because the youngsters are not really paying attention. They don't even want to play instruments; they want to put their record on and scratch that record; they're rather program. And they're gonna have blues in that program—watch!—but it ain't gonna be nothing like what we come up off of; the kids can't feel this type of music 'cause they're so busy listening to hip-hop. But as they get older, and life starts to work on them, that's when the blues gon' come into 'em. 'Cause a lot of the kids now that comes into the clubs [say], "Man, I don't know nothing about this music—I wasn't even growed up in this environment. But this sounds good."
>
> Yeah! 'Cause it's part of life.

Big Bill Morganfield

"I'm on That Journey Right Now"

If you really know the blues, and you hear them and
see their evolution, you know where it came from.
—Big Bill Morganfield, 2016

Please remember, please remember—I'm my daddy's rising son.
—Big Bill Morganfield, "Rising Son" (1999)

Few contemporary artists can discuss "knowing where the blues came from" with the authority of Big Bill Morganfield. Even a casual fan will recognize the name: he is the son of McKinley Morganfield, better known as Muddy Waters, the man who is as responsible as anyone for codifying—some would even say "inventing"—the postwar Chicago blues sound. That sound—resonant with echoes of Delta tradition, updated with big-city amplification and swagger—has been mimicked, imitated, and (all too often) travestied by countless aspirants over the years; Bill Morganfield, like few others can, brings it home.

Bill's life story, appropriately enough, is one of discovery—of his paternity, his musical heritage, and his life's calling. His mother, Mary Brown, came to Chicago as a teenager in the mid-'50s after Muddy had taken a liking to her during a swing through Florida and invited her to join him up north. Given Muddy's "mannish" ways, it was never easy being his girlfriend (or his wife, for that matter), and by the time Bill was born in 1956, she'd met another man, who seems to have been a friend as much as a lover ("I named my child for him," she told biographer Robert Gordon[1]); with his support, she extricated herself from her tempestuous relationship with the blues legend. Still working to put her life together in Chicago, she sent baby William to her own mother in Florida, along with instructions, according to Gordon, "never to tell the child that his father was Muddy Waters."[2]

Bill's grandmother, Verdell Clark, was a loving provider, but she decided not to honor that particular request. "My grandmother refused to not tell me," he affirms. "I've been knowing it all my life. I was a youngster when I first started picking around a guitar. I picked it up because of him; if it wasn't for him, I wouldn't have picked it up. But I said, 'I want to be like my father.'"

That doesn't necessarily mean, though, that he wanted to be a bluesman. "I grew up on Michael Jackson and Stevie Wonder," he recalls. "Gladys Knight, those kinds of people that came through the area, even some of the white guys, Grand Funk Railroad, I remember listening to those guys, Chicago, music of the '70s; Carlos Santana. I remember I had a little transistor radio, and I would sit there with my guitar, and every song that came on, I would try to play it. I would try to play along with every song I heard on the radio. It was actually when I was in high school I got my first real guitar. Maybe like ninth grade, something like that."

It was around this time that Bill finally encountered his father's music and began to understand what all the fuss was about:

> The first record that I had of him, I don't remember what it was called; I saw it somewhere and I got it. I was young, like about twelve, thirteen, or fourteen. I may have just been in a record shop, browsing, I might have seen my daddy's picture on a record. And I got it, and I would put it on the record player in the house: "That's my father doing that!" I would play along with it. I listened to his voice singing; I looked at his guitar playing. It was that slide playing; I was attracted to his slide guitar.
>
> I wouldn't call that my journey's start, because I was playing everything. I just happened to put one of his records on, and I played along with it. And then I would put Al Green's record on and play along with it, and I would put Grand Funk Railroad on there and play along with them, and Chicago, and Santana, and on and on, Otis Redding, all those guys. So I was just playing guitar in general. I remember being at the Boys' Club. I had that one guitar, and I would come from school, and I would be at the Boys' Club and I led the Boys' Club band. I was the leader of that band, I taught 'em all the songs, and we would play little shows for the Boys' Club.

Nonetheless, as he delved more deeply into his father's music, the inheritance and ancestry it represented became more consuming, and it became a more commanding presence in his life. It wasn't exactly the kind of thing a teenager—especially an African American teenager—was expected to be into in those days, but he was undaunted:

> Other kids thought it was kind of funny, initially. I played a lot of different kinds of music; I just liked music. But when I sat down and started trying to learn how to play blues—I ran into one of my old high school buddies [recently], and he said, "It's amazing what you did with this thing. Back then, we thought you were crazy."
>
> I wasn't crazy. I want[ed] to be like my father. I think that's how most kids do, if they have a daddy that's done something that they can be proud of. It's kinda how you do it; you want to be like Dad.

Bill recollects that he was "about ten or so" when he first met Muddy, but he also recalls that Muddy was using a cane then, still suffering from the aftereffects of a 1969 automobile accident, so it's likely that Bill was in his teens—probably not long after (or maybe a little before) that first exposure to his father's music in the record shop. Muddy had come to Fort Lauderdale to play a gig at the War Memorial Auditorium, and Bill's mother Mary, who had moved back to Florida when Bill was about four or five years old, decided to go to the show. They came

Big Bill Morganfield, Chicago Blues Festival, 2017.

back to the house afterward, and they woke up Bill. "That was the first time I can remember laying eyes on him outside of a picture," Bill told Robert Gordon. "We talked, and that night he got rid of the cane. I still got that cane."[3]

At that point, Bill had not yet bought his first real guitar; he was making do with a plastic instrument. "He saw my guitar," Bill remembers; "I always would break that little E string. And when he came by, he noticed that I only had five strings on it. And he told me, 'better get that string for that guitar.'"

It would be years before the two would see each other again. Although he prefers not to dwell on it these days, it's clear that for much of his childhood, the absence of his father weighed heavily on Bill, probably even more so as he grew older and became fully aware of exactly who that father was. "Painful things, painful things," he told journalist Buddy Seigal in 1999. "It's something . . . I wouldn't want for my kids."[4]

"I was hurt for a while," he confirmed to Robert Gordon. "I was deprived of the chance to spend a lot of [my childhood] years with him. Like any son would do with his father."[5] He remembered telephoning Muddy one time. "I said, 'Daddy, I want to come see you.' He didn't say, 'I'm a married man and I got a wife and if you come here, she's going to know what's going on.' He hurt me, broke my heart, he said, 'I don't think it's a good thing to do right now.'"[6]

"I thought my daddy changed his number and didn't want me to bother him," he added. "So for years I didn't try."[7] Meanwhile, refocusing his energies on his own life, he set his sights on college after graduating in 1974 from Dillard High School in Fort Lauderdale. He recalls his college days with pride, as well as some irony: "I was a very smart guy, man, I was an honor student, and I majored in English and I carried around a bunch of books. Even my college classmates—nobody would ever think that I would be a blues musician."

He ended up getting two degrees—a B.A. in English from Tuskegee University in 1979 and another B.A., in communications, from Auburn the following year—and in 1980, he moved to Atlanta, where he attended John Marshall Law School for a year. But instead of pursuing a career in law, he decided to focus on a field more appropriate to his undergraduate major. "I wanted to be a teacher," he confirms. "That was the only thing I knew to do with an English degree, was to teach. I became a teacher in Atlanta; I taught there for several years. I was a coach, too; a basketball coach."

By this time, he had reestablished contact with his father, initiating a latter-day relationship that would continue until Muddy's death in 1983. Appropriately enough, it began with a backstage encounter at one of Muddy's shows. "I had graduated with my first degree," he relates, "and I'd gone over to Auburn University to study communications. I remember we had to introduce ourselves [in class], and I told everybody that my dad was Muddy Waters. My teacher was a musician; he thought that was kind of intriguing. He called me, and he said, 'Your father's going to be in Atlanta, at the Agora Ballroom. You gotta go say hi to him.' He knew I hadn't spoken to him in a while."

> I actually wrote a story about that. I have a story written about when I saw him play the first time. It was a really snowy night. One of my classmates and I drove from Auburn to Atlanta, and it was really bad, the conditions, and I didn't have a ticket to get in, and I went to the door and I told the people, "Go tell Muddy Waters that his son is here." So they went, and the next thing I knew, I was being led to him. He hadn't seen me since [I was] about twelve, but at this point I had finished my first [college] degree, and I just wanted him to know that he had a son that finished college, and I wanted him to know I was doing well.
>
> My daddy, being a proud guy, he told all the guys, "Meet my son." He didn't tell 'em my name; he just said, "This is my son. I want you to meet him." I met [harmonica player] Jerry Portnoy, Guitar Junior, and all the guys. [Guitarist Bob] Margolin, he was there, [drummer] Willie "Big Eyes" Smith, all those guys. I remember him looking at me, he hadn't seen me in a while, and he said "You look just like [another son] Joe," and he stared at me, stared at me, then he stared at me some more. And that's when we really, really started talking a lot more. We talked really regularly until the day he died.

Bill's newfound closeness with his father, though, did not result in any sudden enthusiasm for playing the blues. That wouldn't happen until Muddy died—and when it did, it packed a spiritual force that recalled some of Muddy's own hoodoo-tinged fables of obsession and fate. "When I found out [he died]," Bill told Buddy Seigal, "it was just like somebody pulled my whole skeleton out of my body, you know? It was really strange, because even though we wasn't as close as I wanted us to be, it felt like somebody de-boned me. Or like a part of me had died, in a sense. I was really hurt, hurt for a while there. I wanted to do something as his son."[8]

A few months later, Bill says, he bought two guitars; he gave one to his brother Joseph and kept the other one: "I kept studying, studying, studying, studying, studying . . . that was the start of my journey into the blues." Bill told Robert Gordon that he "went and locked myself in a room for six years, a woodshed, and I learned it. Note by note. Measure by measure. All my dad's records, I learned them."[9]

But even then, it wasn't until he decided to pay a visit to one of his father's most ardent disciples at the Center Stage in Atlanta that he felt the full impact of his mission as a carrier of the Muddy Waters torch:

> I was going to see Johnny Winter to say hi to him, because he and my dad were close. I remember reading where Johnny had said, "Muddy was like a dad to me." So in my mind, I said well, if he's like your dad, then that means you're like my brother. Lonnie Mack happened to be on the bill. I was backstage, walking, and everywhere I was going I was blowing a harmonica, I believe I was playing "Hoochie Coochie Man." And Lonnie heard it and said, "Hey, man, wanna come up and play with me?"
>
> So I went on stage and got a chance to experience it for the first time. I think the people just went crazy, not because I was a great player, but because they were looking at Muddy Waters's son. And it was infectious—not just the blues bug, but the bug to get on stage and perform. So, there we go. That kind of started it.

Bill formed his first professional working unit, the Stone Cold Blues Band, and started gigging around the Atlanta area. "I wasn't really happy with that," he remembers, then he clarifies, "I wasn't happy with me. The other guys were okay, but I thought I could be better. So I stopped, and I started woodshedding some more. Just wanted to get better at it."

> I expanded my territory a little bit, really, after the Kennedy Center tribute to Muddy Waters [in 1997]. There was a guy named Thom Wolke. He wanted to be my manager, so he found out about the event, and I guess he wrote them and said why don't you add [me] to the program. I was the only unknown person on that show. I remember being with Keb' Mo' and Phoebe Snow and Johnnie Johnson and Robert Jr. Lockwood, Koko Taylor and Buddy Guy, Peter Wolfe, Gregg Allman. . . . I remember Robert Jr., old-school guy, I remember him walking up to me during rehearsal, and he just walked straight up to me, I think he had his guitar in his hand, in the case, and he looked me straight in the eye, like he was trying to look through me. And he looked at me and said, "Okay—you're Muddy's son." He and I became good friends from that point, up to the day he died.

Two years later, Bill's debut CD, the prophetically titled *Rising Son*, was released on the Blind Pig label. Executive producer and label co-owner Jerry Del Giudice recruited a studio unit that consisted of four Muddy Waters Band veterans (guitarist Bob Margolin, who also produced the session; pianist Pinetop Perkins; harpist Paul Oscher, who had worked with Muddy from 1967 to 1971; and drummer Willie "Big Eyes" Smith), along with veteran Chicago bassist Robert Stroger. "It was like I was in Blues Heaven or something," Bill effuses. "Man, those guys laid down the sound. That was surreal; just what I heard in my ears was, like, surreal; I couldn't believe what I was hearing."

Some of that sense of wonder can be inferred from the music itself. The set list includes five Big Bill originals (including the anthemic title tune) along with chestnuts from the postwar era, mostly Muddy's but also one associated with Jimmy Rogers ("Sloppy Drunk," actually written by Lucille Bogan and first recorded by her in 1930) and one by Howlin' Wolf ("Baby How Long"). It's obvious from the first verse of the opening song (Muddy's "Diamonds at Your Feet") that Bill inherited a remarkable vocal similarity to his father. At the same time, though, in places he seems almost overwhelmed by the power of the ghosts he's wrestling, sounding mannered—sometimes choked, sometimes gasping, sometimes strained—in his attempts to replicate the kind of emotional intensity Muddy seemed able to convey effortlessly.

(Of course, on further inspection, it's clear that this apparent effortlessness on Muddy's part was actually the result of meticulous craftsmanship. Muddy, summoning skills he'd acquired coming of age in a rural culture that was still largely oral in nature, invoked complex emotions by subtly altering the contours of his instrument—skewing his mouth, repositioning his head, shaking his jowls, "swallowing" some words while projecting others forcefully, affecting a tongue-tied mumble at times and a stentorian clarity at others—techniques that an English major like Bill, schooled in written communication, might not have mastered so easily at first.)

Overall, though, the feeling that we're in the presence of spirits reborn is almost overwhelming—exacerbated by the ghostly echo effect producer Margolin added to Oscher's harmonica, obviously an attempt to invoke the makeshift in-studio echo chamber that Chess used to enhance Little Walter's blowing on Muddy's vintage sides.

Predictably, Bill's emergence was hailed by lovers of blues tradition as an event of near Biblical significance, almost as if the voice of Muddy himself had emanated from a cloud, proclaiming in that legendary juke-rattling baritone: "Behold—this is my beloved son, in whom I am well pleased." This, though, could have created problems of its own—others in positions similar to Bill's have come to feel haunted, if not suffocated, by their famous parents' ghosts (Johnnie Taylor's son Floyd comes to mind; Hank Williams Jr. and Liza Minnelli might also serve as examples). Bill, though, insists that after spending much of his life hungering for just this kind of connection to his father, its realization represented release, not imprisonment.

"That was the only thing I ever really wanted to be known as," he insists. "As his son. Because I was raised away from him."

When I really started to do what I did, it was always done out of pride, to be his son. So I never had any of those conflicts. And of course, I'm a really strong-willed kind of person; I'm going to be who I am, and I understood "God bless the child who has his own." My grandmother used to tell me that. So I never really wanted to be him; I always wanted to be me. I just wanted to be recognized as his son.

I had to go back and grab that stuff. Most people think—ah, that's just three chords. But if you really, really get into it, it's way, way deeper than that. [Many musicians] can't play it that deeply because they think that's all it is. That's all they know—that chord, that chord, that chord—they don't understand that what lays underneath those chords is really what makes that music so powerful and so special. My dad used to say people said how easy his music was to play, and so few of them could play it right.

Over the course of his subsequent CDs—*Ramblin' Mind* (2001), *Blues in the Blood* (2003), *Born Lover* (2009), *Blues with a Mood* (2013), *Bloodstains on the Wall* (2016)—Bill has remained steadfast in his loyalty to that atavistic sound, even as he has become increasingly relaxed in his delivery, and he has assembled wider arrays of sidemen to add texture and variety to his musical landscape. He's also focused increasingly on his own songwriting, revealing himself adept at addressing a variety of topics—sometimes, as on "Trapped" (from *Blues in the Blood*) or "Son Of the Blues" (*Blues with a Mood*), starkly autobiographical; but more often concerning the usual blues themes of erotic obsession, betrayal, and release—in a writerly voice that sounds, for the most part, both contemporary and deeply rooted. His singing voice, meanwhile, continues to resonate with his father's influence, but he has learned to use that similarity as a jumping-off point for self-expression. He now sounds comfortable in his own skin—at home with ancestral spirits, but not possessed by them.

Nonetheless, some lessons have been learned the hard way. "The music business," he notes, "is great, but oh, man, there's so many sharks out there. These guys will eat you up; they're more like leeches, too—they'll bite you, and then they'll suck you dry. A lot of the greats, I mean, some of the best guys out there, they had a taste of the sharks. It's still going on; it's incredible. They put these contracts in front of you, and these contracts got a bunch of words on 'em, and you read 'em, sometimes you read things and not know what you're reading. I call it plantation contracts. Because if you're too smart—I remember my dad's wife saying, 'Yeah, you're mighty smart, Bill. They might not want to [deal] with you.'"

Bill can recount at least one instance where the sharks got the better of him. A CD entitled *Nineteen Years Old: A Tribute to Muddy Waters*, appeared on the Taxim label not long after Bill had begun to establish himself at Blind Pig. "That was done as a demo," Bill explains, "and it turned out to be released as a record. My name is on it, but I have never seen one dime from it. Nothing—royalty payments, nothing. The original songs I wrote on there, those songs—well, let's put it like this: When I look at *Nineteen Years Old*, I say: 'Payin' dues.' You go out there, and the thing about the music business is, you get shocked, and you don't know you've been shocked until years afterward. It's not like a hurt that you get immediately; it takes a little while for you to feel it and realize what you did."

In response, Bill has determined to retain professional and financial control over as much of his career as possible. All of his output since *Born Lover* has appeared on his own Black Shuck imprint. As evidenced on his website, his own name is now a registered trademark; under the aegis of Morganfield Enterprises, he is his own manager and booking agent. This ownership of his legacy will become increasingly important as he expands his horizons even further, attempting to move closer to that chimeric "mainstream" acceptance that most performing artists, regardless of genre, dream of attaining:

"It's a challenge in front of me," admits Bill, who continues to profess his fealty to the tradition that is his birthright, even as he searches for new ways of getting his message across to more diverse audiences.

> I want to get there, and I'm trying to figure out how to get there because it has to be done in a certain way, so that I can keep my fan base that I got. So I'm on that journey right now—I call it my journey to sensibility, my realistic journey of creating something that can be liked by younger people, too, and older people.
>
> The thing about that, though, is as music evolves, as blues evolves, so do the listeners who buy the music. It's about making a difference, touching lives. We all touch lives in our own way. And let's face it: the people who were buying music, who were buying blues twenty years ago, fifteen years ago, some of 'em aren't on the planet anymore. They're gone, so blues being a subculture now, you say to yourself—is it growing? Or is it getting smaller, as far as the listeners? And I don't know what the verdict is on that.

It's a question, of course, that vexes blues musicians and aficionados of all stripes. Still seeking an answer, in 2016 Bill embarked on yet another project, one that raised some eyebrows among his more purist-minded admirers. He composed and performed music for the soundtrack of the Fox TV series *Shots Fired*, a drama that addressed the fraught relations between urban black communities

Big Bill Morganfield, Chicago
Blues Festival, 2017.

and the police, and he also appeared in several episodes. As he explains: "They said, 'What we want to do is create a fusion between blues and hip-hop.' So I got with a hip-hop producer called C-Note [aka The Honorable C.N.O.T.E.]; C-Note has four songs in [the Fox TV series] *Empire*, so he's a really good producer. And we came up with a cross between hip-hop and blues that I think is really, really cool."

One of the songs Bill performed on *Shots Fired*, "Hold Me Baby," was included as a "bonus track" on Bill's 2016 CD *Bloodstains on the Wall*. Updating Bill's keening slide and vocals with electronically tweaked beats enveloped by a swirling aural miasma, it was actually more of a grafting of disparate styles than a true genre meld. Nonetheless, although it no doubt sent chills down the spines of a lot of his longtime admirers, it's possible that Bill is right—it may be just this kind of thing that the blues will need if it's going to make the transition back into anything approaching the mainstream for contemporary African American audiences. If nothing else, a lot of young TV viewers who probably never thought they'd care about anything associated with Muddy Waters have now heard his son's music on a show depicting the hardscrabble reality of urban life as uncompromisingly as Muddy and his contemporaries did with their own "devil's music" over sixty years ago.

But do most of those viewers really know—or care—who Bill Morganfield is? Does it matter to them what his lineage represents? And even if some do, is Bill the best candidate—better, say, than Louisiana's Chris Thomas King, another scion of a famous blues family who has fused his traditionalist roots with what he calls "dirty south hip-hop blues," or southern soul artists like Big Pokey Bear and J-Wonn, both of whom incorporate hip-hop's electronica-spiked impetus in songs whose lyric themes are drawn from the richest lodes of blues and soul storytelling—to facilitate this kind of updating of the blues tradition?

"It's really, really dangerous," Bill admits. "It's not easy. Because I have a strong blues base in fans; I don't have very much of a base of fans in hip-hop or rap. It's hard to imagine losing all your blues fans and then trying to go and get some other different kinds of fans. But, we'll see what happens with the songs I wrote for the show, and if that goes okay, I may try to put together a few more songs in that genre."

Projects like this, he believes, are what it will take if blues is going to retain—or, more realistically, reclaim—its popularity among mainstream African American listeners. "I think you can get 'em back," he asserts, "but you can't get 'em back with just straight traditional straight-ahead blues. Because they won't go for boomp-a-boomp-a-boomp-a-boomp—they won't go for that. You gotta have some beats under that music. If you want to grab the young people, gotta be a whole new sound."

Nonetheless, Bill affirms that he still feels most comfortable with the rootsy sound he inherited from his father and has adopted as his own. In the long run, he's less concerned with pandering to tastes—old-school, new-school, or otherwise—than in remaining true to himself, and to that inheritance. "I do it 'cause I love it," he maintains, "not so much for what the fans want me to do."

I'm at the point now in my career [where] it's kind of exciting, as I try to make that little crossover kind of thing but stay well rooted. I feel challenged. It's kind of like putting more wind in my sails. As my mind is starting to think about it, and listen, and then see how I can do this and how I can do that, I'm almost like in school, in a sense, trying to figure out how to do certain things and how to move my music forward, hopefully, and not backward.

I've always said that blues should evolve. And it has; sometimes it's gone too fast, too far, and some people don't like it, but all things evolve. But I tell you, man, I love that [postwar] sound. It's just "the" sound, to me. I mean, it's part of my heritage; part of my roots, through my father and all that, and I studied it for so long. I wood-shedded and I studied, and I've been in blues so long that it's just part of me."

Kenny Smith

"Bring It Together, Bring It to Life"

"**Y**ou can shuffle, or you can be *shuffling*. To me, that's the difference."

Kenny Smith, relaxing in his home in the Chicago suburb of Evanston, is trying to explain the mysteries of the classic postwar blues shuffle. As one of the few younger-generation drummers who have mastered this deceptively simple technique, he would seem to be a natural authority on it. But as he delves into the topic, his explanation begins to sound more like the ruminations of a New Age mystic than pointers from a Chicago bluesman. "You gotta embrace it," he says in a voice soft yet forceful, choosing his words with a precision that seems to reflect both his musical aesthetic and his approach toward life:

> You can keep time—if you're playing something in 4/4, everybody knows the down-beat is 2 and 4, where you clap; everybody knows that. You can do that. But the key and the goal is, you gotta embrace it. It's going to move like water; a shuffle is going to move like water. It's not going to stay there like concrete. It's not going to stay firmly in one spot. You gotta move with the water, waves of the water. It's all in the body. You can play it, but you need to feel it, and it's got to be in your body.

If Kenny makes this sound almost as natural—and ineffable—as breathing, it's probably because he's been living these rhythms almost since he began to breathe. His father, Willie "Big Eyes" Smith, played drums in Muddy Waters's band in the early '60s, and then again from 1968 until 1980; he later returned to his original instrument, the harmonica, and made a name for himself as a front man (often with his son laying down those family-heirloom shuffles behind

Kenny Smith, dedication ceremony for the Muddy Waters mural, 17 N. State Street, Chicago, 2017.

him). Kenny says that growing up in a bluesman's household was tantamount to being raised by the music itself—to hear him tell it, it's almost as if the blues had a baby (on March 25, 1974) and named it Kenny Smith. "He was always a celebrity to me," Kenny says about his father. "When I really caught on, I'm positive that I was three and a half or four, a lot of friends—I call them family, but a lot of friends and musicians would come over at the time."

They would play music, rehearse in the basement, and I just enjoyed just looking at them playing and having fun, and so that was just about the age when it kicked in. I didn't know they were so famous. I always saw that whole band, the Muddy Waters band [guitarists Luther "Guitar Junior" Johnson and Bob Margolin, harpist Jerry Portnoy, bassist Calvin "Fuzz" Jones, and pianist Pinetop Perkins, along with Muddy himself]. [Harpist] Mojo Buford, I saw him a lot. Always a revolving door of musicians coming in, hanging out, always a barbeque or always a little party.

My father always practiced at home, playing, so I started imitating him when he played, just seeing him playing drums or playing his drum pad. I'd try to sit next to him and try to do what he was doing. I was a diehard—that was it. By the time I was eight years old, I remember saying, "I want to do this." I remember dancing around with my grandmother to a Muddy Waters record; we were just dancing around in the house, and I just remember, I knew Willie was playing on it. I went to several shows and performances they were always having in theaters. We'd go to those— that was the defining moment when I said, "I want to do this." That's when I knew. That was literally what I knew at the time, was the blues.

Kenny says that once the inspiration hit him, he never wavered ("I always think on my own, and that's where my heart was"), not even later, during his junior high and high school years, when he was probably just about the only kid in school with such a strange musical infatuation. "I'd bring a record with my father and them on it," he recollects. "They loved it; they were fascinated by that, too. I have friends that I'm still in touch with, they're proud of me, they're happy, they still love the music. I think that in some ways I influenced them to like the blues, too."

By then, Kenny had also been playing in church for several years: "I was going to church every Sunday, and I would see the guy over there playing drums. I felt the gospel just as deep as the blues. I would just sit there, mouth dropped, just watching him, almost the whole service, just to see how he did [it]. They had the little kids' choir, the Sunbeam Choir. I asked 'em to let me play the drums for a song; that's how it started. After they heard me play, they got me to play a lot more."

But he never wavered from his blues focus. Even before he hit his teens, his father had begun to take him on the road when scheduling and appropriate per- formance venues permitted it. Undaunted by the gruff, often profane camaraderie of the seasoned bluesmen around him ("I'd seen all of that all my life; that was not even an issue, nothing new"), Kenny absorbed both music and life lessons from these early sojourns. "I must've been eleven or twelve," he reflects. "On weekends, if there was a festival, he'd just let me go with him, and that was a blast. I always enjoyed just riding with the guys. They would do a show, and just about at the very end, he would get me up and let me play drums with 'em, with the band. I thought that was so cool."

Just as they had in church, his opportunities quickly expanded. "I remember [my father] sitting down for almost a [whole] set and just letting me get up there and play."

He was just trying to wean me into it. He [also] told me everything I needed to know, far as the drinking and stuff. He told me don't, you know—how to handle those things. He let me know exactly what I was getting into. I said, "Well, I'm gonna give it a good go, give it a good shot, and see what I can do. If I can't make it out there doing it, I'll just keep on playing like I am now, play in my basement, and have just as much fun just practicing in my basement." That was kind of my defining moment in saying that if I don't make it that way, that's fine; music is still going to be with me.

Such was Kenny's enthusiasm that even mundane activities like practicing drum patterns and learning note-for-note, beat-for-beat from records became journeys of discovery: "I would always turn to it and play and focus. I was developing by then, really developing by junior high, so everything was brightly, freshly new. It was like—still, now, I always want to take it in, more and more want to take it in, and learn more: 'Oh, he did it; that artist did it.' And then you go back and, 'Oh, *that* artist really did it. . . .' 'Oh, no; *that* artist is the one who did it. . . .' So it keeps going on and on like that. The more I learned, the more excited I got about playing and trying to really home in on doing it right."

Kenny's first road gig on his own was with Sam Lay in the early '90s. Lay, at that point in his career, "wanted to play drums, but he didn't want to play it all night," as Kenny remembers it, "so he hired me to come out with him and just play drums behind him. I remember him coming to the house, and I remember my father talking to him, and I know he said, 'Take care of him.'"

Not long after, Kenny hit the local circuit with a blues band that had adopted the rather un-bluesy name the Soul Searchers. His fellow Searchers included, at various points, harpist/vocalist Ross Bon, who later fronted the Mighty Blue Kings, and guitarist Nick Moss. He also found himself in growing demand as a freelance sideman around Chicago; word was getting around about this young drummer who carried a legendary surname and was proficient in straight-ahead, shuffle-driven postwar Chicago blues. As always, the joy of playing was made ever richer for Kenny by the thrill of learning and by widening his experience on these gigs:

> I started doing some Rockin' Johnny [Burgin] shows and some Tail Dragger shows right after that. It was at the 5105 Club on Laramie [and North Avenue] with Mary Lane. That was a fun Sunday night show; I did it faithfully every Sunday, and it was a good time. You'd get so many musicians down there. It was great. I met a lot of musicians, and I learned a lot of music, a lot more music and a lot more ways to approach the music.
>
> For me, my brain just feeds off of it. It feeds, and I just want more and more, more and more. Even when we finish this interview, I'll be going and I'll be listening to some more blues, and I'll be taking in a lot, just constantly taking it in.

Since the beginning, Kenny has been a roots man, immersed in the traditional postwar blues he learned from his father and still cherishes. But he's developed big enough ears to appreciate myriad styles, even if he doesn't always venture into them on his gigs. One of his early drumming idols, he reveals rather surprisingly, was the hard-bop jazz genius Art Blakey; today, he maintains, he's up for almost anything a band leader wants to throw at him. "My motto," he maintains, "is, I'll *try* to play anything you ask me to."

> I got that from Willie. I remember I heard something on the radio one time, and I said, "Ah, I just, I'm not liking this music. There's no way I want to play that." And he just said, "You know, you need to know how to play, whether you like 'em or not all the time, you should learn how to play it. Just know how to play it anyway." And I took that and I strived with it, and I said, "Okay, well, I'll take it in, and I'm gonna listen to it and see what I can do with it."
>
> And that's how I got to where I wanted to be more versatile. That's where it popped in. It didn't come by my choice, saying, "I want to be versatile." People just kinda

Kenny Smith, with Willie Dixon looking over his shoulder, Blues Heaven Foundation, Chess Records building, Chicago, 2018.

said, "Try this." And instead of me just saying, "No, I don't do it—" I said, "I'll try it." But any style I play, it's definitely still all based around traditional blues, to me. No matter what I do, there's no taking that away from me; it's still in me.

That preference is obvious in the list of musicians whom Kenny has worked with. His father, of course, used him whenever possible (one of his most cherished recording sessions was 2010's Grammy-winning Telarc CD *Joined at the Hip*, featuring his father and Pinetop Perkins). Other regular calls through the years have come from Bob Margolin (completing the circle that began when Margolin was Muddy's guitarist and a regular visitor at the Smith house); the Cash Box Kings (a long-running Chicago aggregation who signed with Alligator and released *Royal Mint*, their debut for the label, in 2017); Mississippi Heat; harpist Matthew Skoller; guitarist Nick Moss; multi-instrumentalist Eric Noden, and Muddy's sons Big Bill and Mud Morganfield.

These days, most younger adherents of the unadorned postwar style that Kenny reveres tend to be white revivalists. It's not unusual for him to be the only African American on the bandstand, and even when he backs up African American front men like one of Muddy's sons or Cash Box Kings vocalist Oscar Wilson, the audience is likely to be almost entirely white. But he's resolute in his insistence that it doesn't bother him, and he won't get involved in the ongoing debates about whether the music his father helped pioneer has been stolen, appropriated, or otherwise robbed of its identity. (He also refuses to be pigeonholed, as evidenced by his participation on *Chicago Plays the Stones*, a 2018 tribute that featured John Primer, Jimmy Burns, Billy Boy Arnold, and others—along with both Mick Jagger and Keith Richards in cameo appearances—revisiting some of the Rolling Stones' most iconic songs.)

"I keep my mind clean," he asserts. "I keep my mind and my thoughts pure about those issues. When I'm out there, I don't care who you are."

> We can play some good music. That's my goal: try to get out there, play some really good blues. That's the key, and I live by that law, to this day. I'm just happy the blues has expanded to so many different ethnic groups and backgrounds. I'm very happy about that—from all corners of the world. I don't feel like it's been given up [by black people]; it helps everybody. It helps everybody. Everybody got the blues sometimes. Whether you want to deny it or not, everybody got the blues sometimes. So I take it for what that is."

A similar refusal to be corrupted by negativity informs his thinking about his role in bands. Despite his famous name and his obvious gifts for leadership and multitasking (along with maintaining his various gigs around town and on the road he holds a degree in business management, teaches occasional blues seminars at colleges, and shares with his wife Holly the happy duty of caring for their three children), Kenny says he harbors no burning desire to grab the spotlight and push himself forward as a leader.

"It's not all about trying to make the money and look slick on stage," he explains. "If you're really taking the music seriously, it's discipline."

> You need the discipline. If you really take the music seriously, it takes you to some different places, and it keeps you firmly disciplined. When you're on stage, you're a team. You should be a team when you're on stage. You should be family on stage. You should treat every musician on stage with respect. It's not about "me, me, me," it's about us as a family up here, trying to make some really good music. Bring it together, bring it to life. You want to take care of each of your family members the best way you can.

Many musicians, of course, have preached similar things but still succumbed to the ego rush that almost inevitably accompanies basking in applause every night. Kenny insists, though, that this won't happen, even though he has finally started to work on putting together a recording under his own name. Balance, perspective, and focus are more than mere musical values to him: "Like I say, I keep my thoughts out of all of that stuff. I keep my thoughts pure from thoughts like that. I focus, I listen to the music around me, and I try my best to play the best that I can, and I feel good about myself when I'm finished. That's what I do—I just don't let too many things corrupt my head. As I heard in a quote one time, I don't let nobody rent space in my head. Doing my part, preserving, maybe pass it on to someone who's going to carry it on—that's my motivation.

"That's the way I live, period. My music is a reflection of me."

The Taylor Family

"This Whole Thing Is All about Truth"

Remembering Eddie Taylor

A White Castle restaurant now occupies the corner on Chicago's west side where the Domino Lounge once stood. Back in the 1980s, that was a pretty desolate area, but on Friday and Saturday nights the little club at Roosevelt and Western with its front door painted green rocked with the sound of the blues—hardcore ghetto blues, dangerous and raw. The band (usually a trio) churned out rudimentary 12-bar changes behind gristle-and-rotgut vocalists like James "Tail Dragger" Jones and the club's former proprietor Nate "Necktie Nate" Haggins, self-styled Howlin' Wolf tribute artists who'd roar through their sets for patrons who were usually too busy drinking, hip-grinding, and belly-rubbing the night away to complain about the sameness of the shows. Sometimes an instrumentalist/vocalist like harpist Earring George Mayweather or guitarist Johnny B. Moore might front the group, lending a little more variety and musical adventurism to the proceedings.

The night Eddie Taylor walked in, though, things weren't going so well. The band wasn't hitting on much, the crowd had gotten pretty sparse, and Eddie's entrance barely caused a ripple. Eddie, for his part, didn't bother to acknowledge anyone—he simply ambled to the bandstand, strapped on his guitar, and pulled out his slide. That last was a bit of a surprise: He'd been leading his own bands, off and on, for quite a few years by then, but he was still famous mostly as an accompanist, the man whose chording had anchored Jimmy Reed's eccentric timing and added depth and texture to Reed's piercing harp and mushmouthed vocals on such classics as "You Don't Have to Go," "Ain't That Lovin' You Baby," "Baby What You Want Me to Do," and others on the Vee-Jay label in the 1950s and '60s.

He cued the band to play a slow blues and eased into Elmore James's classic "The Sky Is Crying"—and what followed was one of those moments blues lovers fantasize about. As he broke into his first solo, his slidework ascended into realms that even Elmore had seldom envisioned. Piercing, intense, yet enriched with fresh melodic and harmonic nuances, it cut through the night like a beacon, bringing to one of Chicago's most storied blues anthems a depth of musicality and emotional resonance so profound it became a virtually new creation. When the song was over he looked briefly around the room, acknowledged the smattering of applause, packed up his guitar, and walked out the door without a word.

In some ways, that moment symbolized Eddie Taylor's entire career. Over the course of his life he created some of the most memorable blues ever played, yet to the end he was still scuffling, still passing almost unnoticed through the crowd.

Eddie was a man of quiet dignity and pride; his music, as well, was eloquent in its understatement. He preferred to lay precise phrases into the spaces provided by his accompanists rather than assault his listeners with pyrotechnics or dazzle

Eddie Taylor at the Golden Slipper, 325 S. Pulaski Road, Chicago, 1981. Photo © Martin Feldmann.

them with tricks. As an accompanist himself, he had no equal—his chording and single-string complementing, anchored by a metronomelike sense of time, both guided and supported a soloist, even an unpredictable one like Reed or John Lee Hooker, with unerring accuracy.

He was born in Benoit, Mississippi, in January of 1923; his later recollections evoked a childhood drenched in music. His mother, who dated one of Robert Johnson's brothers for a while, was also a lifelong friend of singer/guitarist Memphis Minnie, and Eddie recalled that Minnie "used to nurse me when I was a baby. . . . I used to listen to her play guitar."[1] Within a few years he'd begun to sneak out of the house at night, riding his bicycle out into the countryside to hang around outside jukes and Saturday night frolics where musicians like Son House and Charlie Patton would hold forth; he also befriended local blues celebrities, roustabouts with names like Bull Cow, Popcorn, Little Quick, and Boots. Sometimes, he remembered, he wouldn't even go home—he'd crawl under the porch of a house where a party was going on and fall asleep, with the pounding of the music and dancers inches above his head.

Infatuated with what he was hearing, young Eddie began tearing the wire off brooms in an attempt to fashion primitive instruments for himself; in 1936, his mother finally bought him a real guitar from a Sears and Roebuck catalogue. It was Popcorn who taught him how to tune it; a fast learner, Eddie soon began going into town on Saturday afternoons and busking in the streets—blues for black folks, country ("hillbilly") for the whites. As he honed his chops and started playing farther afield, he met other aspiring bluesmen. One was Jimmy Reed, who'd been raised in the country around nearby Leland. Eddie and Jimmy would sometimes sit under a tree and play together, grinding out the slow-loping blues cadences for which Reed would later become famous. Eddie also met Howlin' Wolf when Wolf was still a farmer who played blues part-time; other early associates included Big Joe Williams and Muddy Waters, Homesick James, Floyd "Dark Road" Jones, Johnny Shines, harmonica prodigy Walter Horton, and both Ike Turner and B.B. King.

In 1949, Eddie moved to Chicago. Soon he was playing in the open-air Maxwell Street Market, one of the prime incubators of the postwar Chicago sound. There he teamed up with guitarist/bassist Jimmy Lee Robinson; the two gigged around town a bit while Eddie reacquainted himself with some of his old compatriots from down home, who'd also moved North to seek their fortunes. Eventually he reunited with Jimmy Reed, and one of the great partnerships of the blues was under way.

Eddie and Jimmy's first appearance together on record was backing up John Brim on "Tough Times" and "Gary Stomp," released on Parrot in 1954. Reed's own first sessions at Vee-Jay, in June of the previous year hadn't included Eddie, but six months later he came back, this time with Eddie in tow, and cut what would become his first chart hit, "You Don't Have to Go." Reed, usually with Eddie accompanying him, went on to achieve a string of hits unparalleled in Chicago blues—all told, he charted nineteen times for Vee-Jay between 1955 and 1965, as compared with Muddy Waters's sixteen for Chess, Howlin' Wolf's six, and Elmore James's four.

Eddie also recorded and/or performed alongside such figures as John Lee Hooker, Elmore James, and Muddy himself, and in the meantime he cut sides under his own name—"Bad Boy" in 1955; "Bigtown [sic] Playboy" and "Ride 'Em On Down" from another session that same year; "You'll Always Have a Home" in 1956, and "Looking for Trouble" in '57, among others—which, although they didn't become hits at the time, are now universally recognized as among the finest in the postwar Chicago blues canon. Both lyrically and musically, they exemplified the blend of downhome rawness and big-city swagger now venerated as exemplifying the Chicago sound of that era.

But for some reason, Eddie Taylor never made a name for himself outside the city until years later, when the white aficionados finally caught up with him. Maybe his musical message was too subtle for audiences at the dawn of the rock & roll era; perhaps he was a prisoner of his own success as a sideman, and his label couldn't (or wouldn't) expend the resources to push an artist whom they considered secondary to Reed, their biggest blues moneymaker. As Reed's career slowed down in the '60s, Eddie faded further into the background. Within a few years, though, he found his career revitalized. In 1968, he went to Europe along with Reed, John Lee Hooker, T-Bone Walker, and others, as part of the American Folk Blues Festival, a tour that helped introduce him to a new generation of fans hungry for a taste of the "real thing." Back in the United States, he became increasingly popular on the predominantly white club and roadhouse circuit— Antone's, in Austin, Texas, became an especially important venue for him in his later years—although even here, listeners weaned on rock and boogie had to learn to listen carefully to appreciate an artist like Eddie, who preferred nuance to overkill.

Even by blues "revivalist" standards, though, Eddie never really became a star. He released albums on such labels as Testament, Wolf, P-Vine, and JSP, sometimes accompanied by old compatriots like guitarist/bassist Floyd Jones, drummer Kansas City Red, pianist Sunnyland Slim, guitarists Louis and Dave Myers, and drummer Odie Payne, sometimes by young revivalists who could re-create the venerated postwar sound note-for-note, even if they didn't always succeed in summoning the appropriate emotional or improvisational fire. He also recorded alongside his wife Vera, a vocalist who'd worked with him occasionally through the years but remained virtually unknown outside of Chicago. (She died in 1999, shortly after recording *You Better Be Careful*, her debut album under her own name, which was released the following year on the Wolf label.)

But Eddie never abandoned his old haunts. He might return from Europe, play for an adoring audience at a trendy North Side blues bistro on a Friday night in Chicago, and then show up the next evening at a rough-hewn neighborhood venue like the Domino, the Golden Slipper on Pulaski Road, or the Delta Fish Market at Jackson and Kedzie. When he wasn't recording or on tour, he presided over a bustling West Side household, where he helped Vera raise their eight children and attempted to face down the economic uncertainty that went along with trying to maintain a career in the volatile, often exploitative music industry. Despite the hardships, though, most of those children went on to express an interest in music, and at least four—vocalist Demetria, guitarist Eddie Jr., and drummers Tim and Larry—have made it their career.

Eddie Taylor died on Christmas Day, 1985. His funeral, held at A. R. Leak Funeral Home on Sacramento Boulevard, was largely ignored by mainstream media; attended mostly by longtime musical colleagues, friends, and admirers, it was a fitting tribute to a man whose music—sparse, expressive and deeply soulful—will live on for as long as there are people who appreciate integrity and honesty in their blues. It is the heart and essence of blues expression.

Demetria Taylor: "Let Everybody Know What I Can Do"

"Everything I do, I do for my mom and my dad."

Demetria Taylor is sitting at a table in Blue Chicago, the downtown club where in about an hour she and her band will be performing "blues with a Millennium sound," as she describes it, for a Wednesday night crowd. Many of the people who'll be dancing and partying to Demetria's music tonight probably recognize her name because she's Eddie Taylor's daughter—this is Chicago, after all, and even casual blues fans have heard of the man who helped create the legendary Jimmy Reed sound. And, in fact, the title song of Demetria's 2011 debut CD on Delmark, *Bad Girl*, was a reprise of "Bad Boy," one of her father's best-known

Demetria Taylor, Blue Chicago, 2018.

records (released on Vee-Jay in 1955); she's far from shy about claiming, and proclaiming, her roots.

But as her band sets up on the bandstand, and as vintage Muddy Waters begins to blast out from the house speakers, Demetria makes it clear that although she reveres the Chicago blues tradition, she's determined to forge her own musical identity. Yes, she concurs, her father and her mother, vocalist Vera Taylor, groomed her to be true to her roots: "I'm out here right now because of my mom and dad," she affirms. "There's never a time I get on stage when I don't talk to God and say, 'Well, this is for you, Mom and Dad.' [Indeed, she'll sometimes conclude a song by pointing heavenward and proclaiming, "I love you, Eddie Taylor!"] I feel like they're the ones who left this legacy for all of us. My mom always told me, 'It's in you, but you got to find it. You got to find yourself. You can sing; you just gotta bring it out.'"

That doesn't mean, though, that she intends to let herself get planted in concrete. "I want to keep going," she continues. "I want to take my father, and everything else I know, take it and do it my way."

Born in 1973, Demetria Taylor grew up in an environment where music from multiple generations and genres blended together. Her parents, of course, were devotees of the Delta-rooted urban blues style her father had played such a significant role in codifying; they passed that on to their children, virtually from birth. "My father used to sit around and tell stories of when he was coming up," she recalls:

> I used to see him on album covers and see him on videos and different stuff. I remember Eddie Shaw, Floyd Jones,[2] [guitarist] Johnny Littlejohn, Sunnyland Slim, people like that, coming around the house. I used to see [keyboardist] Foots [Berry] and Sunnyland, [drummer] Ray Scott, all of them, like [guitarist] Boston Blackie, they used to have a band [at the Delta Fish Market]. I grew up listening to people like Koko Taylor, Bessie Smith, Big Mama Thornton, Eddie Shaw, Howlin' Wolf—I used to be a little girl running around the house: "We gonna pitch a Wang Dang Doodle all night long!"
>
> My friends were into other music; I was into jazz and blues and a little bit of rock—Jimi Hendrix—and they come up and say, "Girl, what is that you're listening to?" I say, "Music." I was into all type of stuff like Anita Baker, Lena Horne, Dionne Warwick sometimes, Michael Jackson, Janet Jackson. As I got older, I just felt, like, that stuff started getting tired, boring to me—not the music, just hanging out with my friends—and I just wanted to do something else different, so I started coming to the blues clubs.
>
> Then I started seeing my brother and them sitting around, my brother [Eddie Taylor Jr.] would play guitar, and they used to have backyard barbeques with my uncle Jimmy Burns, and I started playing drums. I played drums for, like, four-five years, then I stopped 'cause I had carpal tunnel in my hands, and that's when I realized that I wanted to be a singer.

By this time, her older brothers Tim and Larry had launched their own careers, drumming behind some of Chicago's most highly regarded bluesmen both in town and on the road. Her sister Edna, who now sings gospel, also performed on occasion, and Eddie Jr. was honing a guitar style modeled closely on his father's. "Every last one of my mom's kids can do something," asserts Demetria. "All my mom's kids are very creative, and bright and smart. But I just felt like this was something I need to do, just to go my own way and go solo and do my own project.

Eddie done it, Larry done it, so I wanted to do it, too. I wanted to let everybody know what I can do."

In the early 2000s, she began insinuating herself into Chicago's club circuit, both on the predominantly white North Side and in neighborhood venues closer to home. She built up a local following, but recording opportunities remained scarce for a long time. In 2006, she and her sisters Brenda and Edna contributed vocals to Eddie Jr.'s *Mind Game* on the Wolf label (a Taylor family affair that also featured Tim and Larry on drums). It wasn't until five years later, though, that she got the chance to release a full-length CD under her own name. By then, she'd become a regular at B.L.U.E.S. on Halsted ("B.L.U.E.S.," she says, "is the first place that gave me a start, believed in me and started me to singing"). Vocalist Big Time Sarah, a Chicago veteran who sometimes doubled as a barmaid at the club, suggested she call Delmark to inquire about recording opportunities.

As she remembers it, Delmark producer/A&R man, Steve Wagner, came by and was immediately smitten: "That's when he saw me sing a duet with Sarah. I called her up to the stage and asked her to do this song with me, 'Wang Dang Doodle.' We did the song, we finished, they said, 'We gotta record you,' and the rest is history. Six weeks later, we did the CD. Delmark [said], 'We want Sarah to come in with you.' That's how we wound up doing 'Wang Dang Doodle' and 'Little Red Rooster' on the album together."

Her intention, she maintains, was to craft an album that would both pay homage and serve as a declaration of independence: "Every song I've done [on the CD], I've done it in honor of the people I was raised up on. I dedicated the CD to all of them. I love the traditional blues. But I want to go other places with my blues. I want to do the Chicago sound, but I want to do it in my own way."

In that spirit, she offered up tributes to Koko Taylor ("Voodoo Woman" and the anthemic "Wang Dang Doodle" itself); Willie Dixon and Howlin' Wolf ("Little Red Rooster"); Magic Sam ("All Your Love"); and, of course, her father (the title song, which Demetria says moved her so deeply that she cried as she recorded it). Also included were updates of Jimmy Reed's "Big Boss Man," originally released in 1961 (with Eddie Taylor, of course, on rhythm guitar), and Luther Allison's deep-blues ballad "Cherry Red Wine." The opening medley, "I'm a Woman" / "Hoochie Coochie Woman," was another tribute to Dixon and—yet again—her idol, the late Queen Koko. She ventured into more contemporary fare with "When You Leave, Don't Take Nothing," in honor of soul-blues vocalist Artie "Blues Boy" White, who included the song on his 1999 CD, *Can We Get Together*, and vocalist Nora Jean Bruso's "Goin' Back to Mississippi."

Despite her reverence for the postwar tradition, though, both her CD and her live performances indicate that Demetria's true strengths may lie elsewhere. Her voice, high-pitched and occasionally thin, resonates with emotion, but it sounds at least as well-suited to mainstream pop, or maybe contemporary southern soul, as it does to the deep blues she has so far dedicated herself to honoring. Perhaps at least partly for that reason, she's been working to create songs that will allow her to "express the blues in her own way," as Willie Dixon might have phrased it, unencumbered by any obligation to invoke—or live up to the standards of—ancestral spirits. The opportunity to record this new material hasn't arisen as easily as she might have hoped—it's been over seven years since her Delmark debut, and she says she's still working to get herself back into the queue to record a follow-up[3]—but she remains optimistic. "When I do my next CD," she promises, "I want to do all originals. I want to let people know that I got different styles; I'm just not just a lump-de-lump girl. I want to try to develop something that people can know me for who I am. I'm ready to go out there and just let the world know what I can do."

Eddie Taylor Jr.: "I'm Not Changing"

I'm more traditional. I get more feel like that. I don't get no feel from this other stuff. I don't have time for steppin' on no pedals and trying to play a thousand notes. The reason why I'm not changing—what they doin' is gonna soon play out. And when you go in there and play something good, and play it right, it's refreshing. It's old, but it's new to the ears.

I think they're gonna come looking for me in the daytime with a flashlight.

Eddie Taylor Jr. leans back and stares into the middle distance, a muted TV illuminating the darkened living room in his basement apartment in suburban Maywood, Illinois. He's a soft-spoken man, still young by blues standards, yet his conversation reflects a weariness that seems to both burden and goad him, as if the effort it takes to summon brief optimism is itself a victory, reason to believe that better times might still be ahead—or, as the old gospel lyric would have it, "trouble don't last always."

Of all the Taylor children who became professional musicians, Eddie Jr. is the only one who picked up the guitar. Perhaps at least partly for that reason, he remembers feeling haunted by a sense of isolation almost from the beginning, even as he rejoiced in discovering the rich musical tradition his father had represented and his own determination to carry that tradition on.

At first, he recalls, "I wasn't interested in playing no guitar. I was into hip-hop and rap and DJing and all that. It was my little brother Milton that [Eddie Sr.] was trying to teach, but Milton could never get it."

> After my dad died, it just hit me. I started listening to his albums, and I'm like, "Man, this guy can play. He really can play." And he had all, like, Charlie Patton albums and Jimmy Reed albums, Lightnin' Hopkins and Tommy McClennan and Robert Johnson and all them, Willie Nix—the old guys. That's what I came up on. So that's how I started my trademark.
>
> He told [my mother], right before he passed, let him leave his instruments to his kids. His guitar, the big one, I still got it—the 1952 Gibson ES-5—was just sitting in the closet, and I pulled it out. Then, as time went on, she let me get the red one, the '67 355 Stereo Gibson. It was sitting in the closet so long 'til the pickup guard had deteriorated; it just crumbled up. It had green mold all on the pickups."

Being an aspiring bluesman on the West Side of Chicago in the hip-hop era wasn't easy. "I lost all my friends," Eddie admits, " 'cause I turned old fashioned. Once I started getting interested in the guitar, I didn't want to do the hip-hop no more."

> I just stayed all my time in the house, trying to learn the guitar. I'd go to sleep with the guitar on my chest, wake up with it on my chest. I used to cry 'cause I couldn't get it, I couldn't learn, nobody wanted to teach me nothing. Everything I know now, I taught myself how to play. Nobody never showed me nothing. Nobody. I just learned by watching and going out.

In the early '90s, his brother Tim landed a job drumming for Eddie Shaw and the Wolf Gang; it was Shaw, he says, who rescued him from despair. "He come by to pick Tim up, and he heard me in the room pluckin' on my guitar. I didn't really play that good; he just gave me a chance, 'cause I wanted to give up, and he could see I was discouraged. It was frustrating 'cause I couldn't keep up, you know? I didn't know all that stuff that they was [doing], but I guess he just wanted to break me out there. He put me in the band, put me on the road."

His first recording opportunity came a few years later when the Wolf label included him on the compilation *Chicago's Best West- and Southside Blues Singers, Vol 2*. His contribution was a remake of his father's "Ride 'Em On Down" (released on Vee-Jay in 1956), on which his sparse, precisely articulated leads evoked the classic-era sound that Eddie Sr. had helped define. In 1998, he released his first recording under his own name (as "Edward Taylor"), *Lookin' for Trouble: A Tribute to Eddie "Big Town Playboy" Taylor*, also on Wolf. Along with Shaw and a crew of first-call West Side session men, the disk featured his brothers, Tim (drums) and Larry (drums and vocals), as well as his mother, vocalist Vera Taylor revisiting some of the music she and her husband had made together over the years.

Meanwhile, he continued to build his reputation around Chicago, sometimes sitting in on others' sets, sometimes leading his own band of carefully selected traditionalists who could re-create the classic "lump-de-lump" postwar sound he'd embraced as his inheritance and birthright. Even by revivalist standards, his earnestness could be daunting: In his determination to avoid the excesses he disdained so fiercely in others, he became known for turning in note-perfect performances that could sometimes make a room feel more like a recital hall than a juke.

And, in fact, although he has become somewhat more aggressive over the years as his confidence and his catalogue of original material have grown, and

Eddie Taylor Jr., Buddy Guy's
Legends, Chicago, 2017.

despite his insistence that he brings originality to even his most faithful re-creations ("I don't just sit there and copy note-for-note"), his overall approach has remained pretty much unchanged. Occasionally he's expanded his scope to include more modernist fare (for example, a version of Syl Johnson's "[Come On] Sock It to Me" from 2004's *Worried about My Baby*), but for the most part, both his performances and his recordings (at least five more thus far, all on Wolf) have continued to showcase him as a dedicated roots man, convinced that his very allegiance to styles that were codified years before he was born marks him as a courageous individualist in a musical landscape he believes has become overrun with boogie-sodden mindlessness—conformity, as he sees it, disingenuously masquerading as progressivism.

"It's monkey see, monkey do," he avers. "It's like, ain't nobody coming up with nothing different. That's why the music's so boring now. All you hear is 'B-r-r-r-r-r-ooble-ooble-ooble-ooble. . . .' All they doing is stepping on a bunch of pedals. Them new guys out there, I won't call any names, but they don't really do nothing for me."

It's well known, of course, that the majority of listeners who prefer Eddie's style of traditional blues are white—they're often, in fact, the very "purists" accused of appropriating the music's aesthetics and history, trying to keep it from growing. Who, then, is really preserving the legacy, and to whom does it belong? "In some way it [bothers me]," Eddie admits, "and in some way it don't."

> Because we are the most unappreciative people that it is. The white people are more appreciative. They clap, they're more appreciative. But in a black folks' club, they just sit there and look at you. And when you go in there and try to do a deep traditional blues—I don't know if they don't want to be reminded of what they came from, but that's boring to them. They want the Johnnie Taylor and Bobby Bland, that stuff. They don't want that deep stuff. Them people done faded out, or too old.
>
> I understand you got to move with time; it ain't the '50s no more with Muddy Waters playing for the chitlin' circuit. But I don't really care if I even play for 'em, to be honest with you. It ain't like I forgot where I came from, but they just, it's hard to please 'em. I'm not turning my back on my own people, but it's like they don't want to stick together. They don't stick together, they're not supportive, and they just can't get it together. And that's all I really want to say. I don't really want to go deep into it.

The irony is inescapable. The introspective loner who "lost all my friends" when he took up the blues back in the 1980s still feels isolated, but this time from the very blues community he had given up so much to become a part of. It hasn't helped, either, that personal setbacks and tragedies have beset him along the way. In 2002, he was sidelined by kidney failure. His brother Milton stepped up and donated a kidney to him, but in 2013 it also began to malfunction; he's been back on dialysis ever since. His son Eric was killed in a domestic dispute in 2011 ("the guy put a shotgun to his head and blew his head off. Died right on the floor, right in front of us"); two years later, after he separated from his wife, he found himself homeless. "I didn't have nowhere to sleep," he relates. "I slept places with roaches crawlin' on me, rats runnin' across me—you just don't know, man, it was rough. [People] never knew. I always kept myself up, I always had my clothes clean, nobody never knew. I went through a rough time, man. I was going through some stuff."

He's doing better these days, comfortable in his Maywood apartment ("I got peace now—I got my life back"), but making a living remains a struggle—the only regular gig he's had for months[4] has been a solo acoustic set at Buddy Guy's Legends, afternoons and early evenings three times a week, mostly for day-tripping tourists and businesspeople on break—hardly the career he'd envisioned so many years ago when he pulled his father's guitar out of the closet and began teaching himself blues. "I made an announcement last week that I was quitting," he reveals. "I was at Buddy Guy's. I told 'em, 'I'm tired now, man.'"

> I been doing this for thirty years and I ain't got nothing. I'm poor, man. I got one suit in there, couple of ties, old beat-up van back there that somebody gave me. I'm struggling month to month, trying to pay my bills, and I said to myself, this is the life of a bluesman? Living from gig to gig—the only thing I play is Buddy Guy's; I don't play no other clubs.
>
> I've been in Europe maybe about fifty times; there's no more room on my passport. Blues is more appreciated over there. I used to come right off the [plane], go right in the Starlite [a now-defunct West Side club], and play with Willie Cobbs on a Sunday for forty dollars—all night. I went over to Japan, they bow down to me; I came back here, I was nobody.

But that moment at Buddy Guy's, he now admits, was an aberration. After all this time, Eddie Taylor Jr. remains determined to stay the course, continuing to believe that his faith in the music, and the spirit that empowers it, will be enough to see him through. "I'm not gonna quit," he affirms. "You know, I get in my frustrated moments, but—everybody go through their moments. You can't let it get to you. Like Buddy Guy say, you can't let it drive you crazy—you got to stick with it. Things'll get better. You just gotta stick on with it. I'm not gonna quit."

CODA: "AIN'T GONNA CRY"

On March 8, 2019, the Chicago blues world was stunned to learn that Eddie Taylor Jr. had passed away, a little over two weeks before his forty-seventh birthday. He had collapsed while playing in church several days earlier; the official reported cause of death was a heart attack.

In his own quiet way, Eddie Jr. embodied the spirit of defiance and survival that represents the deepest living heritage of the blues. Few artists in any genre—indeed, few people in any walk of life—would have been so resolute in their integrity: Manifesting the same unbending will that seems to run like an inheritance through the entire Taylor family, he insisted on remaining true to the values he held dear—musical, personal, spiritual (as his sister Edna proclaimed during his funeral on March 22, "My brother loved him some Jesus!"— and in fact his last earthly act was making a joyful noise unto the Lord)—even if by doing so he might risk sacrificing wealth, worldly praise, or even personal well-being.

Eddie's discography, consisting almost entirely of sessions recorded for European labels, documents both his fealty to those values and that fealty's cost: as he told me, he'd been overseas and every time he went there he was hailed as a latter-day ambassador of one of the richest musical heritages in the world—yet when he came back home, he could barely find enough work to keep himself in groceries and keep a roof over his head.

Self-pity, though, wasn't his style; he always maintained a public demeanor of optimism and affability, and his music remained shot through with a feeling of hard-earned joy. Like his father, he had mastered the art of mining deep lodes of emotion through understatement and precision, rather than pyrotechnic overkill, and his personality reflected the same quiet strength that ran through his playing.

Eddie's message to the world was, indeed, his music; but even more than that, it was the spirit of unquenchable resolve, toughened by life and burnished by faith, with which he purveyed it. It was, in many ways, the spirit of the blues itself, the same spirit in which the late Denise LaSalle, writing in the voice of the blues in her prose poem "America's Prodigal Son," proclaimed:

"Until America wakes up and accepts me again and gives me the respect that I rightfully deserve, I will be a nomad, a prodigal son, immortal and indestructible.

"But, whenever you want me, America, I am just a musical note away."[5]

Larry Taylor: "I Let Them Live through Me"

"I am an icon of the blues."

Larry Taylor is still relatively young by blues standards, but he proclaims his lineage with the resolve of an elder statesman:

> What makes me the icon and the legend [is] because I started when I was a young man, and I played with the postwar blues masters, and now people of my own generation. Show me any musicians in my generation who have did what I have done and accomplished what I have accomplished. I come after my dad and them, Muddy and them; I knew everybody—all of 'em. I could just go down the line, man. It's not a lot of second generation blues people have the connection that I have. See, I knew everybody. And my point is, now I'm an icon of this blues, and a legend.

A rather sweeping statement, one might think, from a musician who's been a sideman for much of his career and has issued a total of two releases—a full-length CD and an EP—under his own name.[6] But the blues has historically been a field in which it's difficult to measure an artist's importance by relying on such conventional markers as commercial success, mainstream name recognition, or catalog size.[7] To hear Larry discuss his life in music is to be taken on a virtual guided tour of the Chicago blues world from the 1970s into the early years of the twenty-first century—he can recall times when he rubbed shoulders with and/or played alongside virtually every important, semi-important, or diamond-in-the-rough blues artist in the city, and the list of jukes, gin mills, show lounges, after-hours joints, and bistros he's worked in reads like the itinerary for a pub crawl in Blues Heaven.

He was born in Chicago on December 13, 1955. His mother, Lee Vera Hill, met Eddie Taylor when Larry was about two years old and she was fourteen (he still sometimes refers to himself as Larry Hill Taylor). Like all the kids who grew up in the Taylor household, Larry lived with music as a facet of daily life. When his stepfather wasn't rehearsing, or when figures like Howlin' Wolf, Floyd Jones, or Jimmy Reed weren't dropping by, someone was probably playing records or listening to blues on the radio. One Sunday morning, Larry saw Reed playing outdoors in the Maxwell Street Market, accompanied by drummer Johnnie Mae Dunson, and the spark was ignited. "I was a little boy," he recollects, "and I was impressed with her as a drummer, a woman drummer. It all started with Johnnie Mae."

"I didn't have no drums," he continues. "Howlin' Wolf's drummer, Cassell Burrow, left his drums at the house, and I used to take his stuff out of the cases and set 'em up while they was gone, and play 'em."

> I put everything back, but somehow my dad knowed that I had messed with it. And then who comes to the house? It's Cassell. I said, "Oh, I know I'm fixin' to get it now." But Cassell told [him], "No. Let him play 'em. If he know how to put 'em together, assemble 'em, play 'em, let him." So they had no problem with it from then on.

He also remembers "Winehead" Willie Williams, a rudimentary stylist who nonetheless was a master of the deceptively simple deep-pocket postwar blues shuffle, along with another local percussionist called Chicken House Shorty, as among his early teachers and role models. As the years progressed, he gained confidence and honed his chops, listening and learning from these and other musicians, most of them friends and colleagues of Eddie Taylor.

In 1977, *Living Blues* magazine coeditor Jim O'Neal was commissioned to put together a group of young Chicago bluesmen to perform on a bill with Willie Dixon at the Berlin Jazz Festival as "The New Generation of Chicago Blues," an appearance that culminated in Dixon's now-legendary shamanistic delivery of Lucius Barner's "Tear Down the Berlin Wall." Larry was on that revue along with other budding stars such as Lurrie Bell, Billy Branch, Johnny B. Moore, and Dixon's son Freddie. The experience remains a touchstone for him ("We were the people who opened up the doorway for all the young people who's playing today. They got us to thank"), but meanwhile, he was also pursuing his future at home. "My first actual professional gig," he recalls, "was when I started playing with my dad."

> I played with my dad for thirteen years. I played every blues club on the North Side and I played every blues club, a lot of 'em, on the South Side, and all the ones on the West Side from Roosevelt [Road] all the way back over to Lake Street. My dad [also] connected me to other people, like Left-Hand Frank[8] and Brewer Phillips[9] and people like that, Little Arthur [Duncan],[10] James Scott,[11] Moose Walker.[12] I played with a lot of people, man. Big Smokey,[13] all them people. Little Smokey,[14] Hip Linkchain,[15] Willie James Lyons[16]—see, [they were] the players of the blues, and a lot of people don't know that. They wasn't talked about much in history, but these is the people who made the thing.

Larry Taylor, then, by his own account, was a first-call drummer by the time he was in his late twenties, bridging the stylistic and cultural gaps between the predominantly white North Side clubs (where Eddie Taylor had most of his paid

Larry Taylor at home,
Chicago, 2018.

gigs by then) and the neighborhood venues on the West and South Sides, which continued to thrive with a roughshod brio that recalled the fabled halcyon days of the 1950s. On that circuit, musicians who played weekends at corner jukes for loyal followings could legitimately consider themselves "blues stars," celebrities who were recognized on the street, and whose recordings—even if they were only a handful of sides on obscure local labels—might be as prized among their admirers as the better-known records of artists like Muddy Waters, Howlin' Wolf, and B.B. King. This, in fact, is the primary justification behind Larry's insistence on his status as an "icon" and a "legend," and by the standards of the musical world he's moved in for most of his life, it's a difficult claim to deny.

So what happened? Why couldn't he make the full transition into what's usually called "mainstream" acceptance, as his father had done toward the end of his life, and as some of his contemporaries have managed to do in more recent years?

Part of the reason, by his own admission, had to do with personal demons. Even before that Younger Generation tour, he'd already lost five years of his life doing time—first at Statesville Correctional Center in Joliet, Illinois, then at Menard Correctional Facility in Chester—on charges he still maintains were false. He's struggled with addiction at various points, and his intense, brooding nature sometimes crosses into a moodiness that can segue into depression.

But there are also larger issues at play. Larry Taylor is not shy about calling out racism and unfairness where he sees them, whether in the music industry or society at large. He addresses these concerns directly in his 2010 autobiography, *Stepson of the Blues*, and he's no less forthright in his conversation. As a result, he believes, he's been smeared and held back, both personally and professionally. "They try to see me as this wrong guy, this racist guy," he protests. "I'm no racist guy. I got a white girl [keyboardist/songwriter "Barrelhouse Bonni" McKeown]. I got white friends. How can I be a bigot? That's something they choose to fabricate. This thing is all about truth—don't lie on me!"

(Or, as the notes on the back cover of his autobiography put it: "Larry . . . finds himself slogging through a cesspool of greedy, ugly, race-ridden dynamics among musicians and promoters. Trying to speak out, Larry finds his career shut down. But he won't shut up!")

Nonetheless, he remains undaunted. After years of working primarily in others' bands, he's a leader again, often showcasing his singing at least as much as his drumming ("I led my band back in the late '70s, then I cut it off and started playing with other people and became a studio musician. And then, in 2003, I picked up my band, and I been moving on ever since"). He released a new EP, *The New Chicago Sounds of Larry Taylor and the Soul Blues Healers: Real Music for All People*, in 2017, and he's also found inspiration from some unexpected sources.

"We took a trip," he relates, "down south to Clarksdale. This was 2004, when we went to the Handy Awards."

> We was at the hotel there, the Riverside, where Bessie Smith died.[17] I had some experiences—like I could sense and feel the musical ancestors talking and saying things to me. Their spirits come to me, said, "You are one of the chosen ones. Make sure you continue what you're doing with this music, and don't forget it. 'Cause we're gonna be keeping our eye on you—we're going to be watching you." So, what I'm saying is, what makes me such a great musician [is] because their spiritual sprits—I let it flow in me, I let them live through me. And I get great inspiration from them.
>
> I'm a hard-core blues man. And ain't nobody taking that away. Nobody. I don't care what they do. They can't never take that away.

Tim Taylor: "Plug It in the Socket, Hold It in the Pocket"

It's a cold February afternoon, and the heat in Tim Taylor's new basement apartment has just kicked in. He hasn't unpacked his furniture yet, so the only things to sit on are a pair of drum stools in the living room. But Tim is glowing, summoning memories as warm and welcoming as the smile that lights up his face.

"They all used to be over at our home," he recollects, his voice softening as the images come rushing back:

> Howlin' Wolf, Carey Bell,[18] One-Arm John Wrencher,[19] Mad Dog Lester,[20] Big Ben[21]—all these guys used to be in our living room; our mom used to make dinner on Sundays.
>
> And Floyd Jones used to be over at our house every day. He always would bring us bubble gum, a whole bag, like two dollars [worth], every time he would come over to see us. He always kept his Calvert; he loved that Calvert whiskey. Kept him a pint of Calvert under his seat all the time, and he kept him a spit cup in his car—a can. Remember the coffee can? *Ping!*
>
> Man, them guys—Homesick James, man, and a heavyset guy, real heavy, Big Bad Ben. David Lindsey's father. He didn't miss a day coming over there. My dad used to show him a lot of stuff on the guitar. We had so many musicians in our house, man.
>
> Jimmy Reed, I used to love when he'd come over. He'd be walking through the house, drunk, I'd say, "Mr. Reed, you dropped your money." "Yeah, li'l boy, you keep that money, shit. Jimmy don' need no money. You keep that little money." Can you imagine, back in the '70s, picking up twenty and thirty and forty dollars, like three or four times? That was a lot of money back then.
>
> He had epileptic seizures very bad; my father saved his life a lot of times. I had [Reed's] wallet—remember the old wallets that looked like alligator skin? With a string around it. It had all Jimmy Reed bite marks in it, from when he was having a seizure. I think when our house caught afire, all that stuff got burnt up. And it really hurted me that I departed from that wallet, but . . . those was the days, man. I miss all those guys. I miss them so much.

Tim isn't sure exactly why the drums caught his fancy early on ("I don't know," he demurs. "I just loved the drums more than anything"). His father, of course, was a world-renowned guitarist, but he was also a proficient drummer, as was his father's brother Milton, and if Tim needed any further inspiration, his own older brother was close at hand. "Ditchin' school!" he smiles. "I used to go to my brother Larry's house. I'd sit there beatin' on his drums and stuff, and finally I decided I want to be a blues drummer. 'Cause first, you know, I'd call blues 'that old-time broke-down music.' As I grew older and found out the meaning of the blues, and what my father meant to me playing the blues, that's how I started out becoming a blues drummer."

It didn't take long for young Timmy to begin raising hell around the house, banging on skillets and pie tins with any implement he could find; under Larry's tutelage, and with further guidance from his father, he soon graduated to a legitimate drum set. Once Eddie Sr. recognized his son's passion, he did all he could to help cultivate it. "My dad kept telling me to play a shuffle," Tim recalls, "and I was like, 'What is a shuffle?' I didn't know what a shuffle was, so he had me listen to all the old Jimmy Reed stuff [with drummer] Earl Phillips. That's how I learned how to play the shuffle. It was hard for me; when I'd try to do a shuffle, like a Jimmy Reed shuffle, my dad would say, 'No, that's wrong,' and he'd show me."

There aren't many drummers left who specialize in that seductively simple-sounding rhythm, and many who do still fall short of mastering its subtleties

Tim Taylor in his home studio, Chicago, 2018.

(which are far easier to demonstrate than to describe—ask a shuffle drummer exactly how he does what he does, and his answer will often sound more like a Zen koan than a music lesson). "I kept learning the shuffle," Tim continues, tapping his feet and brushing his knees with his hands to show exactly what it was he learned. "It became—it's like, a lot of people try to steal my shuffle. My style of playing is different from any other drummer in the world. My shuffle, I call it 'Plug it in the socket, hold it in the pocket.'"

By the time he was in high school, he was already sitting in at venues like the Delta Fish Market, backing up such stalwarts as keyboardist Detroit Junior ("Detroit Junior used to come to Marshall High School and pick me up every Friday") and guitarist Johnny Littlejohn. His first out-of-town job, as he remembers it, was with Littlejohn, when he was about seventeen or eighteen years old. Not long after that, when his brother Larry couldn't make it to a gig with bassist/ bandleader Willie Kent at the Domino Lounge, Tim offered to fill in. That engagement led to an extended tenure with Kent, which in turn brought Tim his first recording opportunity. In 1983, Wolf Records embarked on a project featuring Eddie Taylor and his wife Vera along with Kent and his aggregation, with Larry and Tim Taylor alternating on drums. The result, released several times over the next few years by Wolf under slightly different titles, turned out to be Eddie's last album featuring himself as leader. Tim also appeared with Kent on *I'm What You Need*, a 1989 LP released on veteran Chicago DJ Big Bill Collins's Big Boy label, as well as at least one more album on Wolf and several on Delmark; he spent some time in his father's band during those years, as well.

In the early '90s, an even bigger opportunity came his way, and again it happened because another drummer was indisposed. "Man, I never will forget," Tim chuckles. "Eddie Shaw was playing out at the Delta Fish Market. He was doing a [tribute] for [Howlin'] Wolf."

> My uncle Jimmy Burns, selling that moonshine up there, he used to sell it out the trunk. So [Shaw's regular drummer], Mot [Dutko], he drunk two half-pints and he fell out. Mot was in the car, man, his feet was hangin' out the window, one shoe on, one shoe off, one sock hanging out the window on his toe. Eddie Shaw couldn't find nobody to play, so I say, "I'll play with you, Eddie." So we start playing.
>
> Eddie said, "You want to do a couple gigs with me?" I'm like, "Yeah!" And next thing I know, I was part of the Wolf Gang. I was part of the Wolf Gang for sixteen years; sixteen long years with Eddie.

Working and recording—again, for both Delmark and Wolf—with one of the blues' most iconic bands was a rare privilege, and Tim would probably have stayed until the end (Eddie Shaw died in Chicago on January 29, 2018). "What happened," he says, "is that I got sickly, and I took off from the band for a while. So he started hiring other different drummers to play. Then I went back with him, playing maybe eight or nine months, and then he got sick, and that was the last time I played with him. The last year I was with him [was] probably about nine years ago.[22]"

Usually, when a sideman leaves a prestigious gig like that, he can parlay his experience into furthering his career, either by forming his own band or by hooking up with another big name. For Tim Taylor, though, it hasn't worked out that way. After leaving the Wolf Gang, he saw his opportunities diminish, and they haven't picked up since. "I've been a good drummer all my life," he laments. "I've never made enough money to buy a home, never made enough money to buy a decent used car. If I don't play with [guitarist] Maurice John Vaughan, maybe one or two gigs a month, I don't play with nobody. I just bought a brand new [drum] set; I got two more sets in the back. I got three sets of drums just sitting here."

Part of the problem, he maintains, is cutthroat attitudes among musicians. "It's a money issue. We'll go play for, like, seven hundred a night; young guys gonna do it for a hundred." And then, of course, inequalities that plague the larger society also make themselves felt in the blues world:

> White [musicians] know how to hook up with the right people, get more recognition, get out there faster. A black person can go into a club, not get hired; a white person go right behind him and get hired. I've never been prejudiced, I've never been segregated or nothing like that, but this world is still messed up.

At the same time, Tim recognizes that his own earnestness can have its costs—he refuses to sacrifice his integrity for a mess of pottage or even a guarantee that he'll be able to afford groceries for another week, and he's willing to pay the consequences for that choice:

> Everybody's not really into the deep, deep Delta old-time blues no more. It's rock; everything is pedals and distortion and fast fingers. I'm a true blues drummer. I can play other things, but I choose to play my traditional blues.
> And you know something else? It's like if only—I wish I could have—I ask the Good Lord every day: Dear God, please just put me with a good band [so] I can play and work, and keep my father's tradition alive.

John Primer

"We're Teachers Now"

You hear the same stuff all the time. Before I even joined anybody, even back in the early days, back in the '60s, I learned all kinda different songs. We had something different to sing every time, every song that came out—Top 10, Top 40—we were there. And then I go back and get 'em—always bring that old stuff, that forgotten stuff, back to the light.

—John Primer

A rich paradox runs through the music of John Primer. Internationally praised for his dedication to upholding the postwar Chicago blues tradition (his band's name, the Real Deal Blues Band, is more than a moniker; it's a mission statement), he nonetheless prides himself on his originality. Like his mentor the late Magic Slim, whose repertoire was so vast that longtime fans would sometimes make bets that his show would include at least one song they'd never heard him play, he applies fretboard and vocal techniques rooted in Chicago tradition to material gleaned from a wide spectrum of sources both vintage and contemporary, augmented by his own creations. He's as likely to serve up an unearthed diamond from a long-forgotten blues or R&B B-side, or maybe a cover of Lonnie Mack's "Satisfy Suzie" or even the 1975 Glenn Campbell hit "Rhinestone Cowboy," as he is to reprise "Sweet Home Chicago," "Mannish Boy," or another of the over-cooked chestnuts—the notorious "set-list from hell"—that audiences never seem to tire of, but which too many performers fall back on to garner easy applause (or to avoid having to come up with anything new). When John does play a song like that, it sounds like what it is: a loving tribute to forebears, infused with fresh improvisational fillips and glowing with admiration, rather than pandering or playing to the cheap seats.

That approach, of course, comes much closer to the spirit of innovators like Muddy Waters and Howlin' Wolf—who aggressively updated, rather than imitated, the music of their idols such as Son House, Robert Johnson, and Charlie Patton—than the rote "revivalism" favored by so many of today's self-styled traditionalists. It's also appropriate for a man who came of age living close to the earth, in a place and at a time when "roots" signified growth and blossoming, rather than stasis.

He was born Alfonzo Primer[1] in the rural hamlet of Camden, Mississippi, probably in 1945 (he has resisted giving his exact age). After his father was killed in a trucking accident, John's grandmother dedicated herself to raising him and his sister. "My mom and grandmother, all of 'em, were sharecroppers," he remembers. "I grew up with all that stuff. Ridin' mules, tractors, pick cotton, pull the corn, chop cotton."

That's not the kind of childhood that usually evokes nostalgia ("It was a poor, hard life. I shared a bed with four other kids. The whole family lived in one house—ten adults and seven children. Everyone worked in the fields to put dinner on the table"[2]), but despite the hardship, John has at least some fond memories of his early days. "Music was my life," he attests:

> When I was born, and I was old enough to know what music was all about, I loved music. Dancing and stuff, trying to listen. I remember I was a little kid, maybe one or two years old, I saw all them catalogues from Sears, and they all had guitars in them. We'd get one every month. I would go to the mailbox, bring the book in the house, and I would just get the book, lay on the floor, turn to the guitars and just stare at those all the time. Go out and play, come back and get the book, get [back] down on the floor.

In the time-honored Southern tradition, John made his own first guitar by hand. He remembered it in a 1991 interview with the late Lois Ulrey, which appeared in Issue 2 of Ulrey's *Magic Blues* magazine: "One string upside the house. My grandmother's broom, I took the wire off it and made me a guitar upside the house. She kicked my butt for doing it, but I still would do it when she'd go to town or somethin' like that on Saturday. I'd fix me one upside the house and play me some music. That's my first instrument."[3]

There wasn't much actual guitar music around to learn from, though. Most of the singing he heard in church was a capella, sometimes accompanied by a vocalist who "play[ed] the bass with his mouth," probably in the fashion of gospel quartet singers like the Southern Sons' Cliff Givens, who was renowned for imitating the sounds of a string bass. Occasionally someone might come "walkin' down the road playin', or guys come by my grandmother's house with a guitar," and there were some juke joints nearby, but the boy never summoned the courage to do more than "peek through the cracks—we weren't allowed to go in there. Afraid to go in a juke; people fight."

John's music lessons, such as they were, evolved primarily out of friendships and family relations. "I had a friend," he remembers, "we were seven, eight years old, sharecroppers; he was living a couple miles down [from me], he had a guitar, his dad played guitar and stuff. We'd mess with that guitar." He also had a cousin named Percy Flax who played guitar and gave him a few pointers. For the most part, though, music came into his life via records and radio:

> Muddy Waters, Lightnin' Hopkins, all that Bukka White stuff, B.B. King, Jimmy Reed, John Lee Hooker. Probably the first blues stuff I listened to was John Lee Hooker, 'way back. All these other famous blues guys back then, I learned 'em. Blues or gospel. WDIA come out of Memphis, we could get it down in Camden. At nighttime we'd get, out of Nashville, Randy's Record Mart. Friday, Saturdays, all type of music on there. At night it would come out, come strong—"Randy's Record Mart! WLAC! Nashville, Tennessee!"[4] Country music? Oh yeah, I loved it. Most [of what] you'd listen to back then was country-western music, cowboy songs and stuff like that.

In 1963, John moved with his sister to Chicago. He didn't come for the music; he was growing into manhood, and he wanted to get a job and better himself. But he did purchase a guitar not long after he arrived—the fulfillment of a life-long dream. He told Lois Ulrey that once he had the instrument (an acoustic) and learned how to play it, he "rehearsed all the time, every day, sometimes at night. I didn't miss a day from rehearsal."[5]

From there, it was inevitable that he'd begin to insinuate himself into the still-robust neighborhood blues scene on the West Side, where he lived at the time. "A guy named Mr. Little," he remembers, "and a guy named Riley. They were blues guys but they never played nowhere hardly, they'd just sit home all the time [and play]."

> All the kids would go over there after school, Friday night or after school in the day-time, at night, and play blues. [They] didn't have an amplifier. Had TVs and stuff like that hooked up; we'd play guitar through that. Had guitars, not name-brand, raggedy old guitars, somethin' for us to beat on, but they worked. We'd all be there,

ten or twelve of us be there at night, learning how to play, playing blues and stuff. [The late guitarist] Michael Coleman, all of us. Later on when I was old enough, I started playing with this guy named Pat Rushing on Maxwell Street [the famous open-air market off Halsted on the Near West Side].

We used to rehearse a lot; we had this band we created, the Maintainers. Pat moved into a building at Spaulding and Roosevelt, I believe. He would be drunk, playing at home all the time, all day and all night, drinking. We started hanging with him, playing, go play at house parties and stuff. There were clubs all up and down Roosevelt [Road]. One night at Bow Tie's on Roosevelt, [Rushing] and his wife got into a fight; [she] hit him upside the head. "Won't be back here tomorrow!" We only played there one night.

Pat Rushing was a pretty elemental guitarist, but John says that the Maintainers played a variety of music, including contemporary R&B, along with blues. He

John Primer, Blues Heaven Foundation, Chess Records building, Chicago, 2018.

also encountered other young guitarists who were working to update the Chicago tradition:

> This little band I used to see on Maxwell called the Transistors—Melvin Taylor, Sam Goode—I lived not too far from them. I went around where they were rehearsing, so Sam told me, "Hey, I'm going to the South Side tonight on 39th Street"—Peyton Place I think was the name—"I know this band, they're looking for a guitar player." We stopped in there that night, it was [guitarist] John Watkins, Dino Alvarez on drums, I think it was Dion Payton playing guitar, Murphy Doss on bass. So I sat in and played with 'em that night. John Watkins asked me if I was looking for a gig. "I play at this club called Theresa's." I said, "Yeah? Never heard of it." "We're rehearsing down there Sunday. I'm getting ready to leave. I can't take this bullshit no more."

Theresa's Lounge (or Theresa's Tavern—the name on the sign varied over the years), at 4801 S. Indiana Avenue, was by then already on its way to becoming one of Chicago's most legendary South Side blues venues. Long the home base of harmonica ace Junior Wells (former Muddy Waters sideman; originator of such blues classics as "Messin' With the Kid," "Hoodoo Man," and "Come On In This House"), it was the kind of place where, on a given night, virtually any of the still-active "living legends" of Chicago blues—James Cotton, Buddy Guy, Louis Myers, J.B. Hutto, Big Walter Horton, Sunnyland Slim—might drop by to have a drink, sit in for a few numbers, or maybe even hold down an evening's gig when Junior was on the road. At least partly because of its proximity to the University of Chicago, it became one of the first South Side clubs to draw a significant white clientele, and it eventually became an almost obligatory stopping-off point for blues tourists from overseas. Almost by accident, John had stumbled into the gig that would set him on the course toward international recognition—he remembers the year as 1974:

> That Sunday I went down there about two o'clock. I'd never been over to the South Side. Afraid—Blackstone Rangers, gangs—I don't know! Theresa's was on 48th Street; I got off at 49th Street. "Oh man! I got off at the wrong stop!" So I'm shakin', walking up [to] 48th Street. I go inside, John Watkins is in there rehearsing. Theresa's sitting at the bar with her hand in her pocket, half-asleep, nodding. And John was playing [Wild Cherry's] "Play that funky music, white boy. . . ."
>
> And all of a sudden I saw a beer can, [it] flew back—wham!—and she said, "Motherfucker, please don't play that shit in my place!" And John looked at me, he said, "See? That's what I'm talkin' about." She was real strict about the blues. She didn't want them playing no rock & roll up in there. So Monday night I came down there, [told] Junior Wells, "John Watkins told me to take his place; he quit." Junior looked at me, said, "I don't care. I don't care."

John took that to mean he was as welcome on Junior's stage as Watkins had been (Junior's oracular pronouncements sometimes required some deft exegesis), and he decided to take the job. Thus began the first in a remarkable series of apprenticeships and associations that would mark his career for the following two decades. Most successful blues artists can cite a mentor, usually an older musician whose style they absorbed, or who taught them how to navigate the sometimes-treacherous byways of a professional musician's life. Few, however, can match the record of John Primer. Between the 1970s and 1995, when he finally struck out on his own, he had the opportunity to play alongside, and learn from, at least five of the most gifted and influential blues artists of his—or any other—era. A gig with Junior Wells, of course, was a living lesson in blues history. The lead guitarist in Theresa's house band during that same time was Sammy Lawhorn, a highly skilled fretman who had also worked in Muddy Waters's band. Although hampered by an alcohol problem, Lawhorn continued to showcase his dazzling technique and deep blues sensibility for years after he left Muddy, usually from his chair on the bandstand at T.'s.

Lawhorn was renowned for his mastery of the whammy bar; he could use it to make his instrument moan, weep, and shiver with near-vocal expressiveness. But that was the only electronic gimmick he'd touch; blues feeling, to him, was summoned from the hands and the heart. He passed that low-tech, high-passion ethic on to John. "I learned a lot from Sammy," John relates, "a lot of style from Sammy. 'Gon' play the blues? Play the blues! Don't use no gadgets and stuff like that. If [you] wanna be a blues player, don't use no Crybabys and all that phase-shiftin' stuff. Throw that away. Put it in the garbage!' I learned a lot of the old blues, all that Robert Johnson stuff, the way I play it, that's what I learned from Sammy."

John also says that it was Lawhorn who inspired him to take up the slide, which has since become one of his trademarks. His tenure at T.'s, though, was much more than a graduate course in blues traditionalism. Owner Theresa Needham may have chafed at the fusion-oriented tendencies of young Turks like John Watkins; nonetheless, her house band played eclectic sets, both on their own and while backing Junior Wells, whose James Brown–influenced blues-funk fusions endeared him to South Side audiences as much as they rankled white purists. That eclecticism suited John perfectly—his sets at T.'s might include offerings like Tyrone Davis's "Turning Point" or Al Green's "Sweet Sixteen," and he was always ready to plunge into some throbbing, on-the-one funk when Junior decided it was time to get his Godfather on. In fact, at least one song John has continued to include in his repertoire, "Rhinestone Cowboy," dates back to those days—he picked it up from a drummer at T.'s who went by the stage name "Stawr."

That gig paid the rent—John remembers that he and the band often played seven nights a week, whether Junior was in town or not—and the constant stream of out-of-town visitors meant valuable exposure to a wider audience, but it was still "just" a club gig, unlikely to bring a young guitarist anything more than local celebrity. But word was getting around about the exciting new guitar player at Theresa's, and in 1979, Willie Dixon recruited John to join his band, the Chicago Blues All Stars. His first gig with Dixon was in Mexico City.

"Playing with Willie Dixon," he has remembered, "was a huge opportunity for me. Willie did a lot for me when I was starting out. He got my passport and took me to Mexico City. This was the first time I had ever been out of the United States before. I learned how to play many of the old traditional songs from him. I met . . . Muddy Waters in Mexico City while I was playing with Willie Dixon. He heard me play and asked Willie about me."[6] Dixon, a savvy businessman, also "pulled John's coat" about that aspect of music ("Willie taught me the importance of writing my own songs and protecting them"[7]), a lesson that's held him in good stead as a songwriter through the years.

After his stint with the All Stars, John returned to Theresa's and resumed his old job as Sammy Lawhorn's second-in-command behind Junior Wells, until yet another career-changing opportunity fell into his lap. In 1980, Muddy Waters's band quit en masse, disenchanted with their financial situation and at odds with Muddy's manager, Scott Cameron. Muddy needed to recruit a new crew in a hurry, and he hadn't forgotten the young fretman who'd impressed him in Mexico City. He dispatched harpist Mojo Buford, an old compatriot of his, to Theresa's.

"Mojo came down there," John remembers, "checkin' me out a couple times. So he came to me, asked me do I want to play with [Muddy]. I said, 'Yeah!' 'We're going to rehearse tomorrow on Lake Park [Ave.] at the house, in the basement'— [Muddy] wasn't living there anymore; Charles was living there, his son—'I'll pick you up at 10:00 tomorrow.' I was ready; ready to go."

Playing lead guitar for the man most consider the premier architect of the post-war Chicago style might have seemed like a daunting proposition, but John had been well schooled. After all, both Junior Wells and Sammy Lawhorn were Waters alumni, and Dixon had worked closely with Muddy during the Chess Records glory days; each in his own way had prepared John for this moment. At T.'s, he had also honed the art of negotiating his way among the diverse, sometimes unpredictable musical directions Wells and Lawhorn would chart. Watching them closely, observing both their strengths and their weaknesses, he learned how to conduct himself, on stage and off, as a professional.

Touring with Muddy gave John the opportunity to see the world, and to be seen, as never before; and, of course, being associated with a such a living legend was "a dream come true. . . . I was in shock that this was happening to me. Playing with Muddy was like playing with a king."[8] On purely musical terms, it was also an invaluable chance to delve further into the music's roots and study the technique of one of its all-time masters (when John plays slide these days, it can sometimes sound as if Muddy himself is guiding his hands and fingers). Muddy was also one of the blues' most accomplished vocalists, and listening to John sing, especially when he takes on a Waters classic like "I Be's Troubled" [a.k.a. "I Can't Be Satisfied"], "Take the Bitter with the Sweet," or "Mannish Boy," it's easy to believe he absorbed a lot of Muddy's phrasing, timbre, and enunciation. He insists, though, that his tenure with the master did not have much of an effect on his vocal technique—that happened much earlier. "I picked up a lot of stuff from Muddy [on records] in my younger days," he says, "when I was growing up, back when I was eight or nine years old. My voice, the way I sing, is my natural voice."

In 1982, when illness forced Muddy off the road, John again found himself looking for a musical home. And again, events conspired to ease his transition. A little earlier, Magic Slim's longtime rhythm guitarist, Coleman "Alabama Junior" Pettis (who also went by the name Daddy Rabbit), had left Slim's band, the Teardrops, due to health problems of his own. Pete Allen had taken over the job for a while, but now Slim was looking for a replacement. John recalls that he learned of the opening almost as soon as he came back to Chicago from his final tour with Muddy's band:

> I stayed with [Muddy's] band after Muddy got sick. We played a little bit, me and the band, a few gigs. [Magic Slim's drummer] Nate Applewhite was working at Theresa's at that time; if Slim was in town, he'd be working at Theresa's, too. Pete Allen and Nate had some kind of confusion and Pete quit, and I came in behind Pete.

Magic Slim (née Morris Holt) was a massive man, whose music—fierce, even belligerent in its intensity—and pugnacious stage persona ("Oooh, it's gonna be a mess, I tell ya! I'm madder'n a one-eyed Russian and crazier'n a constipated Gypsy!") could be almost overwhelming, even in a rowdy South Side juke. Some might have considered returning to those hardscrabble jukes something of a comedown after touring with an international celebrity like Muddy Waters, but

John insists he never saw it that way. "It was cool with me," John maintains. "I liked what I was doing."

> Playing in the small clubs, it was cool. [The money] wasn't the same, but it's my job, the music, y'know, so I felt good playing small clubs. [Slim] asked me, "How many nights you wanna work?" I said, "I don't care, how many you want." So we were working seven nights a week. He'd keep the band working; sometimes he had two gigs [in one day]. See, what it is, you're never too big to go back where you came from. That's the point—don't never forget about where you came from.

He didn't stay off the road for long in any case: "As soon as I joined the band, I think we played at Florence's [at 55th and Shields] a couple gigs, and we went on tour for six weeks. I played with Slim something like thirteen years, 1982 'til 1995."

By this time, John had codified his style, based in the postwar blues he'd mastered at T.'s and with Dixon and Muddy, but spiced with up-to-date rhythmic and chordal colorations (at least partly the legacy of Sammy Lawhorn). It was rootsy, yet sophisticated enough to appeal to listeners weaned on rock, soul, and R&B. Always eager to learn, he absorbed additional lessons from Slim during his time with him, and they weren't all musical ones. "I learned a lot from Magic Slim," he says. "How to go on the road and stuff, how to treat your musicians, pay your musicians, be fair with them, treat 'em right. Because without them, your musicians, you ain't nothing. You're out there by yourself. Lotta people thought [Slim] was mean; he'd talk, 'I'm gon' kill the bass player, the guitar player, the drummer. Gonna buy y'all a black suit!' [But] he was cool. I worked for him all those years, we never got in an argument."

But even as he enjoyed his tenure as a Teardrop, John was working to develop his own musical identity.[9] His first recording under his own name was 1991's *Poor Man Blues* on the Austrian Wolf imprint; he followed that up with several more over the next few years, and by 1995, with his catalogue expanding, he knew it was time to make the big move and establish himself as a front man. "I hated to leave the band," he admits. "We had such a good thing going for us. But I did [a] new CD, called *The Real Deal*; helped me out a lot. [I figured,] be there so long as you can, then you gotta go. Let somebody else learn."

That's not a casual statement coming from John Primer. Having had his own career enriched so deeply by mentors, he takes very seriously his own responsibilities as a role model for young musicians. "We're teachers now," he attests. "I'm a teacher now. Teach you 'bout the blues." This includes encouraging his charges to absorb what they can from him and then learn to fly on their own:

"Somebody wanna move along, let 'em go. Think you'll make more [money]? Go ahead. Somebody else [comes in], teach them how to play it. Keep the blues goin'."

Of course, the blues is a business as well as a living legacy. It's no secret that road gigs are getting scarcer, and even in cities like Chicago many venues are either cutting back on live music or closing their doors entirely. John believes that club owners and promoters, for the most part, are doing the best they can, but that doesn't make it any less of a struggle, even for an established veteran like him.

"It's hard," he admits. "Life is hard—everything is so hard out here. To me— I'm speaking to my experience—when I work, I be treated fair. Because I ask for a price, and if I don't think it's right, I won't take it. They kinda go along with you, try to help you best they can. It's tough right now. A reason why they don't

John Primer, dedication ceremony for the Muddy Waters mural, 17 N. State Street, Chicago, 2017.

pay local bands much [is] because we are local—there's a lot of us here playing music. To me, small clubs, they're doing the best they can. They try to keep all of us working, they keep us from starving. They're not taking advantage; it's just the way you got to look at it; they're keeping you from starving. I wish we'd get paid more; maybe one day we will, y'know?"

With that in mind, John has little nostalgia for the neighborhood jukes where he and most of his colleagues cut their teeth. Yes, he acknowledges, a club like Florence's was "a party every Sunday." On the other hand, "back in the days, a club, they pay you, it all depends. If nobody come in, you wouldn't get paid. Or they'd short us or cut us, y'know. Back then, money wasn't guaranteed. If you get hired at [North Side clubs like] B.L.U.E.S., Kingston Mines, one of them, Buddy Guy's or Blue Chicago, the money is guaranteed. You don't have to worry about, 'Hey, I wonder if I'm gonna get paid by the end of the night.' No, you gonna get paid."

Like most musicians, though, John prefers to talk about his love for the music and his dedication to keeping it alive and strong. In recent years, he's been featured around Chicago in some unique and challenging settings, especially for a bluesman as dedicated to tradition as he is. In 2007, he played some gigs with pianist Yoko Noge's "Japonesque" project, which melded the traditional Japanese folk music called *min'yo* with Chicago blues. Featuring John and veteran blues bassist Bob Stroger along with Noge on vocals and piano, Avreeayl Ra on trap drums, Tatsu Aoki on shamisen (a Japanese stringed instrument), and Hide Yoshihashi and Amy Homma on Japanese Taiko drums, the music spanned centuries and cultures, as Stroger and John laid straight-ahead blues riffs over the Eastern harmonies and multitextured rhythmic cadences of Noge and her cohorts.

Equally challenging were his 2008 appearances with the Chicago Sinfonietta under the conductorship of Paul Freeman, which performed *Three Songs for Bluesman and Orchestra*, a composition by noted blues producer and critic Larry Hoffman. John says that despite the "strange" feel that sometimes permeated these gigs, lending his style to such atypical settings "really was kinda easy; it wasn't too stressful. Just a lot of rehearsals."

Nonetheless, what he loves most is to front a no-nonsense blues aggregation that shares both his love for tradition and his dedication to keeping that tradition fresh by bringing in original ideas while still hewing to the time-tested melodic, harmonic, and rhythmic bases that have long given "Chicago blues" its unique identity. It's an approach that's been evident on his recordings from the beginning: His 1991 debut, *Poor Man Blues*, was a set of eleven original composi-tions, and if he was still honing his chops as a lyricist ("His original songs aren't particularly interesting," wrote one critic, somewhat patronizingly, "but they function as good vehicles for exciting jams. . . . Primer may not add anything new to Chicago blues, but he has a great time playing, and it sure is fun to listen to him play"[10]), the personnel he chose—including ex-Teardrops "Alabama Junior" Pettis and bassist Nick Holt, along with younger-generation Chicagoans like harpist Billy Branch and the fiery guitarist Michael Coleman—foreshadowed his ongoing dedication to both honoring heritage and celebrating fully in the "now," and the set's overall ambience reflected the mixture of unforced emotionalism, musical dexterity, and joy that continues to be his calling card.[11]

"Unforced," in fact, is probably the operant term. It's all too common for musi-cians who profess dedication to "keeping the blues alive" to sound mannered, insisting on note-for-note accuracy, loath to depart from the hallowed text (one vocalist even recalls being castigated by her sidemen for daring to sing a song in a different key from the original[12]), transforming a music of celebration and defiance into a stilted exercise in pedagogy. John, though—even when his music sounds as if it could have been written and recorded almost any time over the last sixty-five or seventy years, as on his mostly acoustic *Blues on Solid Ground* (issued in 2012 on his own Blues House label)—has mastered the art of attack-ing every note, every phrase, and every word with the aggression and delight of one who's discovering its wonders for the first time; not retreading the past but rediscovering, and reigniting, inspiration.

"I just love what we're doing," he enthuses, reflecting on both his music and the life he's led negotiating the unpredictable highs and lows of the business. "Love it. It's all in my bones, in my heart. I love to play music. When I pick my guitar up and step out, ready to play something on stage, I feel motivated. I feel good. I don't be drinking, no alcohol—it just gives me a natural high.

"I was born with it. I can tell the world I was born with it. I know I was. Oh, man! Music—I just dig music. I still love all music, can listen to it and enjoy it. Any type of music. Right now."

Shemekia Copeland

"I Know What My Purpose Is"

Shemekia Copeland exploded onto the scene in 1998 at the age of nineteen with *Turn the Heat Up*, her debut on the Chicago-based Alligator label. Reaction was immediate: "Shemekia Copeland's promise is as limitless as her talent," raved *Living Blues* magazine, adding that "her voice is pure, beautifully unaffected, and powerful," and lauding her stylistic range and "unshakeable confidence"[1]— admirable qualities in any artist, remarkable for one so young on her first bolt out of the gate. As she began touring more, things only intensified: adjectives like "sizzling," "storming," and "incendiary" began following her around like starstruck groupies alongside such descriptive bromides as "no-holds-barred" and "take-no-prisoners"—some reviewers even dragged the dreaded "red-hot blues mama" out of storage to describe her.

Overheated as some of the encomiums may have been, they captured her pretty well—but in some ways, they also missed the mark. Despite the intensity Shemekia poured into virtually everything she sang (even on ballads she sounded like a warrior wrestling demons into submission), there was already a sense of worldliness to her. She seemed to be singing from the depths of hard-won experience, bespeaking an "old soul" informing the youthful passions that surged through her songs and lyrics. That the blues was witnessing the arrival of an accomplished new storyteller seemed undeniable: Shemekia Copeland was singing "grown folks' music" before she was out of her teens.

It's a persona she has claimed for as long as she can remember, and by her own account, it was bequeathed to her by her parents, especially her father, the late guitarist Johnny Copeland. Johnny Copeland attained international celebrity in the 1980s after white listeners finally caught up with him, but by then he'd spent decades recording and touring, primarily in the South and Southwest (the sides he cut for such labels as Mercury, Golden Eagle, Atlantic, and Wand, among others, are now prized by collectors). Although considered a modernist for his time—he was part of the generation of Texans, also including such firebrands as Johnny "Guitar" Watson, Albert Collins, and Freddie King, who fused elements of postwar blues, R&B, and rock & roll into a sound that could appeal to multiple generations and diverse audiences—he was also a dedicated roots man. In 1985, two years after a revelatory tour of Africa, he returned to Abidjan to record *Bringin' It All Back Home*, a multicultural celebration that included both African and American musicians. Eight years later he appeared on pianist Randy Weston and trombonist/arranger Melba Liston's *Volcano Blues*, further honoring the blues as an African-rooted world music. Other outings, such as his 1996 release, *Jungle Swing*, also invoked African themes.

Copeland, who moved from Texas to New York in 1975, welcomed the accolades of the white audience that was "discovering" him during those years, but he resisted any efforts to patronize him or his music. Like B.B. King, Jimmy Witherspoon, and others who made clear their distaste for the all-too-common stereotypes of bluesmen as crude and unsophisticated, he commanded—and demanded—dignity and respect, both on stage and off. He wouldn't sell his CDs at his shows, he once said, because that would mean relegating the blues to the status of "third world music," unworthy of its rightful place in respectable record outlets alongside soul, R&B, and pop.[2] His daughter, immersed from infancy in these values, had little choice but to follow his lead.

"I was such an old soul," she attests. "Let me tell you something: I'm growing younger! Remember that story, 'Benjamin Button'? I would swear to you that when I was born, I was born an old lady."

She was born Charon (pronounced Sha-RON) Shemekia Copeland ("my dad wanted me to be called Shemekia Charon, and my mom wanted me to be called Charon Shemekia") on April 10, 1979. The family lived in Harlem, close to where St. Nicholas Terrace dead-ends at 127th Street. "When she was born," her mother, Sandra Lynn Copeland, has remembered, "[Johnny] said to me that she would never do anything but sing the blues. He said, 'Don't let her do anything else but

Shemekia Copeland, Meyer
Theatre, Green Bay, Wisconsin.

sing the blues, because that's what she was born to do.' And I said: 'Where did
that come from?' Because I wanted my daughter to be a lawyer."[3]

Indeed, the earliest music she remembers hearing was blues, along with old-
school soul, gospel, and country; when her parents weren't playing records, her
father was writing songs and rehearsing at home. She'd stand behind the couch,
imitating his singing as best she could, and he eventually began using her as his
sounding board—if she liked something he came up with and tried to sing it, he
knew he had a keeper. Hardly the soundtrack for a typical New York childhood,
especially in the rap/R&B-besotted 1980s, but she loved it from the beginning,
and as she grew older she embraced it even more:

> It was my "normal" to listen to that music. When I came home [from school], that's
> the music I played. I didn't even bother with the radio, because I was not into popular

music. The funny thing was that I was so secure, even then, [the other kids] just accepted that I was different from them. I was odd, but I didn't get teased for it. I was never bullied or anything like that. I went through the same little insecurities that all girls grow up going through, just trying to figure out who you are as a human being, and maybe it was a little more difficult for me because I knew I was different, but I was okay with it all at the same time.

Despite her father's ambitions for her, though, she says that in her earlier years, at least, she didn't expect to grow up to be a blues vocalist ("I never thought I could sing," she admits). On the other hand, she often tells the story of the time she sang Koko Taylor's "I'm a Woman" for her class at grammar school, and her teacher, taken aback by the lyric "I can make love to a crocodile," dutifully reported the incident to her mother. (Sandra Lynn merely shrugged and encouraged her little girl to keep singing the music she loved.) When she was about nine years old, Shemekia made her debut on the stage of Harlem's Cotton Club when her father called her up from the audience to sing. A few years after that, he talked her into doing a Cotton Club show of her own, a gig that proved both inspirational and humbling. She closed with Jackie Wilson's "(Your Love Keeps Lifting Me) Higher and Higher," but before she could finish, her dad gave her a lesson in the venerable art of head-cutting—he took the stage and promptly took the show:

> I was in the process of introducing everybody, and I brought my daddy up on stage, and my dad came up there, and he put his arm around me, and I gave him the mic— big mistake! He didn't do anything except be who he was . . . this amazing performer. And he grabbed the mic, and he said: "Your love lifted me higher!" It was amazing. I can't really explain it but it was just amazing. And he just crushed me.
>
> And I was like: God, I got some work to do.[4]

Nonetheless, she insists that it wasn't until she was at least sixteen and had been singing on her father's shows for quite some time, that she finally decided this was what she wanted to do with her life. She also makes clear that much of her early reticence had less to do with insecurity ("My family gave me the strength to be able to make my own decisions and do what I want") than her own inviolable sense of self-worth, grounded in the values her parents had taught her. "My father was very spiritual," she affirms. "My mom is, and my family all around me. My grandmother was, before she died, and so we are very spiritual."

> I remember when I was about nine or ten, and my father took me to see [the late Chicago vocalist] Big Time Sarah. She was this really great entertainer, got the crowd going, getting guys' heads, puttin' 'em in her breasts and shakin' 'em, all those kinds

of raunchy things. But even as a child, I just knew myself enough to know—I said to him, "If I ever have to do this, I know I'll never become a singer." And he said, "You don't have to do that, sweetie. There's a lot of different styles of blueswomen out here. That's not the only way; not everybody does that."

I mean, it was cool; I loved it. But I just knew I could never do it. I knew that, even then.

When Shemekia was about fifteen, her father was diagnosed with congestive heart failure, and over the next few years he endured a grueling series of surgeries. No longer able to sustain himself over the course of a full show, he began featuring her as his opening act. She leapt at the opportunity to help him, but she soon realized there was a deeper purpose behind his refusal to give up the stage. "I believe he did all that [final touring] for me," she maintains. "No way he could have felt like getting up there, all those nights that he got up there. He needed me to help him out, but he was doing it for me. And now I realize that. I realized that a long time ago . . . just a strong man. I pray I have that strength."

At one point, Sandra Lynn Copeland remembers, when Johnny was in intensive care, he seemed to be going through a crisis. "Shemekia sat down beside him and she started to sing to him. And as she sang to him, the machines started to level off. His breathing became very soft. I looked up and saw tears . . . a nurse walked in and she said, 'Don't stop. Whatever she's doing, it's affecting the other patients too.' At that point, I'm going, 'Omigod, this is what she was meant to do.'"[5]

By 1997, when Alligator Records president Bruce Iglauer saw her perform at Chicago B.L.U.E.S. in New York, she was already well on her way to becoming a seasoned entertainer. Iglauer, who had seen her on one of Johnny's shows a few years earlier, says he "was instantly knocked on my butt. . . . I was kind of shocked that somebody that age could have that adult soul in that young body. I literally couldn't believe how good it was."[6]

Along with veteran producer/songwriter John Hahn, who had known Shemekia since she was about eight years old when he was working with Johnny on a recording project and had already become her manager, Iglauer set up a session to record some demos. Pleased with the results, he signed her to a contract, and by the following year, *Turn the Heat Up* had been released. Although the overall feel of the album reflected its good-timey title, Shemekia was already showing encouraging signs of depth: she delivered "Ghetto Child," for example, an uncompromising slice of social commentary penned by her father ("I'm just the ghetto child, in this so-called free land") with a stentorian force that bespoke despair, outrage, and resolve. It immediately became a showstopper for her, and it has remained so to this day.

Although Johnny Copeland never got to see his daughter blossom into a full-fledged recording star, she made sure he knew that his dreams for her were in good hands. As soon as she cut those first demos with Hahn and Iglauer, she rushed to the hospital to play them for him. "He would listen to those songs," her mother relates, "and tears would run. And I would ask him, 'What's upsetting? Is it something that you don't want, or did it sound bad? What's the problem?' He says, 'No. Her heart is in it.'"[7] He died on July 3, 1997.

Shemekia's own territory, meanwhile, continued to expand. Most of the blues world welcomed her with open arms—many out of respect for the Copeland name; almost all in response to her dauntingly outsized talent—but she encountered a few who resented the idea of such a youngster, especially a woman, striding so brazenly onto their turf. "I got into this one argument with [a veteran Chicago vocalist]," she relates:

> He doesn't know me from Adam, didn't know my father, didn't know where I came from, but he was trying to tell me, "I don't care how strong you might think you are; some man will end up—a man can get you strung out and do this to you and do that to you, all these women get strung out on this and strung out on that, and runnin' behind men and da-da-da—" And I just looked right at him and said, "That's not gonna happen."
>
> I don't think he's used to a woman talking to him like that. But I said, "That's not gonna happen." And he said, "Well, how do you know it's not gonna happen to you?" I said—and I have never had to talk to anybody that way—" 'Cause I ain't never had no dick that good, to make me lose my mind or make me stuff something up my nose or anything like that. It's never gonna happen. Never. And I can confidently say that to you." And he said, "Well, it happens to everybody." And I said, "Well, I guess if you don't know, you should phone God up and ask him." Then walked away.
>
> And then I cried. Because I was so upset that I had to speak that way to him. And I was so upset that he was that ignorant. If I wasn't confident, if I wasn't raised by my mother and father who taught me to value myself, and taught me to never put anybody up on a pedestal, I don't care who he is, 'cause he's just a man—if I wasn't raised that way, he could've somehow knocked me down. But he doesn't know me, and he doesn't know my strength.
>
> But that day, he learned that you will respect me. Period. It was just that simple.

Shemekia's sophomore outing, *Wicked*, released in 2000, garnered a Grammy nomination for Best Contemporary Blues Album of the year, and it furthered her reputation as a gifted, if still-developing, stylist. Although her full-bodied

bellow remained her calling card ("Wild, Wild Woman" finds the singer promising a prospective erotic conquest that he's a "lucky man," but in the face of all
that power we don't know whether to envy the guy or pray for him), she also
demonstrated a jaunty, New Orleans–flavored sassiness on "If He Moves His
Lips" (featuring a guest vocal, mostly spoken, by R&B legend Ruth Brown) and
a maturing ballad style on such outings as her father's "It's My Own Tears" and
"Up on 1–2–5," another vignette of ghetto despair, this one written by John Hahn
and Joe Hudson.

For the most part, though, she was still living up to Alligator's motto, "Genuine Houserockin' Music." At John Hahn's urging, Mac "Dr. John" Rebennack was
enlisted to produce her next release, 2002's *Talking to Strangers*; guitarist Steve
Cropper then stepped in to oversee her following album, *The Soul Truth*, released
in 2005. As expected, those R&B veterans helped infuse a new, funkier element
into her sound, but out in front her vocal delivery remained pretty much the
same—tantalizing hints of depth and nuance, all but overwhelmed by the ferocity
of her attack. Although she didn't say so publicly at the time, in retrospect she
realizes she'd veered dangerously close to a rut.

"I needed time," she admits now. "I needed time."

> I made my first record—two years later, the next one. Two years later, the next one.
> Two years later, the next one. You make a record, you're touring, and then you're
> back in the studio—it doesn't allow for life to happen. You're too busy touring and
> making records. We tried to make it sound different by getting different producers.
> . . . But really, what needed to happen, was I needed some time to figure out what it
> was that I wanted to say. I was so young, I was making records, I didn't even have
> time to breathe.

It couldn't have been easy to leave Alligator, at least arguably the driving force
in the contemporary blues market. To make matters even more complicated,
Bruce Iglauer was a longtime family associate who had featured Johnny Copeland,
along with Albert Collins and Robert Cray, on 1985's Grammy-winning *Show-
down!* and had helped nurture Shemekia's solo career virtually from the beginning.

Nonetheless, she left, and almost immediately she felt her world expanding.
The young woman who could still say, as late as 2005, that "I'm never alone; I'm
always with someone," and then gush about how thrilling it had been to actually
take a taxi to a restaurant in Chicago to have lunch by herself,[8] blossomed into
a world traveler and a savvy observer of national and international affairs: "So
many things happened in my life! Here I am traveling to Kuwait and Iraq [on the

2008 Bluzapalooza tour[9]], getting involved in a long-term relationship, moving to Chicago—I wanted to change completely and do something different."

Up until that point, she says, she hadn't thought much about including social commentary in her music. To her, songs like "Ghetto Child" and "Up on 1–2–5" were simply vignettes drawn from experience—no polemic or ideological message intended:

> "Ghetto Child," for me, was my life. I wasn't thinking "political" at the time. I was a kid who had seen many of her friends murdered and killed; I never thought of it as a "political" thing. It wasn't until I got older that I understood that. Now, it's like— whoa, it hits me hard. But then it was just, here I am, this kid who would watch her friends go, and I'm like, "I'm just a ghetto child. I grew up in the ghetto, my friends grew up in the ghetto, this is the perfect song for me." But I didn't realize how deep it was until I aged.

It was during that 2008 Bluzapalooza tour, in fact, that she began putting her personal experiences into a larger perspective. When Barack Obama won the U.S. presidential election on November 4 of that year, she remembers, "I found out he won, in Kuwait in a mess hall . . . and I couldn't even show excitement of any kind. You can't talk politics over there, you can't say anything, you have to keep quiet at all times about anything like that."

> And so here I am in Kuwait, standing in a mess hall, find out that he won, on a big screen, and I can't even cheer or applaud or say [anything]. Silence in the mess hall. Silence. And it was just the most eerie, strange feeling. And then, here I am going through the airport in Kuwait, and a young guy from there said [she lowers her head and whispers]—"Obama! Obama!" You know, like, really quiet, under his breath to me, because obviously I'm American and he wanted to show excitement, and they were like [whispers again] "Obama!" And I thought to myself, "Wow!" It was crazy.
>
> So I just experienced so many things that I wanted to sing about. I never much got into what was happening government-wise; I wasn't old enough to vote until the second Bush election, but I wasn't into it at all. It was after that [Kuwait experience] that I got into it. And when you start getting into that—oh, god! A whole other world opens up to you.

Worlds were opening musically, as well. After leaving Alligator, Shemekia signed with Telarc, a California-based label known for the eclectic reach of its roster. At the same time, she buckled down to her homework. "I did four records [for Alligator] and then decided I wanted to have voice lessons," she admits with a wry smile. "I figured, maybe I should try to learn how to sing now! And then working with [producer] Oliver [Wood], also showing me that the subtleties of my voice can be just as powerful as the power in it, also helped a lot. And how Oliver, myself, and John have grown over [her subsequent] three records, for me, is just amazing."

Although it wasn't billed as such, her 2009 Telarc debut, *Never Going Back*, represented both a comeback and a musical rebirth. Under Wood's production, her sound had deepened and expanded into a blend of roots-rock, progressive folk/alt-country, and pop, along with the hard-driving blues that remained her primary stylistic jumping-off point. She delivered Buddy and Julie Miller's excoriating "Dirty Water" ("You can try to lock up the truth, but the door won't shut / 'cause the truth just comes out like blood from a cut") like a call to arms; she called out religious hypocrisy ("Sounds like the Devil") and wrong-doing men ("Limousine") with equal fervor; she offered up anthems to selfhood in the face of perils both existential ("Born a Penny," Joni Mitchell's "Black Crow") and social ("Rise Up," "Broken World"); she exulted in her spirituality on offerings like "The Truth Is the Light" and "Big Brand New Religion," the latter a kind of riposte to the hucksters she'd called out in "Sounds like the Devil." Characteristically, she both tapped and tweaked her blues roots with an ironically up-tempo reading of Percy Mayfield's suicidal "River's Invitation" and an airy, folklike take on "Circumstances," a hard-bitten ode to perseverance and survival written by her father and featured on *Flyin' High*, his 1992 album on the Gitanes label.

The centerpiece, though, was "Never Going Back to Memphis," a dispatch from the dark underbelly of Bluff City hipster life written by Hahn and Oliver Wood and cast in an ominous minor-key dreamscape. Cinematic in its vividness, it was a tour de force both musically and lyrically, and by Shemekia's own account it was as revelatory to sing as it still is to listen to: "That's when I got into storytelling," she enthuses. "I love that. I love telling stories. That's what we were trying to do, and then we've just grown with that, with every record."

The blues world was taking notice of that growth. On Sunday, June 12, 2011, the final night of that year's Chicago Blues Festival, the late Koko Taylor's daughter, Joyce "Cookie" Threatt, bestowed one of her mother's tiaras on Shemekia and pronounced her the new "Queen of the Blues" in front of a cheering crowd at the Petrillo Music Shell. Contrary to some rumors at the time, the crowning was entirely Cookie's idea (she has said that her mother considered Shemekia her heir apparent, and Koko herself indicated as much to me during a 2002 interview[10]) and had nothing to do with the Alligator label, which released its anthology,

Shemekia Copeland: Deluxe Edition, that same year and would re-sign Shemekia a few years later.[11]

Since Taylor's death in 2009, the issue of who—if anyone—should be considered the new Queen of the Blues had become a contentious one, with several different "coronations" and crownings in the ensuing years leading to hurt feelings and bitterness in some quarters. Shemekia, summoning the same equanimity that has maintained her since she was a teenaged *wunderkind* thrust into overnight stardom, refused to be pulled into the fray.

"That was a total surprise for me," she affirms. "I didn't know anything about it. Oh my god—it was a wonderful honor, and I was grateful for it."

> Koko didn't ask for that title, and neither did I, but when you receive something like this, you accept it graciously. Some young girls coming up will probably know about her through me, just as I learned about so many other singers through her. To me she'll always been the Queen of the Blues, because she was my queen. I never call myself that. That's the one thing Koko always was—gracious. You don't necessarily have a title to have a purpose, or to know what your purpose is. And I know what my purpose is.

33⅓, released on Telarc in 2012, earned Shemekia her second Grammy nomination and represented yet another upward arc in her trajectory—her voice sounded surer and more relaxed than ever, and her thematic scope continued to expand. Included among the usual blues-themed odes to eros and demands for fidelity were outings like "Lemon Pie," a caustic denunciation of social inequality and fat-cat politicians; "Somebody Else's Jesus," a throwdown to false-bottomed religionists that picked up where "Sounds like the Devil" had left off; and, most stunningly, "Ain't Gonna Be Your Tattoo," a graphic parable of domestic violence and survivorship penned by Hahn and Wood. The woman who had once eschewed "political" material now embraced her newfound role as a voice of social conscience.

"When *33⅓* came out," she says, "doing songs about domestic violence and doing songs about religious hypocrites—that was right up my alley."

> A woman came up to me at one of my shows, and she said to me, "I had been in an abusive relationship for many years; I was on my way home in a car after getting into it with my boyfriend, and I had [Chicago radio station] WXRT on, and that song came on." And she said, "I never went back to him again."
>
> She was crying. I was crying. Everybody was crying. And I just thought, if it's just her life I changed, it's one person, that's fine with me, I've done it, my whole career was worth it.[12]

In 2015, after re-signing with Alligator, Shemekia dropped *Outskirts of Love*, her follow-up to *33⅓*. Offerings this time included everything from Solomon Burke's deep-soul classic "I Feel a Sin Coming On" through a hard-crunching version of Albert King's Memphis-brewed blues/funk hybrid "Wrapped Up in Love Again" and her father's dark-night-of-the-soul meditation, "Devil's Hand," to inspirational outings like Jessie Mae Hemphill's "Lord Help the Poor and Needy," "The Battle Is Over" (composed by Maurice "Mighty Mo" Rodgers and Jerry Winn but best known for Sonny Terry and Brownie McGhee's 1973 version), and Creedence Clearwater Revival's hymnlike "Long As I Can See the Light."

Once again, though, it was the topical fare that cut most deeply. The title song, peopled with lost souls wandering the night in search of solace, was both stark and celebratory in the great blues (and rock & roll) tradition; "Cardboard Box"

Shemekia Copeland, Meyer Theatre, Green Bay, Wisconsin.

found Shemekia and guest vocalist/guitarist Alvin Youngblood Hart portraying a homeless couple wringing irony-toughened philosophical resolve out of their predicament ("Life is rough, it only gets worse / We all end up in a box, I just got mine first"); "Drivin' Out of Nashville," on its surface a honky-tonk romp buoyed by Pete Finney's shimmering pedal steel guitar, was actually the tale of a singer who responds to her producer's sexual harassment with Bonnie Parker–style brio ("I'm drivin' out of Nashville with a body in the trunk"). Everything paled, though, next to "Crossbone Beach," a nightmarish scenario of date rape and retribution, again cowritten by John Hahn and Oliver Wood. Shemekia's vocals made the protagonist's anguish come alive with visceral force; Robert Randolph's steel guitar solo, meanwhile, was an aural manifestation of her plunge into terror and dissociation.

Outskirts garnered Shemekia another Grammy nomination, but by then—despite her putative vow to pace herself—she was already looking toward the future (a gaze that became even more purposeful after the birth of her son, Johnny Lee, on Christmas Eve of 2016). "I'm smart enough to know these [topical] songs are not going to make me popular," she said;[13] nonetheless, that's clearly a direction she wants to pursue further:

Zac Harmon did a great song called "Stand Your Ground" [in honor of Trayvon Martin and Black Lives Matter], that John and him wrote together. Definitely, I don't see why that would be off the table for me. And I don't like the way the elderly get treated in this country, either. That pisses me off; I just thought about that not too long ago—"I want to say something about older people in this country." There's a lot of things like that, that I would talk about. [Violence in the streets] has been happening ever since I was a kid in my neighborhood. This is not brand-new; they've been killing kids forever.

Perhaps surprisingly, though, she seems relatively sanguine about at least one issue that some of her contemporaries find especially disturbing—the "whitening" of the blues, both on record and in performance. She is her father's daughter, of course: she's well aware—and fiercely proud—of the cultural heritage her music represents. But she sees her message as universal, and she's realistic enough to know that a messenger needs to cast as wide a net as possible if she wants to be heard.[14] "In order to preserve the past," she insists, "in order to preserve the heritage, we have to open it up and let whoever wants to do it, do it."

If it wasn't for the Rolling Stones, nobody would know about Muddy Waters and Howlin' Wolf. If it wasn't for Stevie Ray Vaughan, [they wouldn't know] Albert King, Freddie King, all of these guys—well, some would, but most of 'em wouldn't. It was those guys who put them back on the map. I think artists, black artists, are very accepting of white artists who play their ass off and are soulful. My father loved Stevie Ray Vaughan. Stevie was a good person, and he had a great respect for the music and the artists who came before him. Some don't, but he did—I know he did. I think young people are smart enough to know that it came from someplace, that there's a tree.

I look out into my audience, there's mostly white faces out there. I'm grateful for those faces, because [without them] I wouldn't be able to work. I don't think anybody on the black circuit would know who I was, because I guess I just don't do that style of music. And you know what I think? I think people need to get out of their—black people need to get out of that whole "soul circuit" trap, and I would say the same for whites: Get away from the white, rock-edged—check out everything! When you start to separate things and just stick to one genre, you just screw yourself. There's so much music out here—you're missing out on a lot of things.

In fact, about the only thing that seems able to coax intolerance (and even a hint of militance) out of Shemekia Copeland is intolerance itself, especially when it comes to music. Not unlike the genre-blending blues musicians of her father's generation who incorporated elements of rock & roll, country, R&B, deep soul, and more into their styles while never forsaking their essential identity, she is steadfast in her insistence that it's her very determination to explore and evolve that represents her deepest blues pedigree:

Too many people, I call 'em Blues Nazis, they focus so much on whether or not you're playing a shuffle or a slow blues, and "Keep it blues!" [That] keeps this genre in a box so we can't evolve; we can't grow. And I refuse to let that happen. Just because you change things a little? Just because you steal from all the people who've stolen from you? Yeah, now I'm taking it back! Can't I do that? Why am I still not a blues artist? Because I'm taking a little bit back? They used us, so why can't I take a little bit and put it into what I'm doing, and have it still be blues? It makes perfect sense as far as I'm concerned.

Jazz, opera—what haven't I done yet? Nancy Wilson, Ella—love it! I don't care if it's Pavarotti or a Brazilian samba. It's blues, 'cause I'm a blues singer, so anything that comes out of my mouth is gonna be blues.[15]

Sugar Blue
"The Music Must Progress"

If you listen to so many of these quote-unquote "blues artists,"
all they're doing is regurgitating stuff that was cutting-edge in
the 1940s and '50s, and even the '60s. Come along and change
the precepts and change the construct, and all of a sudden they
can't play the music anymore, so they don't want to hear it.
Excuse me? The music is only dead in your mind—not in mine.

—Sugar Blue

Few contemporary bluesmen have come by their art as honestly as Sugar Blue. Few revere their mentors and forebears more deeply; few are more passionately committed to carrying on the music as living African American vernacular tradition, rooted in slavery and oppression but charged with power and liberating spirit ("From this crucible the Blues was born," he has written in a prose poem dedicated to the late guitarist Honeyboy Edwards, "Screaming to the heavens that I will be free, I will be me!"). At the same time, though, fewer still have crafted a style as unremittingly forward-looking, even transgressive—forged, according to his critics, in defiance of the very roots he professes to honor and carry forward.

Blue gives little shrift to such arguments. "Purists?" he snorts. "I don't recognize these people. The blues is only limited by your concepts and your abilities, and what you are able to invest in the music."

To see Sugar Blue in action is to witness a man in the act of "investing" virtually every fiber of his being. With sweat pouring down his face, his eyes jammed shut and half-hidden by his trademark slouched beret, he hunkers over his harp like a parched man drawing sustenance. The sound that erupts out of that harp defies blues convention—quicksilver skitters, runs, turnarounds, and octave leaps; a tonal range that builds from growling depths through shrieking ascents into jagged, high-end declamations. Even more radical, perhaps, is his apparent determination to challenge and deconstruct the emotional, as well as the melodic, harmonic, and rhythmic contours of blues tradition. Even when his lyric themes invoke desperation, or when he's reprising a melancholy classic like the Big Bill Broonzy / Little Walter standard, "Key to the Highway," in both his playing and his singing he seems to steel himself against, if not actually mock, the sorrowful vulnerability that, to many, remains the sine qua non of blues expression.

It may not be surprising, then, to learn that Blue's formative experiences in New York included sitting in with such jazz futurists as Sun Ra and Rahsaan Roland Kirk, or that he spent time woodshedding and jamming on the city's 1970s-era loft jazz scene. At the same time, though—and here, perhaps, lies the key to both his artistry and his penchant for attracting controversy—this young aspirant with an ear toward the avant-garde was also a bona fide folkie, busking on the streets of Greenwich Village, studying vintage blues 78s, absorbing the music of harmonica masters like Jimmy Reed, Big Walter Horton, Little Walter Jacobs, both Sonny Boy Williamsons, and Sonny Terry ("I studied them like a student working on his doctorate").

Ironically—or, perhaps, fittingly—Blue's very stage name grew out of an encounter with a disgruntled listener. "It must've been about one or two o'clock in the morning," he remembers, "and we were playing on a street corner under this old lady's window, old Italian woman. She opened the window and started cussing us out in Italian—we had a raucous crowd around us—and the old lady threw out a box; I guess she was trying to bean me. And the box exploded, and it was full of old shellac 78s. They all shattered, except for the one record on top, and it was called 'The Sugar Blues' by Sidney Bechet. And I had been looking for a name, so when that happened, I looked at it and said, "Hmmm. Sidney Bechet— S.B. 'Sugar Blues'—S.B. Sonny Boy—S.B. Okay, that's it—I'm Sugar Blue."

. . .

He was born James Whiting in 1949, into a Harlem household where music, theater, and literature—the fruits of the Harlem Renaissance—were a daily presence and inspiration. His mother, Joyce Savage, had been a member of the celebrated Brownskin Models, a revue that presented elaborately costumed dance routines, songs, and musical comedy on cross-country tours from the mid-1920s until 1954, when its founder, actor/playwright Irvin C. Miller, retired.[1] By the time James was born, his mother had also retired from show business, but he still "grew up surrounded by her musical friends." (According to family lore, Billie Holiday stopped by to visit when he was a few months old; when she picked him up, he burped Pablum onto her gown. Unruffled, the Lady simply removed one of her trademark gardenias from her hair, covered the stain, and went on to her gig[2]). His childhood, as he remembers it, was "steeped in stories of the Harlem Renaissance."

> Langston Hughes was, and is, one of my favorite poets and authors, and Zora Neale Hurston, Ralph Ellison. So I was kind of an artsy-craftsy baby. And as far back as I can remember, I wanted to play an instrument, and I wanted to be in show business—like Mom, y'know? And she was always telling me, "No, you don't want to be in this business. It's a real rough road, and you make very little money, and it's really hard to [balance] a life." And I was like, "I don't care! I want to be in music."

His first instrument of choice was the saxophone, but he soon gravitated to the harmonica (inspired, at least partly, by seeing Stevie Wonder at a show his mother took him to when he was about twelve years old). A chance encounter with a street musician named Sweet Papa Stovepipe ("He's singing and playing his guitar, I'm playing backup as best I could, and he'd stop and take a nip out of his bottle and start telling me stories about when he was a young man") helped motivate him to delve more deeply into the blues, and by the time he'd reached his late teens he'd gravitated to Greenwich Village, where the remnants of the fabled '60s-era folk boom were still thriving. With a repertoire that included everything from songs by Bob Dylan, Woody Guthrie, and Buffy Sainte-Marie to the pre- and postwar blues classics he'd been studying on vintage recordings, he was able to make decent money playing on the streets.

But he didn't limit himself, even then. When he wasn't busking, he was insinuating himself into some of New York's most forward-looking jazz circles—that's how he met Sun Ra and Roland Kirk, among others—and, not to be constrained by even his own progressive aspirations, he also picked up pointers from veterans of earlier eras. In fact—and, yet again, ironically—these encounters with old-school horn men helped him develop elements of the harmonica style—scalar, emphasizing major-key whole-step intervals rather than blue notes and flatted fifths—that some blues traditionalists now criticize. "I was trying to imitate,"

Sugar Blue, Buddy Guy's
Legends, Chicago, 2016.

he asserts, "as close as I could on a diatonic instrument, things that saxophone players and trumpet players were doing."

> And I didn't have all the half-steps, so I just approximated as much as I could. I remember [former Basie tenor saxophonist] Buddy Tate telling me, "Man, if you want to play music, you've got to master that instrument." He said, "Do you know how to go, 'Do, re, mi, fa, sol, la, ti, do?'" I said, "Yeah, I know that." He said, "Well figure that out on the instrument, and that'll give you some facility that you don't have." I started working on it, and it gave me an assurance, a knowledge about how to move around on the instrument. And it served me well.

Most importantly, though, he made the acquaintance of Victoria Spivey, a legendary figure from the "classic blues" era whose career had spanned upward of forty years and had included collaborations, as both pianist and vocalist, with the likes of King Oliver, Louis Armstrong, and Lonnie Johnson. Her recordings—"Black Snake Blues," "Dirty Woman Blues," "T.B. Blues," et al.—were (and are) among the disks most highly sought by collectors.

In her sixties by then, Spivey had forged a new career for herself as a label owner. Her Spivey imprint, which she'd cofounded with jazz historian Len Kunstadt in about 1961, was famous for its line of blues and jazz albums featuring a remarkable array of artists spanning numerous styles and generations. Blue's first encounter with her on the streets of New York, as he remembers it, was "like a scene out of *Sunset Boulevard*."

> Len was her driver; they were married, but she never treated him like that. She treated him like her chauffeur, and he didn't mind; he loved it. So they pulled up in a 1949 torpedo back Cadillac—pristine, looked like it just came off the showroom floor—and she stepped out, and she was dressed in this old 1940s style, great big blowsy skirt, a picture hat and platform shoes, and she looked like she'd stepped out of a movie. And I'm like, "Who in the hell is this?"
>
> And so she's standing there, and we're playing, and after we finished she says, "Hello. My name is Victoria Spivey, and I am the Black Queen of America."
>
> I'm like, "Yes, ma'am!"
>
> "And oh, that's my driver."
>
> So she said, "I want to record you."
>
> And I'm like, "Record me? Okay! Why not?"

The music that arose out of those collaborations, released on the Spivey LPs *Spivey's Blues Parade* (from 1970) and *New York Really Has the "Blues Stars"* (issued in 1975),[3] captures the young aspirant in the bloom of early inspiration. He showcases a tubular, occasionally squalling tone that recalls "Easy," Big Walter Horton's famous 1953 harmonica tour de force on Sun Records, and a moody ballad style on which the influence of saxophone masters like Lester Young—or maybe Stan Getz, with whom Blue would eventually collaborate—is evident. They're bravura performances—Blue's dexterity and tonal suppleness are already formidable—but there's little evidence of the genre-busting iconoclast that he would become.

Spivey helped him expand his social network, as well. "Victoria Spivey introduced me to Willie Dixon," he remembers. "Also, Victoria introduced me to Bob Dylan."

> She told me, "I want to introduce you to my son Bob." Dixon was on stage—this was at the Bottom Line—and she took me over to a dark corner. We got up close, and—"Hey! That's Bob freakin' Dylan!" And she walks up to him, she says, "How you doin', son?" And Bob says, "Oh, I'm fine, Mama Spivey." And she says, "I want to introduce you to the best young harmonica player in New York City. And he's

gonna play on your next record." And he looked up at her, and he looked at me, and he said, "Yes ma'am." Which is how I ended up playing on a Bob Dylan record [the song, "Catfish," was originally intended for Dylan's 1976 LP *Desire*; it was eventually issued on *The Bootleg Series, Vols. 1–3, Rare & Unissued 1961–1991*].

In 1974 or so, seeking further inspiration, Blue made a pilgrimage to Chicago, where he wandered awestruck through the city's blues scene, exulting in the chance to see—and even meet and play alongside—some of the artists he'd idolized for so many years. "Big Walter was playing on a regular basis," he recalls, his sense of wonder still palpable, "and One-Arm John Wrencher, Easy Baby,[4] Eddie Taylor—I remember having the opportunity to play with Eddie Taylor, and I knew that Eddie Taylor was the foundation for a lot of the things that Jimmy Reed had done. And I got to play with him and talk with him and hang out with him!"

At one point, he recalls, the Aces, Little Walter's former backup band and a famed aggregation in their own right, walked into a club where he was playing. Guitarist Louis Myers, who was also an accomplished harp player, praised Blue ("I have played with some of the best harmonica players in the world—Sonny Boy Williamson, Little Walter—and I never heard nobody riff a harp like you do") and invited him on a whirlwind tour of some of the city's best-known West and South Side clubs including Theresa's on Indiana Avenue, where Blue thrilled to the music of Junior Wells, Buddy Guy, and former Muddy Waters guitarist Sammy Lawhorn. They ended up at an after-hours joint "in a basement in a tenement, [where] they were goin' at it, man, and they were selling pints and stuff. Those were some great times, man, hanging out with all of those incredible players."

Upon returning to New York, Blue hooked up with veteran R&B journeyman Rex Garvin and guitarist Johnny Copeland (recently arrived from Texas), among others. When pianist Memphis Slim, who'd moved to Paris years earlier, came to town for a brief residency at the Top of the Gate on Bleecker Street, Blue went to see him. "I sat in," he recalls. "He liked what I was doing, and I asked him, 'Well, if I came over to France, do you think I could make it?'"

He said, "If you've got the chutzpah to come on over, I'll help you." And about two or three weeks later, I was on the airplane going to France. I had always been in love with the French language, and Paris in particular, because of the great singer and stage actress from the 1930s, Josephine Baker. My mother loved Josephine Baker. You could say that Josephine Baker was her idol. And [Blue's girlfriend] Cecile Savage was a French girl, and so we started busking like we'd been doing in New York, playing in the Metro and on the street corners, getting shooed away by the gendarmes.

I remember when I first saw Memphis Slim in Paris. He pulled up to a joint in a Silver Ghost Rolls-Royce, and he stepped out of it, and the suit matched the vehicle. I was like, man, this guy is too cool! And after he stepped out, two beautiful young French girls popped out from behind him—I said, "I like this country!"

Blue played club gigs with Slim (ever the eclecticist, he also worked alongside such jazz masters as Getz, Steve Lacy, and Lionel Hampton), and over the next few years he recorded *Cross Roads*, his debut under his own name, and the sessions that became *From Chicago to Paris* (released on the Blue Silver label after he returned to the States in the early '80s). Never less than fearless, he also hooked up with the Rolling Stones ("He's a very strange and talented musician," Mick Jagger told *Rolling Stone* magazine's Jonathan Cott[5]) and laid down the now-iconic harmonica line that propels the Stones' "Miss You," from their 1978 LP, *Some Girls*.

After touring with the Stones for a while (he appears on *Emotional Rescue* and *Tattoo You*, as well as *Some Girls*), he changed course again, returned to the States, and headed for Chicago. Once more he was heeding the advice of Memphis Slim. "Slim," he remembers, "had already spoken to [Willie] Dixon about me, so I almost had a gig before I got here." Dixon, of course, was one of the most venerated carriers of the traditionalist postwar blues flame, but he welcomed the iconoclastic young improviser into his Chicago Blues All Stars. "Willie Dixon had really big ears," Blue attests. "He was more progressive than a lot of people thought. He said, 'When I'm playing, when we're doing the rhythm and stuff, I want you to play what I tell you to play. But when it come time to solo, I want you to do what you do.' So he would let me go—boom! He said, 'Take off,' and I did. It was a wonderful learning experience. I used to talk to him about songwriting and his motivations for lyrics, and stuff like that. And he'd sit down and talk to me about it, and tell me stories."

When he wasn't blowing harp with Dixon (he appears on Dixon's 1988 Grammy-winning *Hidden Charms* LP), Blue was haunting the city's blues meccas, once again cherishing the companionship and mentorship of Junior Wells, James Cotton, and others whose music he'd admired since childhood. He eventually broke free from Dixon to form his own band, and he came into full flowering as a recording artist between 1993 and 1995, with outings on Seven Seas (Japan), DeAgostini (Italy), and Alligator (the Alligator LPs were leased from Seven Seas; *Blue Blazes*, released on Alligator in 1994, was a reissue of 1993's Seven Seas LP *Absolutely Blue*). Although he wouldn't record again until 2007, he toured consistently, both domestically and overseas, solidifying his stature as a dominant force in the music by virtue of his live performances alone.

Unfortunately, though, another, more sinister force was becoming dominant in Sugar Blue's life, a saga he relates with characteristic bluntness in "Krystalline" on 2007's *Code Blue* (released on his own Beeble imprint). It's a vintage Sugar Blue performance, searingly intense yet stripped of pathos or self-pity: "She took all of my money," he sings, "Left me shivering alone / I woke up broke and hungry, my friends and family gone / You're a strange white lady, tell me, honey, what's your name / She said, baby I ain't no stranger—Just call me Krystalline Cocaine."

"I was hip to cocaine long before [the Stones]," he attests today, dispelling any suggestion that their high-velocity lifestyle might have fueled his addiction. "Long before that. I spent a lot of time in what I came to discover was a very deep depression, and I spent a lot of time self-medicating, as many Black people do. You live with a foot on your neck long enough, you gotta find some way to avoid the pain of it. And for many of us, it was through substance."

It's difficult to determine whether his addiction had a significant impact on his playing—he was already known as a volatile improviser, prone to unpredictable flights of ecstacy or fury as the mood struck him and, if anything, those characteristics became more pronounced as the years went by—but the inevitable chaos that came with it took a heavy toll, emotionally and financially and, very likely, creatively as well. At the very least, it certainly helps explain the twelve-year gap between *In Your Eyes*, which appeared on Alligator in 1995, and 2007's *Code Blue*.

A high-strung man under the best of circumstances, Blue found that his attempts to palliate his anguish were only feeding on themselves, sucking him into a vortex that threatened to destroy him. "There came a point," he has said, "where I decided, it's either I'm going to get off, or I'm going to die from this shit. . . . Everything that I had worked for as a musician up to that time was about to go down the toilet and me along with it. So it really wasn't a difficult decision to make."[6]

In the late '90s, Blue entered a recovery program at the Crossroads Centre, the self-described "luxury drug rehab center" on the island of Antigua that Eric Clapton had founded in 1997.[7] It was there that he wrote the lyrics for "12 Steps," his ode to recovery, which finally surfaced on *Voyage* in 2016 ("I had been looking for the music to deliver the song," he says, "to make the song complete. We sat down with this incredible bass player, Joewaun Scott, he's one of the baddest young bass players around, and he came up with this bassline, and it was just, like, 'Yes!' It just gave the life to the song that we were looking for."). But, as is often the case, he couldn't maintain his sobriety after he returned to Chicago;

it took another period of rest and introspection, this time in Switzerland, to get him back on track.

In about 2004, he made the acquaintance of Ilaria Lantieri, a bass player (and erstwhile physician) from Milan, Italy, who soon became his full-time bassist and life partner, as well as a font of inspiration and stability (it was she who helped convince him to start recording again, which led to *Code Blue* and the three CDs that have followed it). Their 2012 wedding at 2120 S. Michigan Avenue in Chicago, the famed Chess Records studio building (now the home of Willie Dixon's Blues Heaven Foundation), was officiated by Minister Rose Reed (Jimmy Reed's daughter) and attended by blues dignitaries ranging from Marie Dixon (Willie's widow and Ilaria's maid of honor) through harp legend Billy Boy Arnold, Eddy Clearwater, Jimmy Johnson, former Chess recording artist and songwriter Cash McCall, Ronnie Baker Brooks, vocalists Sharon Lewis and Deitra Farr, and Howlin' Wolf's stepdaughters Bettye Kelly and Barbra Marks, among others. True to the universalist spirit Blue embraces in both his music and his life, the ceremony included (along with the traditional Christian service) a Cherokee marriage ritual; the bride and groom jumping a broomstick; and an Italian good-luck toast of prosecco and biscotti.[8] Blue and Ilaria's son, James, was born the following year.

Like his newfound steadfastness as a husband and father, Blue's music since his return to recording reflects the resolve of a man who's been blessed with a second chance and is determined to make the most of it. His improvisational fearlessness remains unbowed; his lyrics, meanwhile—illuminated, perhaps, by the clarity of vision that accompanies sobriety—have both deepened and expanded. Offerings like "Let It Go" ("Homeless mothers bare and cry / for hungry babies born to die") and "NOLA" ("Innocents killed by NOPD guns / the Ninth Ward slaughter /drowned in black waters") from *Code Blue*, and "Life on the Run" ("Another young man shot down out of hand / vigilante justice, the law of the land") from 2016's *Voyage* show that his passion for social justice and his defiance in the face of its enemies remain steadfast.

At the same time, a new tenderness has revealed itself. In recent years, Blue has reunited with Sarah, his daughter from an earlier relationship, who is now in her twenties, and this, along with his marriage and James's birth, seems to have opened his music, as well as his heart, in ways that might have seemed inconceivable just a few years earlier. Juxtaposed on *Voyage* alongside outings like "Life on the Run" and the sardonic, world-toughened "One" ("One man's heaven is another man's hell / One man's risen and another man fell . . . one

man's enemy is another man's friend / one man breaks and another man bends")
are creations that even many of Blue's staunchest advocates would probably
never have anticipated—sun-drenched odes to happiness, with Blue's harmonica
recorded acoustically to accentuate the sweetness of his tone, and the songs'
lyrics reflecting optimism both palpable and hard-won. "On My Way (Sarah's
Song)" is a repentant father's promise to his daughter (and, one suspects, a
healing man's promise to himself); the lilting, Spanish-tinged "Sunshine" is an
unabashedly romantic love song ("The sun is shining from up above / looking
down on the one I love"); the disk's centerpiece, "Love Is Everywhere"—a breezy
confection that culminates in a warming shower of coos and gurgles from baby
James—could easily have been cloying ("I'm feeling proud, happy and scared
. . . I'm going to be my baby's dad"), but in the context of the overall disk and
Blue's own life, it stands as one of the most courageous admissions of softness
and vulnerability he has ever dared express. The ironist who once referred to
himself as the "Gucci Gucci Man" (on 1995's Alligator release, *In Your Eyes*) has
finally found a way to let the sunshine in, and bask in it.

But if the music has softened, the man has not. He still bristles at accusations
of "inauthenticity," accusations he equates with an overall cultural and historical obtuseness on the part of (mostly white) critics and other purists, who may
reify the music for its universality ("everyone gets the blues") but seem unable or
unwilling to acknowledge it for what it is—at its core, first and foremost, living
Black cultural history, as relevant to Black life as it has always been, adaptable and
fluid as Black people themselves have had to be through generations of oppression and disenfranchisement, changing and shape-shifting in order to survive
and remain strong. "We've been running towards the future," he asserts, "and a
lot of folks are trying to run backwards—culturally, philosophically, politically."

> That is because arrogation is their quest. They are trying to separate the creators
> from their art, just like they separated the Indians from their land. What's amazing
> about this musical construct is that it has grown and changed the musical under-
> standing and mores of people around the world. And that is the strength of the Black
> spirit, and that is why there are so many that would like to arrogate it, because they
> understand the power of it, and they want it for themselves. Unfortunately, by the
> very act of arrogation, they take themselves away from the power and the beauty of
> the music and the people that made it. And they could have it; all they would have
> to do is be a part of it.
>
> Because Black people have always been a people that have welcomed any and
> all—even people like Dylan Roof:[9] "Yes, come on into the prayer meeting! Sit down!
> Celebrate Jesus!" There are many folks in the blues that are just like Dylan Roof;

they want to come in and destroy what was, what is, and what will be. And they will never be truly a part of the spirit of that music.

When people stop denying what has been [and] what is, then we can change what will be. Until that time, we are stuck in the same trap that people made for themselves, and for us, a hundred years ago or three hundred years ago. I will never be a part of that because that would put me back in chains; that would put me back in the time of Jim Crow. No! No! The music must progress, as the situation that we live in must progress.

Progress, though, also means honoring the past and acknowledging roots, demanding that history and heritage be recognized. Blue, a lifelong cosmopolitan whose personal and professional associations (and achievements) have been so varied that they almost put terms like "diversity" and "multiculturalism" to shame, nonetheless remains unbending in his determination to name, and resist, what he considers white appropriation of African American music and culture, especially—but by no means only—in the blues.

"Let me tell you," Blue says, his voice and eyes hardening. "I use the acronym: B.L.U.E.S.—Blacks Living Under Egregious Suppression."

I came up with that, okay? And I think it's more true now than it ever was. It's a damn shame, but it's really very difficult nowadays for a Black man to make any green playing the blues. And I love and appreciate the fact that so many people have been moved and motivated to play the music, but when it gets down to the soul of it, the root of it, all they can do is approximate. They cannot really express the root and the source of the music because they haven't lived the life.

Excuse me, but if you were born and raised with white privilege, there's no way that you're really going to be able to do anything but approximate. You cannot really, completely relate a Black experience. And the blues experience [he pounds his fist on the table for emphasis] is a Black experience! Anybody that doesn't want to accept that fact is really telling you who they are. And ain't nothin' good about that. Because it's really a flagrant arrogation of our culture and history.

And that being said, I appreciate the people that love it and the people that try and do it, but when it comes down to it, if you really want to hear the blues, you better be sittin' in front of a Black man.

Strange words, some might say, from a musician whose first major commercial break came with the Rolling Stones (arguably the archetypical white-boy blues band), who has recorded mostly for labels marketed to white aficionados, and whose audiences have been predominantly white for most of his career (even extending back to his busking days in the Village). Blue, however, sees no con-tradiction: "Keith and Ronnie and Mick and the rest of those cats, man, they did some good for the music, and they took the history and the root and re-created themselves—rock & roll. [Keith] is very profoundly rooted in the blues. And if you listen to practically anything they did, I mean from *December's Children* to *Some Girls*, it's all Black music, basically. I mean, like, 'Miss You'—disco! Ain't nothing but the blues, man."

He's even willing to give the Stones a pass on abominations like "Brown Sugar" ("Scarred old slaver knows he's doin' all right / Hear him whip the women just around midnight"), insisting that such lyrics roll off him like "water off a duck." But it does return him to his original argument that most white blues musicians, by necessity, are "approximators" rather than creators: "As much as I like the fact that [the Stones] love the blues, and I like the fact that they sort of spread the culture and, in a sense, gave it a larger audience, they didn't create anything.

Sugar Blue, Chicago Blues
Festival, 2018.

They just imitate. If you listen to Robert Johnson do ['Love in Vain'], and you listen to the Stones do it, and if you listen to 'Little Red Rooster' by the Rolling Stones, and you listen to it by Howlin' Wolf—excuse me, man, you got to know, if you have any sense of what the music is, you know where the power is."

As for audiences, he dismisses any potential conflicts or contradictions with a characteristic bon mot: "An audience is a collection of ears. I'm not responsible for what's in between 'em."

And in fact, not unlike other Black blues and jazz artists who have insisted on the cultural and ethnic identity of their music and yet worked and established life-long friendships with white musicians who've earned their respect, Blue extends that "welcoming" spirit to any artist—as well as any listener—willing and able to meet and celebrate the music on its own terms. "If you can play, and you know where you're coming from and you know what you're doing, and you have respect for the root, then I have respect for you. If you don't, I don't care what color you are, I got no time for you. I've played with Japanese, Italians, Brazilians—musicians that really are deserving of the name don't cotton to any of that bullshit. If you respect, understand, and appreciate where the music came from, then it is your music, too. And if you don't, it ain't."

For his part, Blue has peered over too many precipices and stared into the darkness too often to allow it to envelop him again, even in a world (and an America) where darkness seems to loom more ominously every day. He's forthright about the struggles he's endured to achieve and maintain sobriety ("It was difficult to do, and it's a fight I have to deal with every day"), but he's just as effusive about the light he feels has finally broken into his life, and the joys—as well as the challenges—that lie ahead. The optimism that permeates so much of *Voyage* represents more than an artistic departure for him—it's a manifesto of victory forged through struggle, a victory he's determined not to let slip through his fingers.

"I feel good," he concludes. "I'm happy about my family, I have a wonderful wife, a beautiful daughter, and a marvelous young son. I don't really have time, anymore, to be drowning in misery. I've got a life to live and a child to raise, a wife to love, and so the music that I'm playing now reflects how I'm feeling, and the way I am today."

Nellie "Tiger" Travis

"There's a Queen in Me"

> I grew up in a prejudiced world. I grew up in that world, and it's worse
> up here now than it was down South. It never stopped with our own
> kind, and it never stopped with the other kind. I used to get mad and
> hold a grudge at people, because I think they were wrong for treating
> me the way they did. But when all of that happens like that, it's just
> a blessing. I've received blessings behind that. And I just eventually
> forget about it—Well, I don't forget it, but I forgive and keep moving.
>
> —Nellie "Tiger" Travis

N ellie Travis, born in Drew, Mississippi, during the height of the Civil Rights movement ("I was born there in the sixties—that's all you need to know") and raised in the historic community of Mound Bayou,[1] views the world through eyes that were both hardened and widened early on. Today she's feted as one of the most upbeat, good-timey entertainers in contemporary blues (or, in her case, the blues/R&B/pop hybrid known variously as "soul-blues" and "southern soul"). Her 2013 recording, "Mr. Sexy Man" ("Heeey, Mr. Sexy Man—What yo' name is? What yo' name is?"), became a club hit and juke-joint anthem almost as soon as it was released—it even spawned its own line dance—and its ongoing popularity has continued to sustain her in performances throughout the South, as well as in northern outposts like Chicago, where she's lived since 1992. (After years of generating sales on its own, "Sexy Man" finally made its way onto a full-length CD, *Mr. Sexy Man: The Album*, on the Wegonsee label, owned by producer/songwriter Floyd Hamberlin Jr., in 2017.)

But there's a depth to Nellie that both her admirers and her critics seem often to have missed. Her voice, rich with texture and paradox—pleading yet adamant;

tear-choked yet effervescent; raw yet radiant—sometimes seems almost like a stealth weapon: on its surface it may sound unremarkable, but within a few bars of a song it sneaks up and grabs you by the heart.

Nellie's childhood in Mound Bayou was typical, in many ways, for an African American girl coming of age in mid-twentieth-century Mississippi. Her grand-mother, Alice Travis, was a devout Christian who tolerated few secular amuse-ments ("It was always church and Sunday school. . . . She taught us a lot of old standards, you know, stuff that I still live by today"). Nellie's first real exposure to popular music, as she remembers it, was in high school, when she joined the stage band as a trombonist and began participating in talent shows. She also became a cheerleader and joined the basketball team, making Rookie of the Year her first season on the varsity squad.

It was a loving, close-knit household, but life was not easy. Among Nellie's earliest memories are "the struggle my grandmother went through, with having eighteen kids. . . . I had to pick and chop cotton for school clothes."[2] She'd board one of the trucks that rolled into town before daybreak during harvest season and travel with her grandmother out to the surrounding plantations, where the pay for picking cotton might range anywhere from $2.50 to $5.00 per hundred-pound sack, and the sunup-to-sundown hours were brutal. The most wounding experiences, though—the ones that would haunt her for years, and whose effects still haven't entirely healed—occurred closer to home.

"I was laughed at, at school, because I was poor," Nellie remembers. Even today, she says, "I'll start having flashbacks of my hard times, when I was laughed at because my grandmother would take my pants from last year and make 'em a skirt, or expand the leg out because we couldn't afford to [buy] anything, and then to have to listen to—I never understood about me being so poor that the girls didn't like me. That went on for years as a part of my life." The humiliation only intensified after Nellie attained what should have been one of the crowning glories of her high school career:

> I was the Queen of my school—Miss JFK. I ran against the popular girl at school, and after I won, they intended not to get a float for me. I went to school that morn-ing to see my float, and there was no float, and the home economics teacher said, "Oh, you can just ride in the car with Miss Eighth Grade Science Club."
>
> But I'm the Queen of the school! So I went home. I got in the bed. I was mad, I was crying. . . . My grandmother asked me what was wrong, and I told her, and she's like, "You're not going out like that." She went out and bought posterboard and glitter and stuff, and she made me some signs, and at that time my girlfriend was

Miss Football Queen, and her boyfriend had just bought this beautiful brown '79 Thunderbird, and she rode on one side of the car and I rode on the other.

After graduating, Nellie stayed around the Mound Bayou area for a few years, but she'd already become determined to pursue a career in show business, even if she wasn't sure exactly what form it would take. "I always wanted to be a beauty queen, and I wanted to be in acting," she affirms. (In fact, she had been a finalist in Mississippi's Miss Teen pageant when she was about fourteen, but when she went to Jackson for the event, she discovered that only one other African American girl was among the contestants, and none of the white girls would speak to either of them. "I got discouraged, and I never went back.")

Some years earlier, veteran R&B songwriter and producer Ed Townsend, whose credits included hits by Brook Benton, the Shirelles, Dee Dee Warwick, Peaches & Herb, and others, had moved to Mound Bayou to regroup after seeing his career sabotaged by mishaps and personal demons. While there, he began writing the song that became "Let's Get It On," Marvin Gaye's iconic 1973 hit. "Let's Get It On" catapulted Townsend back into the big time. In 1984 he returned to Mound Bayou and recruited a band of young musicians with the goal of educating them about the music business and helping them get their start.[3] Quite a few were John F. Kennedy Memorial High School alumni; Nellie was one of them.

Inspired, she named the band SSIP (for "Mississippi"), and they got down to business rehearsing and honing their chops. Things started out promisingly: SSIP laid down some tracks at Sounds Unreel Studios in Memphis and opened a show in Clarksdale for Townsend's old protégé Dee Dee Warwick. He then landed them a slot opening for Ray Charles at Delta State University in Cleveland, Mississippi, about ten miles from their home base in Mound Bayou. This was going to be It—the big break, their springboard to fame.

> "I was upstairs practicing, getting ready," Nellie recalls, "and [then] Ray didn't do the show." Ed had sent Ray most of the money; his price was $22,000, and they owed him seven. So we're upstairs, me and the other girl that was going to sing with me, and my sister came up and she said, "You didn't hear?" I'm like, "What?" "There's not gonna be a show." Oh, my heart was crushed. My heart was crushed! Ed Townsend took our music that we had done—he had written a lot of stuff—and he never told us what happened, but by him being Ed, it just blew his mind for whatever reason, and he just walked away from it all.

After an attempt to land a gig as a backup vocalist for singer/comedian Joe "Poonanny" Burns fell through, Nellie decided it was time to seek her fortune

Nellie "Tiger" Travis, Motor
Row Brewing, Chicago, 2016.

elsewhere; since many of the soul and R&B figures she idolized were based on
the West Coast, she headed for California.

"I went to LA with the attitude of being a star," she relates. "I was going to
sleep on Quincy Jones's doorstep and make him hear me. After I got there, I saw
it wasn't so easy. I began working at a club in Compton—'Neither One of Us,'
Gladys Knight, that was the hot song I was doing in L.A.—and I stayed out there
for six years. I ended up working [as an office temp] more than performing."

"I learned that [L.A.] is no place for a country girl," she told *Blues Blast* magazine in 2017. "Everybody I met was with a record company or this or that. It was
all a myth, a lie. I did not meet anyone who was able to get me somewhere."

I did the audition [for a proposed Marvelettes tribute project]. The producer was
from Memphis. He told me to turn around—and I'm wondering where this is going.

Then he left and disappeared in the studio. Finally I start going through the studio, calling his name. He suddenly comes out of this room and I see three young ladies lined up against the wall naked. He tells me I made the audition, that I have a great voice and [I'm] the right size. Then he says, "You know, in this business, you have to suck dicks to make it."[4]

Realizing that Babylon wasn't going to be any better for her soul than it was proving to be for her career, Nellie set her sights on Chicago, where both her mother and her sons' father lived. In 1992, with her situation becoming bleaker by the day, she sent the boys to live with their dad; not long after that, she made the trip herself—partly to be at her ailing mother's side, partly to resume her career search in what she hoped would be a less toxic environment.

She didn't have long to wait. Lee's Unleaded Blues on South Chicago Avenue had a history going back at least to the 1970s, when it was known as Queen Bee's and booked some of the South Side's leading lights, including Junior Wells and guitarist Lefty Dizz. In the early '80s, a businessman named Ray Grey purchased the place, installed his wife, Leola "Ms. Lee" Grey, as proprietor, and renamed it Lee's Unleaded Blues ("Ninety-three octane! That's pure blues—ain't no lead in it!"[5]). A soft-spoken, abstemious woman, Ms. Lee ran the club like a combination prefect, party hostess, and mother hen. Under her watch, such well-known Chicago blues artists as vocalist Artie "Blues Boy" White, bassist/vocalist Queen Sylvia Embry, Lefty Dizz, guitarist L. V. Banks, and Scotty and the Rib Tips (led by guitarist Buddy Scott) performed on weekend nights for standing-room-only audiences.

To enter Lee's was to step into living Chicago blues history, and that's exactly what Nellie Travis did not long after arriving from California. She has said that she was originally hesitant to take on the local blues scene, because up to that point she'd been primarily an R&B stylist. As she remembers it, Lee's was almost a school for her: "I would listen to the guys singing songs at Lee's Unleaded, and I would write down the lyrics. Half the time the lyrics were wrong. People sang it wrong and I didn't know any better."[6]

For all that, though, the first song she sang when she finally got the chance to sit in at Lee's with Scotty and the Rib Tips was her old standby, Gladys Knight's "Neither One of Us." Encouraged by the response she received, she next journeyed to the Kingston Mines, one of the North Side's most popular blues tourist attractions, where—again, fortuitously—Howard Scott and the World Band were holding forth. The World Band is one of the many configurations of the musical Scott family, a Chicago institution whose legacy extends back to the doo-wop era. Over the course of the past sixty-plus years, various Scott-led ensembles have recorded with, played behind, and/or toured with some of the city's (and the country's) most prestigious soul, blues, and soul-blues acts. (Buddy Scott was an original member of the family aggregation, but since he was more of a straight-ahead bluesman he ended up forging his own career.)

Eclectic and versatile, the World Band was ready to give Nellie the backing she needed: "As soon as I opened my mouth, the place went crazy, which is exactly what I [had] envisioned happening. After I did two songs, the manager called me in the back and told me they wanted me to start next Tuesday."[7]

Nellie held down the gig at the Mines for the next five years or so, developing her chops and her confidence, and she frequented as many other blues venues around town as she could, building her reputation and establishing contacts in the time-honored hustling tradition. In 1997, Koko Taylor booked her for a prestigious New Year's Eve gig, along with Artie "Blues Boy" White and veteran soul singer Ruby Andrews, at her banquet hall on 159th Street in south suburban Markham. But then, in the midst of what should have been a triumph, Nellie found herself shattered.

"That whole morning, I had an ill feeling," she recollects. "I didn't know what it was; it was just a gloomy day [for me], and it was a beautiful day outside. My mother was determined to come out that night. She called up her cousins, 'You all gotta come and hear Net sing'—they called me Net—'you gotta come out and hear her sing.' I wore her red gown that night; I performed in her gown. It was about 11:30. She was standing up videotaping me, and she dropped dead with a massive heart attack."

Nellie froze in midsong, screamed "Mama!" and plunged into the audience to take her mother into her arms.[8] "I knew she was dead when she dropped. Everybody was pulling me away—I said, 'No,' because I could hear the sound. I knew."

Koko Taylor responded with a characteristic blend of compassion and resolve. "She basically adopted me as her blues daughter," Nellie says. "Koko took me on as a child—as one of hers. . . . Koko [became] my mentor, my mom, and my friend."[9]

In 2000, during a sojourn in Japan, Nellie and her guitarist, Shun Kikuta, recorded the album *Heart and Soul*, released on the Bluesox label and featuring her dusky vocal stylings on a set that alternated postwar blues standards ("Got My Mojo Working," "The Thrill Is Gone") with soul and soul-blues offerings both vintage ("I'd Rather Go Blind," originally the B-side of Etta James' 1967/'68 hit "Tell Mama") and recent (Denise LaSalle's "Dirty Old Woman"), along with some tantalizing examples of her range and versatility (Tracy Chapman's "Give Me One Reason," the Staple Singers' "Let's Do It Again").

She also got to showcase, for the first time, her gifts as a songwriter: "I've Got Amnesia," which she says she wrote during a European tour after suffering a panic attack ("I had come down a mountain, and to see the streets were so narrow that one car had to wait and let the others pass, [and] the only thing on the side was the deep blue sea with no sides or nothing—I got really afraid, so I just laid on the back seat and I started humming this song"), is a vignette of domestic payback, cast as a deep-soul ballad and infused with what would soon become her characteristic blend of angst, aggression, and coquettishness. As she explains the storyline: "One day I get lonely and decide to call a friend of mine, and the friend comes to my rescue. So whenever my man comes home, I'm gonna act like I fell and bumped my head, like I got amnesia, 'cause I don't want to know who he is anymore."[10]

Having a full-length recording credited at least partly to her (it was billed as by "Shun Kikuta and Nellie Tiger Travis") should have been the realization of a lifelong dream. Nellie's reaction, though, reflected a wariness, even a defensiveness, no doubt borne from years of hurt and disappointment, that remains with her to this day: it sometimes seems as if the protective shell she's built around herself is capable of letting in only so much light at a time. "*Heart and Soul* was basically [Kikuta's] CD," she has said, "but as far as I'm concerned it's mine, because I did most of the work. . . . They catered to Shun on his album and put him in higher places, but not me."[11]

In any case, she never looked back. That same year, she and producer Vintz Famus gathered a crew of first-call Chicago session musicians and recorded *I Got It Like That*, which she issued on her own Tiger Belle imprint. Again, the primary focus was straight-ahead blues, although she also displayed her gifts for soul balladry (a reprise of "I've Got Amnesia"), urban contemporary pop-R&B ("Thinking of You") and deep-gospel testifying ("Thank You").

Whether serendipitously or by design, though, her next move was to drastically remake both her music and her persona. In about 2005, at the urging of vocalist Stan Mosley, Nellie began working with Floyd Hamberlin Jr., a Chicago-based producer and songwriter with a proven track record in the contemporary soul-blues/southern soul genre. The CD that resulted, *Wanna Be with You*, issued on Hamberlin's Da Man label, abandoned the rootsy-sounding production of her earlier CDs almost entirely: Instead of 12-bar blues, it highlighted songs couched in easy-rolling two-chord vamps, propelled by sprightly dance rhythms rather than shuffles, seasoned with faux-string swashes and synthesized horn lines, and driven by programmed beats (although at least occasionally, as on the churchy ballad "Teary Eyed," an acoustic piano brought some life-affirming freshness to the proceedings).

The transformation worked. Over the course of the next year or so, no fewer than four songs from *Wanna Be with You*—"If I Back It Up," an ode to dance-floor booty-shaking; "You Gone Make Me Cheat," a frustrated woman's throwdown to an unsatisfying lover; the soap opera–like "Baby Mam Drama"; and, perhaps most impressively, "Super Woman," the plaint of an overburdened working-class housewife starved for love and understanding—made local and regional southern soul radio charts, and Nellie suddenly found herself in demand on a circuit that, until then, had scarcely been aware of her.

Her next two releases—2008's *I'm a Woman* and its 2009 follow-up, *I'm in Love with a Man I Can't Stand*—were recorded and issued under the auspices of Dylann DeAnna's CDS label, and they continued along the same lines as *Wanna Be with You*. The programmed production, for the most part, remained punchy and clean, even sensual on steamy outings like the unfortunately titled "Let's Get It Poppin'" (from *A Man I Can't Stand*). The material was strong as well, with some of her most moving ballads ("Don't Ever Leave Me Again," the wrenching "Don't Talk to Me") and pointed social commentary ("M.O.D. [Man on Drugs]," effective despite its uncharacteristically cheesy production) sharing space with amiably goofy fare like "Slap Yo' Weave Off," with its signifying lyrics diluted by a sing-songy melody and Nellie's own irony-drenched croon. (She had originally balked at recording "Weave": "I'm like, 'I don't wanna do that mess—the song is silly!' And Floyd said, 'Silly' sells.") As if to prove she still had it in her, she even tore into some deep-pocket 12-bar blues on "I'm a Tiger," which she cowrote with label owner DeAnna and producer Carl Marshall and included on *I'm in Love with a Man I Can't Stand*.

By 2009, it was beginning to look as if Nellie's determination was paying off. Songs from her Da Man and CDS outings were making noise all over the South, yet she was also one of the few blues-based artists who seemed able to cultivate loyal followings among both white and black audiences, at least partly because she structured her shows to reflect those audiences' diverse tastes—heavy on the 12-bar shuffles for the white folks, more emphasis on smoother, sexier sounds and dance tunes for the African American southern soul crowd. When Koko Taylor died on June 3 of that year, Nellie was one of her many disciples and acolytes who felt as if a torch had been passed down.

But there's a reason why some folklorists and historians invoke Eshu-Eleggua—Yoruba trickster, Guardian of the Crossroads, lord of irony and paradox—as a guiding spirit of the blues. Events soon conspired to both burnish Nellie's reputation and resurrect demons she thought she'd long since laid to rest. In November, five months after Koko Taylor passed, Nellie was preparing to do a show at Mr. G's Supper Club on 87th Street in Chicago when she received a call from Verlene Blackburn, longtime personal assistant to legendary WVON deejay Pervis Spann. Spann, who was also one of Chicago's pioneering African American club owners and music promoters, had a long-running gimmick on his shows where he'd crown someone (usually B.B. King) as the "King of the Blues," and someone else (usually Koko herself) as the "Queen." (Various "Crown Princes" and "Princesses" were also honored over the years.)[12] His audience never seemed to tire of the routine, and the artists accepted the honor with appropriate noblesse oblige, along with perhaps just a hint of good-naturedly ironic forbearance:

> "His secretary called me," Nellie remembers. "She said, 'Mr. Spann wanna know where you're gonna be tonight; he's gonna come out and see you.'"
> And I'm like, "Wow—that's really special, because he's been sick." So that night, before I got through singing, she came up and said, "Nellie, can I say something on the mic?" At this time she's bringing Spann up. So she came up, she said, "Ladies and gentlemen, this is the seventh person that we're crowning, and Mr. Spann is crowning Nellie 'Tiger' Travis the new Queen of the Blues." And the band was like—I was like—I just broke down and started crying. 'Cause it was a shock. Nobody had a clue, period. And I'm like, "Oh my god!"
> Everybody—Oh, they went crazy. Ronnie Baker Brooks was there, everybody went crazy. They took a picture, they sent me a plaque later, you know, with me being crowned. It was just amazing."

Nellie wasn't the only one, of course. About a month earlier, in Belzoni, Mississippi, soul-blues star Denise LaSalle had been crowned "Queen of the Blues" in a ceremony overseen by Helen Sims, president of the Mississippi Delta Blues Society ("The void left by Koko Taylor's death," Sims stated, "can only be filled by Denise LaSalle"[13]). And there was more to come: in 2011, Koko's daughter, Joyce "Cookie" Threatt, would crown Shemekia Copeland with one of her late mother's own tiaras and name her "the new Queen of the Blues" on stage at the Chicago Blues Festival.

Controversy was inevitable. Nellie, whose first reaction had been exultation, was devastated by the ferocity she encountered. At one point, after being invited to participate on a panel honoring Koko's legacy, she was verbally attacked on stage ("This is all on video and everything, and I'm sitting there with this fake-ass smile that was hiding a whole lotta tears"). On other occasions, she maintains, she was sabotaged when she attempted to sell her merchandise at her shows. Off stage, she endured hostility and even personal threats, sometimes from people closely associated with Koko herself (or maybe one of the other newly crowned queens)—all of which, Nellie maintains, arose primarily out of jealousy.

At times she tried to convince herself it didn't really matter—"I realized that it is not about a title," she told *Blues Blast* in 2017; "I am a queen either way"[14]—but disingenuousness has never been her style, and it certainly didn't work in this case. The pain, and the scars it reopened, ran too deep:

> It was a joke. The joke was on me *again*. I went through that in high school, remember? So it was on me *again*. I went through that *again*. Another "Queen" shit I went through that hurt me! And I'm sitting there saying, "Why are people so bitter?"
>
> That part of my life hasn't been out since, probably, in mid–high school. I had to let it go because all of that would come back at me, and I would be a hurricane. There was a side to me once upon a time, and it's only because of how people was treating me—I had to let it go because I saw danger for people, and danger for myself, because I would have been in prison somewhere.
>
> I mean, it's such a hateration nation, the nation of the blues. . . . I've stayed humble through this, I've cried through this, I've hurted through this, I've wanted to quit through this, through all of this. . . . I still talk to 'em, but I just, you know, treat 'em with a long-handled spoon.

Her response was 2011's *I'm Going Out Tonight*, released on the CDS subsidiary Benevolent Blues, which found her surrounded by all-natural instrumentation, recasting herself again as a straight-ahead blueswoman. The disk featured "Koko," a reprise of "Queen of the Blues (A Tribute to Koko Taylor)" from 1999's *I'm in Love with a Man I Can't Stand*, along with a new song, "There's a Queen in Me," which many listeners interpreted as another riposte to the haters, but which she insists was simply a long-overdue proclamation of pride and self-worth. As if to drive the point home, she delivered the Kokolike "Tornado Wrapped in Fire" ("In your eyes, I once was a low flame / But now I'm a tornado wrapped in fire"), written for her by CDS president Dylann DeAnna, with a smoldering mix of outrage and hurt.

It wasn't until two years later, though, that the fire really ignited. Floyd Hamberlin, still working closely with Nellie, came up with a hook—that pugnaciously sultry "What yo' name is?" siren call—and grafted it onto a tale of lust-driven

dance-floor intrigue, goosed by an earworm-like guitar riff and laid over a throbbing techno-driven beat. The result, "Mr. Sexy Man," took the southern soul world
by storm. Almost overnight, it became Nellie's theme song; the subsequent video
and line dance only solidified its place in the southern soul-blues firmament. On
that circuit, a hit can remain current for years, and by her own account "Mr. Sexy
Man" has kept Nellie working steadily ever since. "When I work in the South,"
she told *Living Blues* magazine in 2016, "it could be 5,000 to 6,000 people when I
do a concert. . . . They be out in that sun all day long waiting to hear 'Sexy Man.'"[15]

She dropped a few tantalizing single tracks over the next few years, but it
took until 2017 for the long-awaited *Mr. Sexy Man: The Album* to emerge. Like
several of her previous outings, it was somewhat compromised by less-than-
stellar cover art (it could almost pass for a thrift-store cutout or even a bootleg),
but the production sounded refreshingly clean for a southern-soul album, with
plenty of robust instrumentation (musicians included guitarists Sir Walter Scott,
his nephew Kenneth "Hollywood" Scott, and Mike Wheeler) to offset the usual
synth-groove boilerplate. The songs themselves were as thematically varied and
emotionally complex as any she'd ever recorded—listeners expecting a set of

Nellie "Tiger" Travis, Women of the Blues Tour, BB's Jazz, Blues, and Soups, St. Louis, 2016.

coochie-popping "Sexy Man" clones were in for a surprise. Tucked alongside such party-friendly fare as "Textual Harassment," the double-entendre "Fix a Flat," "Cold Feet" ("I got cold feet in a warm bed") and the title song were ballads— "Tired of Being Alone" (not the Al Green classic), "I Woke Up in Love," "I Used to Run to You," "Walking in the Rain in Memphis"—that ranked as among the finest of her career. "I do my greatest work with ballads," she has said, and this set bore her out—notable in a genre in which novelty songs and dance tracks seem increasingly to be state of the art.

Nonetheless, the soul-blues/southern soul circuit remains a challenge to negotiate ("I always try to stash a little money back," she admits, "in case things don't go right"); for an artist like Nellie, who clearly aspires to cross over into the "mainstream" as a contemporary blues entertainer without losing her core African American following, the challenge is even greater. A 2017 appearance on Jimmy Fallon's *Tonight Show*, during which she performed "Slap Yo' Weave Off" backed by Questlove and The Roots, received mixed reviews. It was part of a satirical closing segment during which Fallon jokingly ran through several suggestions for a new theme song; Nellie got to sing one verse. Moreover, she was there in the first place only because Fallon had earlier targeted "Slap Yo' Weave Off" for ridicule during one of his snarky "Do Not Play This Record" routines, and it was only after she picked up the gauntlet and summoned her online admirers to hit him up with demands for an appearance that he (or his producers) decided to book her. Nonetheless—still ensconced, perhaps, in the same emotional armor that has been her bulwark her since childhood—she refuses to see it as anything but a triumph, maintaining that Fallon's antic dance moves as she sang her "silly" song were enthusiastic, not mocking, and that his comments that night—"I love it. It's a catchy song"—were sincere.

There also remain challenges closer to home—not least of which is the uncertain future of the music itself. Nellie is far from alone in recognizing that cultural appropriation, although perhaps not discussed as widely (or publicly) in the blues community today as it has been in the past, remains of vital concern. At the very least, the conflicting definitions of blues "authenticity" between its legion of white aficionados and its smaller, if no less avid, African American fan base, make it extremely difficult for an artist to market herself successfully across the board. Nellie may have been more successful at this than most, but it remains a problem, and the underlying cultural and social dynamics of the phenomenon portend concerns far more ominous than mere demographics or market share.

"I see blues evolving into a white scene now," she maintains, echoing the concerns of fellow Chicagoans Sugar Blue and Sharon Lewis, older-generation artists such as Bobby Rush and Denise LaSalle, and many others.

> It's gonna end up being rock, it's going to be all white music, just like the Rolling Stones, and they're going to be filthy rich offa that shit. They're taking it from us—or we're giving it to them, I'll put it that way. If you look at half our Black kids are killing each other, and even without them killing each other they're not into the blues music. If we embraced our culture more, our standards for music, if we embraced it more—the only way we can do something about it would be to stop patronizing that garbage that they're playing. Let their own kind patronize it; they're supporting each other. We don't do that. And until we do, it's gonna be their music.

She also recognizes that it can be hazardous for artists to speak out publicly on this topic; several who have done so maintain that bookings and even recording opportunities have become scarcer since they made their voices heard. "Oh, I know—it's a threat," Nellie affirms. "They will blackball you. So that means you still got us by the nuts. You know the story of Leadbelly, right? How tragic was that? You imprison me . . . and then you get me out of prison when you want to throw a party? That story, I cried—that was so sad. And that's the kind of shit they want to take it back to."

There's nothing left to do, then, but soldier on, girded by faith, goaded by both the caress of praise and the sting of criticism—still summoning, after so many years, the defiance and resolve of an eighteen-year-old girl from the other side of the tracks in Mound Bayou, Mississippi, wounded but unbowed, perched atop a 1979 Thunderbird adorned with glittering posters that had probably cost her grandmother more to make than she could really afford, waving and smiling into the faces of her erstwhile tormentors, thoughts and emotions roiling inside her which decades later would erupt into song: "I've paid a lot of dues, it wasn't easy, no / You got to keep on keepin' on 'til you reach your throne. . . . There's just one thing you need to see: There's a Queen in me."

Floyd Taylor

The Chosen Son

"Call this 'southern soul'? I'm gonna retire!"

Floyd Taylor, his laptop open, relaxes in a motel room in Chicago, playing a demo of "All of You, All of Me," one of the tracks on *All of Me*, his upcoming [2010] CD on the California-based CDS label. The mix is mostly synthesized, and the song bounces with an incessant, somewhat nervous-sounding rhythm. But it's also shot through with a sensual warmth that not even Floyd's tiny laptop speakers can muffle. His voice on it sounds rich and muscular, conveying both gentleness and rough-cut passion—that tough/tender, sex-machine-with-a-heart-of-gold machismo that never seems to lose its appeal for the women who comprise the bulk of the southern soul audience.

Floyd, though, doesn't want to talk much about "southern soul," at least not when he's looking toward the future.

"Now what I did here," he explains, "was, I went and got a little Teddy Pendergrass and put a little Johnnie Taylor twist on it. That's what I did."

This song here is directed at the female species. Because it says everything that a woman wants from a man and wants a man to do, know what I'm saying? That's a soul song; it's not a "southern soul" song, it's a soul song. And that's the market I'm aiming for. Malaco [his former label] turned this record down. When labels don't let an artist be an artist, then you got a problem. I'm not satisfied. Some of those cats, they may be satisfied. But I'm like Malcolm X; I'm not going to eat a chicken wing and say I'm full.

Satisfaction does not come easy to Floyd Taylor. Born in Chicago in the mid-fifties,[1] he was raised by his mother, Mildred Singletary, a God-fearing woman who recognized his musical gifts early on and made sure he put them to good use by singing in church. But it was his father, deep-soul legend Johnnie Taylor, whose influence would end up possessing him most powerfully.

Johnnie Taylor's legacy is among the richest in R&B. Born in Crawfordsville, Arkansas, in 1934,[2] he sang gospel as a teenager in Kansas City and moved to Chicago in the early fifties. There he sang both doo-wop and gospel; in 1953, he joined Sam Cooke's[3] old gospel quartet,[4] the Highway QCs, whom Cooke had left about three years earlier for the nationally renowned Soul Stirrers. Taylor remained with the QCs until 1957, when the Soul Stirrers themselves recruited him to replace Cooke, who had just made his famous crossover into secular music. The connection with Sam remained strong: The Stirrers, with Johnnie at the helm, were the first act to record for SAR, the label Cooke cofounded with J. W. Alexander, in 1959.

Johnnie was—to put it mildly—a free spirit, even by the somewhat disingenuously permissive standards of the gospel world. In 1960, after a police investigation following an auto accident found him to have been driving under the influence of marijuana, he unrepentantly left the Stirrers to become a Baptist preacher ("The Reverend Johnnie Taylor [Formerly with the Soul Stirrers]").[5] By the following year, though, he was recording for SAR as a secular artist. His first chart hit was in 1963 on the SAR affiliate label Derby, but he didn't really hit his stride until 1966, when he joined Stax and quickly hit No. 19 with his debut for the label, an Isaac Hayes/Dave Porter blues called "I Had a Dream." He remained with the Memphis soul powerhouse until 1975, recording such now-classic numbers as "Who's Making Love," "Steal Away," "Jody's Got Your Girl and Gone," "I Believe in You (You Believe in Me)," and the jazz-tinged "Cheaper to Keep Her," among others; all told, he charted on Stax twenty-four times. In 1976, having moved to CBS, he leapt aboard the disco bandwagon and came up with the biggest-selling hit of his career, "Disco Lady." Johnnie's last Top Ten hit was "Love Is Better in the A.M. (Part 1)" on Columbia in 1977.

By 1984 he'd joined Malaco, where he quickly rose again as one of the top stars in the new southern soul (or, to his evident displeasure, "blues" or "soul-blues") field. "Good Love," which peaked at No. 39 in 1996, was his most successful latter-day recording, but some of his most important songs from his Malaco days never saw chart action at all. (His LPs fared somewhat better: *Good Love!*—his eighth for Malaco, hit No. 1 on the Billboard blues album chart, and No. 15 on

Floyd Taylor, Chicago Blues
Festival, 2012. Photograph
© 2012 Linda Vartoogian/
FrontRowPhotos. All Rights
Reserved.

their R&B album chart, in 1996). "Last Two Dollars," from *Good Love!*, and both
"Big Head Hundreds" and the prophetic "Soul Heaven" from his 1999 album
Gotta Get the Groove Back remain ubiquitous on southern soul radio, on jukeboxes,
on club deejays' computers and turntables, and in the repertoires of bands and
singers both well-known and obscure—they're probably better known, at least
in the southern soul world, than some other artists' million-sellers from those
same years. It could be argued, in fact, that the sometimes fractious and volatile
Taylor is more universally beloved now than when he was alive.

It's a daunting legacy to live up to, and much of Floyd's professional life has
been shaped, even consumed, by his attempts to make peace with it. "It has a
double-edged sword," he admits. "It could be a blessing, and it could be a hinder."

Either way, though, it's his legacy, his mark, and sometimes his burden. And he's determined to honor it and bear it on no one's terms but his own.

Floyd is a bit vague about exactly how involved Johnnie was in his life when he was young, but he does remember the first time he heard him sing. He was about five years old, and his father came by the house to rehearse. Exactly which songs Johnnie worked on that day has been lost to memory, but they were most likely gospel—this would probably have been in the late fifties, when Johnnie was still a Soul Stirrer. Floyd was taken by his father's voice, but he was not overawed. "My impression," he maintains, "was, like, just a guy that was singing. That's all."

Even later, he insists, after Johnnie had crossed over and it was almost impossible to turn on the radio and not hear one of his hits, Floyd didn't treat it like a big deal. "Y'know, my friends never, we never discussed that. I mean, I never was the kind of kid that bragged about what my father did. And even though they may have asked me questions about it, I just shrugged it off."

But beneath the cool, a passion for following in his father's footsteps was simmering. Floyd remembers seeing Johnnie perform at Chicago's fabled Regal Theater when he was about twelve years old; the headliners that evening were Smokey Robinson and the Miracles, but it was Johnnie's explosive showmanship and joyful demeanor, the way he seemed to galvanize himself by galvanizing the crowd, that stayed in Floyd's mind. A few years later, he got to experience that feeling for himself, performing on a talent show at DuSable High School, "and the rest," as he has put it, "is history."[6]

That history, though, didn't come to fruition right away. By his late teens, Floyd was singing in a ten-piece ensemble called the Peace Band, a group that patterned themselves after Kool & the Gang but also covered pop hits like Elton John's "Bennie and the Jets." The Peace Band gigged around the South Side, developing their repertoire and honing their stagecraft, working such well-known clubs as the High Chaparral and the Burning Spear. For a singer still in his teens, being on that circuit meant growing up pretty fast—but that was nothing next to what happened after he received an unexpected invitation from his father. "It came about," Floyd says, "because he knew his son wanted to be in the business. He called me one day, and he said, 'I got a job for you. Come on.' That's all. Short and cut, just like that. I worked a whole summer, when I was out of school, doing tours that he was doing, the Kool Jazz Festival—San Diego. And when it was time to come [back] to school, I just came back home. And on weekends, I would just travel with him occasionally and do some of the dates with him."

Floyd's job on his father's show was to sing background. More importantly, though, he learned. But the lessons were not going to be spoon-fed:

> I had not one rehearsal with the rest of his backup singers. I learned on the fly. I'm like, "Aren't you going to—" He says, "No, this is the way you're going to learn it. On the fly, just like I did."
>
> My dad was the kinda guy that [would say], "Listen—you wanna be in this business? You gonna get it just like I got it. If I'm going to hold your hand, you're not going to learn anything about this business. You gonna work for it." He often told me, "I could take you, put you in the best studios, get you some of the best writers, but what would [you] have earned? One of your records take off, you get a couple million dollars, you're not gonna appreciate it. Because you didn't earn it. And you gonna blow that shit." I always thought that was— "What? Dad, please!"
>
> But now that he's gone, I'm glad he didn't spoil me. I appreciate every dime I got. When I hang that mic up on that stand and say "Good night," I'm unemployed until the next gig. Tomorrow's not promised to you no way, but in this business it's really not promised to you. So I was glad that he did that.

Floyd remained a member of the Johnnie Taylor revue, off and on, until 1999. He was ready to strike out on his own long before then, he says, and his father encouraged him to do so; but when he tried, he discovered that the very name that had seemed to work magic when he'd heard it announced on stages and bandstands across the country now seemed to be working against him.

"When you're someone's child and they're famous," Floyd explains, "in this business, it automatically clicks in. People are really looking at you. It's like living in a bubble, man. It can be a struggle—it's a lot harder for kids that have parents in the business. 'Cause you're scrutinized, man. I was never able to fit into a clique because I was the son of Johnnie Taylor."

The upshot was that Floyd remained a backup singer for a lot longer than he thought he would. In the 1980s, he began to record demos of his own, but when he auditioned them for record companies, the answer was always the same: "'Hey, you sound too much like Johnnie Taylor. We can't use you. . . .' After [the] rejections, my dad said 'hey, you want a job? Come on out here. I need you to sing background again.'"[7]

The frustrations weren't limited to recording. On Chicago's South Side, tastes were usually flexible enough for him to garner praise when he did a show, even in blues clubs. But when he traveled to other parts of town, he often found himself facing white audiences with more arbitrary definitions of blues "authenticity."

This, in turn, resulted in demands he could not tolerate: "I didn't sing that kind of gutbucket blues that they wanted to hear, and I wasn't gonna let them work me like that every night, for the kind of money that they were paying. It was too much of a clique thing . . . and if you wasn't in the clique and wasn't in the game that they was playing and singing the kind of music that they wanted to hear, then you didn't play there."

"A lot of folks," he adds, "think this shit was just handed to me. They don't know what I was going through, back here in the city of Chicago."

On Wednesday, May 31, 2000, Johnnie Taylor died, reportedly at home and from a heart attack, in the Dallas suburb of Duncanville. Thousands of mourners, including such luminaries as Aretha Franklin, Bobby Womack, and Al Green, attended his funeral at Dallas's Good Street Baptist Church a week later. Among those who sang for him at the service that day was his son.

"There," Floyd recalls, "me and Malaco actually got connected. They heard me singing at my father's funeral. They asked me if this was what I wanted to do, and I gave them the look, 'Are you kidding? Of course this is what I wanna do.'"[8]

Overnight, Floyd Taylor had become hot property. He remembers getting offers from Columbia, United Artists, Universal, and Sony, as well as Malaco, after his father's death. No doubt at least some of these new musical suitors simply wanted to cash in on the Taylor name. But even if it felt at times as if this sudden bandwagon was really a hearse, Floyd wasn't about to let it pass by. "It didn't bother me," he maintains, "because I had a dream that I wanted to live. And, I mean, you're being exploited anyway. The record labels make all the money, and you have to get out here on the road and make your living the best way you can. So you're being exploited anyway. What's the difference?"

Not much, apparently. Floyd says he wrote down the names of all the companies that had approached him and "literally threw them into a hat." Malaco was the one he drew. Once he arrived there, it became clear that his patronymic would be among his strongest selling points. "Here comes the real deal," trumpeted an early Malaco press release "the heir, the Legacy. . . . Floyd Taylor."[9]

Legacy, in fact, was the title of Floyd's first Malaco CD, released in 2002. Its promotion both reflected and intensified the "in-his-father's-image" campaign implied by those early publicity notices: "Johnnie Taylor fans will not doubt the well from which this voice is drawn. Floyd Taylor does not deny he sounds like his father when he sings. He sounds like him when he talks, laughs, singes, shouts, whispers, and cries. . . . Now comes his time in the spotlight. . . ."[10]

For all that, though, the CD did not contain any Johnnie Taylor covers, and despite the similarity between Floyd's voice and his father's, *Legacy* was clearly the debut of a young artist determined to use the gifts he'd inherited to forge his own way. At its best, it exemplified Floyd's stated ambition to be "a good storyteller."[11] There were also encouraging hints of forward-looking musical innovation. His blend of languorous sensuality and punk-rapper insouciance on "When We Touch," for instance, set to a sparse arrangement ignited by carefully inserted trigger-drum explosions, exemplified the bracingly modernist flavor that Floyd brought to the table. On the other hand, in places it seemed as if Floyd—or, perhaps, his label—was still searching for a truly new and distinctive musical personality to present. Several tracks skirted close to unimaginative boilerplate—lyrics lacked depth, rhymes were strained (it's a testimony to Floyd's vocal prowess that in his hands, a song like "Old School Style" could survive even a couplet that rhymed "Chill out with some sweet Marvin Gaye" with "I know how much you like foreplay"), and the results were neither hot enough to be sexy nor callow enough to invoke youthful innocence.

But whatever its shortcomings, *Legacy* was an impressive debut; its weaknesses, such as they were, reflected some of the uncertainties plaguing southern soul in general, rather than any problems with Floyd himself. If it sounded in places as if Johnnie Taylor's spirit had been resurrected, it also sounded as if that spirit was exploring new realms of expression and singing through a fresh voice. The follow-up, *No Doubt*, dropped in 2005, and like its predecessor it was both a trip down memory lane for nostalgists (it included a cover of Johnnie's 1966 hit, "I've Got to Love Somebody's Baby") and an affirmation that Floyd was his own man, or at least was moving in that direction. His sinewy baritone, enriched as his father's had been by colorations that Johnnie himself had absorbed from Sam Cooke, was charged with new urgency by his rap-honed phrasing and, in at least some cases, the lyrics' uncompromising honesty.

"Baby, I've Changed," for instance, was a stark portrait of a street-tough player reaping his just deserts as an uncredited female vocalist delivered a litany of his transgressions in a grief-choked, sobbing torrent of anguish: "What about the STD that you brought home to me. . . . Don't make me call the cops, stop knockin' at my door. . . . What about the arguments and when you knocked me down / You didn't even care about the baby that I lost . . . my bank account, my money that you spent." But Floyd also proved himself capable of a disarmingly self-deprecating irony, as in "Hit It Right," written by Malaco staff writer Rich Cason, in which the singer complained, over a spiky neo-R&B groove, that "being a playa just ain't the same" in an age when "independent women done changed the game . . . she got things today, make her scream her own name / Eveready's got her shaking from her head to her feet / How in the hell can a real man compete?"

You Still Got It, his third Malaco disk, released in 2007, featured the tribute "I Miss My Daddy." It could easily have been lachrymose, if not morbid, but it turned out to be one of the most moving songs in the Floyd Taylor canon—and a surefire housewrecker in live performance. Floyd says he came up with the idea himself; at the very least, it's obvious that songwriter Rich Cason listened carefully to Floyd's reminiscences when he was putting "I Miss My Daddy" together. There are some surprisingly candid personal memories ("Just because you wasn't always there / I want you to know I understood / It wasn't easy for you, but I know you cared / You did the best that you could"). Yet Floyd also summoned a grittiness that made it seem as if he was putting forth a manifesto of his determination to prevail on his own and declare his independence as both an artist and a man.

But like its predecessors, *You Still Got It* was both successful on a track-by-track basis and characterized by a sometimes uneasy feeling of trying to balance genres and aesthetics that didn't necessarily mesh. "They wouldn't let me be myself," Floyd maintains, as if concurring with that critical appraisal. "They wanted to call all the shots. And if you want an artist to be successful, you have to give him some leeway in there, and when you don't give an artist no leeway, and you got him pigeonholed, then it's time for [the artist] to go."

Looking for a more amenable environment ("I'm not a 'southern soul' singer; I'm a singer," he insisted even then), he decided to sign with CDS, a West Coast label that has absorbed quite a few southern soul-blues artists who formerly worked for more established imprints like Malaco and Ecko. Although production credits on *All of Me*, Floyd's 2010 CDS debut, went to Simuel Overall (aka Simeo), Earl Powell, and Sidney Jones, Floyd maintains that CDS allowed him the full creative control he asked for when he signed, so it's safe to say that what ended up on the disk represented his own preferences pretty closely. Perhaps the most striking thing about it is the way it balances old-school soul sensibility with contemporary sonic texture, often more seamlessly than a lot of Floyd's latter-day Malaco output did. Ballads like "All of You, All of Me," with Floyd's boudoir baritone murmurs riding atop a spring-loaded percussion track washed with strings, shared space with dance floor workouts like "I'm 'Bout It 'Bout It," probably the most infectious song Floyd ever recorded, in which Floyd uses his leathery voice almost as a percussion instrument to drive the cadence as aggressively as the programmed beats. " 'Bout It" became a club hit virtually from the moment the CD was released and it remains so today.

With its roomy, R&B-seasoned studio production and deep-soul vocal stylings, *All of Me* should have been Floyd Taylor's breakthrough recording. But despite the relative success of "I'm 'Bout It 'Bout It" and maybe one or two other tracks, most of the focus on Floyd, especially in his live performances, continued to emphasize his uncanny, even eerie, resemblance to his father, especially when he revisited Johnnie's trademark hits—which he continued to do in his shows, often at the exclusion of his own best material. Despite the richness of his own still-burgeoning catalog, and despite the local and regional success some of the songs from that catalog enjoyed, he seemed unable to extricate himself from the grip of the "legacy" he professed to cherish, even as he struggled to transcend it:

"You wrestle with that shit up there," he says yet again, returning to both the topic and his own ambivalent feelings about it. "Because you want the people accepting you for who you are."

> And that's a pain in the ass. "Are you liking me for me, or are you liking me for my father? Are you just being generous?" 'Cause if I'm not doing this shit right, don't just pat me on my head and send me to my room. I wanna know if I'm doing it right. It ain't no joke. The only reason why they think it's a joke, they haven't experienced it. [Another singer] asked me, "Do you just try to sound like your dad?" No. It's in the DNA. It just comes out that way. It's not like I sit at home and say, "How can I sound like my dad?"
>
> Now what I will do is, I will put a record on, and I will listen to how he phrase. And if I can phrase it that way, or phrase it better, then fine. But yeah, that was my college education, my father. Why not? A lot of black men don't have a father who gets lucky enough to leave [his] children something back here that they can carry on. I'm thankful my father was able to leave something, and that I can try to take advantage of it.

It takes its toll, which may account for the harshness that creeps into his tone as he reaffirms his determination to break free—which he believes he'll do only when he finally shakes the label of being a "southern soul" or "soul-blues" entertainer, the same labels his father chafed under during the final decades of his life:

> I'm trying to get away from the chitlin' circuit. I really am. Because the chitlin' circuit is nothing [like] what it used to be when my father was out there. Everybody on the

chitlin' circuit now is just like crabs [in a bucket]. They see one get up, they try to pull him down; they don't wanna see one make it out of there.

One thing I like about those cats on the other side of this business is they work with each other. [Regardless of] how you say those rappers are, those cats work with each other. They help each other. These assholes on this chitlin' circuit do not try to work with each other at all. Because they are so afraid that one is gonna get one dollar more than the next one. I don't have no respect for none of 'em out there, except those old guys: Bobby Bland, Bobby Rush, Denise LaSalle. The rest of 'em—kiss my ass. And I mean that, and you can print that, too. 'Cause don't none of 'em put no food in my belly.

On a roll now, he seems unable to stop, his frustrations erupting into caustic personal attacks. A major southern soul hitmaker with whom he's shared bills? "Singin' brother—stupid up here [he points to his head]." Another star, perhaps the most commercially successful on the circuit? "Can't sing a goddam lick." A veteran artist whose career extends back to the glory days of the deep soul era? "Hell of a singer. Also, brain ain't doin' upstairs." A younger stylist who has earned the kind of crossover R&B recognition that Floyd aspires to? "Can't sing a goddam lick, and ignorant to the bone."

It would be easy to write it all off as hubris or bluster, or to wonder why this man who derides some of his colleagues for their own self-pity ("What're you crying about? You ain't paid half the dues them [earlier] folks have paid") sometimes seems so close to succumbing to bitterness himself. But maybe it's not such a mystery. As much as Floyd Taylor loves "this business" and revels in being an entertainer ("You look out there and see people smiling and having a good time, you've taken their mind off their problems for a little while. That's a big reward"), there seems no end to the conflict, no end to knowing that his most treasured inheritance, as well as his most valuable professional calling card, is also the weight that he sometimes fears may prevent him from ever flying truly free. And then there's the unthinkable—what if there's no escape? What if that very inheritance, the success it has afforded him, and the suffocating "soul-blues"/"chitlin' circuit" label are inextricably intertwined?

So there's no option except to persevere, summoning the same blend of optimism, dedication, and fatalism that spurred him to turn that first, long-prayed-for recording opportunity into a swashbuckling, throw-a-name-into-a-hat gamble. And if it means risking a reputation for being arrogant or standoffish in a world where personal good will can often mean the difference between success and oblivion, that's just a risk he'll have to take.

"I don't hang out," he admits. "After a show, I'm gone." Anyway, there are more important contacts to cultivate:

> When I met you [in Merrillville, Indiana, where Floyd had appeared on Memphis-based promoter Julius Lewis's star-studded "Blues Is Alright" tour], I went out that night. I was so tired after I did that concert, but I knew I had to go out there and promote this record. I could hear that bed callin' me. I knew I needed to lay down. But I know I got to get this record promoted, too.
>
> We took this song ["All of You, All of Me"] to a steppers' ball. I was nervous as hell, because, see, this is my project; I financed this whole thing. When folks actually got out and started dancing on this thing and asked for it again and again, I was like, 'Oh, man!' Those folks were in their early thirties, middle forties, you might even have had some early twenties up in there. I've been on the computer, tracking this record. Down south, it's burning up. Soon as mainstream radio looks at the database and see what this record is doing, then they're gonna put it [on]. So it's a good record, and it's in the Lord's hands. So there it is.

Floyd leans back and narrows his eyes. He's been out and about all day; soon he'll probably step out again into the Chicago night to shake hands, slap backs, cajole club deejays into playing his track—"working his product" in the time-honored tradition, hoping that the city's fabled status as a northern outpost of the chitlin' circuit—and, as always, his father's revered place on that circuit and in the city where he first rose to fame as a gospel singer—won't sabotage his attempts to break it into the mainstream R&B market: "If this here [he pats his heart]—you gon' do it," he concludes. "You gonna get thrown out of clubs, you're gonna get told 'no' all the time—you just got to have it. I fly home [to Jackson, Mississippi] tomorrow. I'll sleep a day; I'll get up and hit the streets. Friday, I'll be in Dallas. Saturday, I'll be in Beaumont. Sunday, I'm supposed to fly all the way to Minnesota. But that's going to be one gig that I cancel. Because my body is telling me, and when my body tells me, I usually listen to it and shut it down. But like I said from the beginning, [and] I can't say it enough: you got to love this game, man. If you don't love it, you don't get nothing out of it. You gotta love it."

. . .

About a year after that conversation, Floyd has returned to Merrillville as part of Lewis's traveling revue (this time billed as the *Chi-Town Blues Festival* and featuring such luminaries as Millie Jackson, Denise LaSalle, Bobby "Blue" Bland, Theodis Ealey, and Sir Charles Jones, along with Floyd himself). *All of Me*, despite

Floyd Taylor, Chicago Blues Festival, 2012. Photograph © 2012 Linda Vartoogian/ FrontRowPhotos. All Rights Reserved.

its promising jump out of the gate, didn't make the mainstream R&B splash Floyd had hoped for, and once again his performances on this tour have consisted almost entirely of his father's hits.

"How's the CD going?" I ask him.

"It's going."

. . . silence . . .

"It's a good product," he adds, as if reciting from a script. "It's a very good product, and I'm very proud of it, and I'm looking forward to this next project that I'm about to embark on."

He won't reveal what that project is, but he's already left CDS to pursue it. Arrogance or confidence? Burning bridges or blazing trails? Floyd Taylor won't venture an answer, and it's likely he'd never even ask himself the question, for to do so would be to admit the possibility of doubt. He's still gambling, still meta-phorically tossing names into a hat with a player's bravado, insisting he remains undaunted.

"If you have it in your heart," he asserts again, "and you put God first, ain't nothing gonna ever hold you up. And that's where I'm at. I'm just trying to put some realness back in the game."

Coda: "There Was a Party in Soul Heaven . . ."

In 2013, Floyd Taylor released what turned out to be his final recording, *Shut Um' Down*, on the Artia label. The songwriting was strong, but the studio production, contemporary-sounding as it was (except for a rather anomalous cover of his father's 1982 hit "What about My Love"), seemed oddly subdued, and Floyd's voice sounded grainier than it had in the past. The cover photo showed him looking uncharacteristically tired, a bit puffy, and clad almost carelessly in a rumpled shirt.

In retrospect, it seems clear that his health was already failing by this time. On February 20, 2014, he died of a heart attack.

Floyd's younger brothers T. J. Hooker-Taylor and Johnnie Taylor Jr., along with his sister, Tasha Taylor, continue to carry on the family name; they're gifted singers, but as of yet none of them has found a way to fully escape their father's shadow (although Tasha, with her formidable stylistic range and theatrical flair, has carved out the most distinctive musical personality).

For his part, Floyd never achieved his dream of mainstream R&B stardom. Many of his finest musical accomplishments remain virtually unknown (he sel-dom, if ever, performed material like "Baby I've Changed" or "Hit It Right" on his shows). Nonetheless, he was one of his genre's most formidable talents. This chapter was originally planned for my previous book, *Southern Soul-Blues*. I include it here as a tribute to an artist of merit and lasting value who, as is so often the case, never got the opportunity to attain the recognition and rewards he merited during his lifetime. Too often, especially in the blues, we end up missing people after they're gone more than we appreciated them when they were here.

Deitra Farr

"If You Don't Create, the Music Will Die!"

You can't just jump out from nowhere. You gotta get the root.
But don't stay in the root—build from the root.

—Deitra Farr

Deitra Farr has never trod a conventional path, even though her upbringing was similar, in many ways, to that of most of her blues contemporaries. Born in Chicago in 1957, she grew up listening to soul, R&B, and gospel, along with the blues that her father loved. Unlike many, though, she wasn't raised in the sanctified church. In fact, she wasn't particularly religious at all until she was about eleven years old, when she discovered the Catholic faith and immediately felt at home there ("I don't know why, I just felt the pull of it"). Nonetheless, it was church that provided her with her first opportunity to sing in public.

"At that time," she remembers, "there was a spirit at that church [Holy Angels on Chicago's South Side] of doing real revolutionary type things. And one of 'em was, 'We're gonna have a gospel choir.'" And I jumped right in there—I said, "Wow!" I had never sung outside of the bathroom. We had a wonderful thing going on. Everybody was black people, and we just—the choir director gave us all these good gospel songs, and they said, "This is not traditional Catholic-type music, but this is our heritage." And I jumped in on that, and that's when I got a chance to sing. Eventually the older people in the church started to complain. They wanted us to sing traditional Catholic hymns, so we had to go back to doing that. We had one year of gospel music, and that started everything for me. That gave me the chance to actually sing in front of somebody other than my mother.

As it turned out, it also resulted in her first lesson in the vicissitudes of stardom; her choir director decided to step in at the last minute and sing "Trouble Don't Last Always," the song that was to have been her featured number on a program ("My first break, and it's snatched from me!"). By then, though, she'd gotten the bug. Pretty soon, having no compunction against "crossing over" from the sacred to the secular, she began testing the waters on the local club circuit. Her voice eventually caught the ear of drummer Jimmy (aka "Jimmi") Mayes, and he took her on as lead singer for his band, Mill Street Depo. She made her first recording, "You Won't Support Me," with them in 1976. Sounding much older and worldlier than the eighteen-year-old neophyte she was, she immersed herself in the persona of a single mother castigating her children's father for abandoning his family.

But again, the way the deal went down provided an ominous glimpse into the dark side of the business she was unwittingly setting herself up to get into. "That was supposed to be a demo," she says. "I had left the group [by then]. My dad called me up and said, 'I heard you on the radio.' 'You did what?!' I was real angry about that. 'You guys put out an album without talking to me?' I've forgiven everybody for their sins, but I'm tellin' you, this business is just—it's not cool sometimes."

Eager to expand her territory and her music, she began to investigate the Chicago blues scene a few years later while attending Columbia College, where she majored in journalism (she graduated in 1981). The blues veterans were as enamored of her vocal prowess as Mayes had been, and by the mid-'80s she was gigging around town, and sometimes on the road, in the company of some of the music's most legendary figures—Sam Lay ("Sam snatched me right out of the Kingston Mines in 1984: 'I never heard a young girl sing the blues like that before! You wanna go on the road with me?'"), Sunnyland Slim, Louis and Dave Myers, and others. She became determined to follow in their footsteps, to embrace the music's heritage as they had done, but—also as they had done—propel it forward, keeping it alive as a contemporary music, reflecting contemporary aesthetics and concerns.

Some others, though, weren't so welcoming. "I didn't fit the stereotype," she maintains. "Customers would say, 'You don't look like a blues singer!' I was 110 pounds, I was real little then. So right away I don't fit the physical characteristics of a 'blueswoman.' Then I had the nerve of going to college, too? And graduating?

I remember [a club owner] saying once that I was too educated to be a blues singer!"

This is what I had to face. [But] those older blues people really embraced me. I would've given up if it weren't for them. People like Sunnyland, Eddie Taylor, Johnny Littlejohn—all those guys who are not here any more. I can [still] hear Sunnyland— I would be walking in the door, and he would be, "Deitra! Come up here!" And I didn't even want to go up there, because [the club] wouldn't hire me, and I made it a policy I wouldn't even sit in.

When I started, I went to Erwin [Helfer][1] for help, and he was very close to Mama Yancey.[2] I met her, I believe, at his house; they did gigs together. And we just hit it off. I would go to her house, she'd send me to the liquor store and we'd drink, we'd sit up and talk—Oh, I was just crazy about her. People would see this old, frail woman [and say], "What could she do?" But then, when she opened that mouth—Oh Lord! This big voice would come out. I think she was on the very first [Chicago] Blues Festival that we had, and she didn't have anything she wanted to wear. So I said, "Well,

Deitra Farr, Chicago Blues
Festival, 2017.

I'll go downtown and get you a dress." And she told me what size, and the color. I said, "Mama, you don't wear that size." "I know what size I am!" She was right! She looked smaller than she actually was. I think Irwin told me she was buried in that dress.

She continued to grind it out on the local scene, accepting gigs when they were offered—she remembers Blue Chicago and the Wise Fools as being among the few clubs that welcomed her—but it wasn't until 1990, when Blue Chicago owner Gino Battaglia "sent me and my band to Dusseldorf to represent the Chicago Tourism Bureau," that opportunities really began to open up. "It was an acceptance that I needed," she attests. "I felt like sort of a reject in Chicago. When I started going to Europe it just seemed like, 'Oh! I'm at home here! They like me as I am!'" Although she believes her reputation as a globe trotter has been somewhat inflated, she continues to perform outside the United States on a regular basis, and she's never forgotten the exhilaration and relief she felt at the reception she received when her overseas sojourns began.

She lived in Rome for fourteen months in the early 2000s, and she says that if it hadn't been for the international turmoil in the wake of the 9/11 terrorist attacks, she'd probably still be there. Nonetheless, life in a foreign country could be lonely ("The first isolation is the language barrier. The second isolation is that people are into their families, and you ain't in the family"). More disturbingly, although she prefers not to dwell on or even discuss some of the more egregious incidents that have occurred, she discovered that racial prejudice was alive and well in even some of the most cosmopolitan European regions. "There's this romantic thing about Europeans not being prejudiced," she acknowledges, "but they got just as many racists over there as they do here. When I was living in Rome, I had a reserved ticket to sit next to [an Italian woman], and this woman didn't even want me sitting next to her on the train."

Back home, Deitra finally returned to the recording studio in the early '90s. By this time, her voice had matured into a resonant alto, gospel-seasoned ("I used to go see Thomas A. Dorsey[3] at the Pilgrim Baptist Church, because I was off into that, the history of how spirituals began to sound the way they do, and why it's so close to blues") and charged with bluesy immediacy. She sang on Chicago guitarist Dave Specter's 1991 debut, *Bluebird Blues*, and she also appeared on *Chicago Blue Nights*, an anthology on the Japanese DIW label. From 1993 to 1996, she was lead vocalist of the Chicago-based roots-revivalist band Mississippi Heat (led, ironically enough, by French harmonica player Pierre Lacocque). She recorded two albums with them: *Learned the Hard Way* (1994) and *Thunder in My Heart* (1995).

Her debut recording under her own name was *The Search Is Over*, produced by singer/guitarist Johnny Rawls and released in 1997 on the British JSP label; she also appeared with Bonnie Lee, Karen Carroll, Mary Lane, Melvina Allen, and Zora Young on the anthology *Chicago's Finest Blues Ladies* (Wolf) in 1998.

Over the next several years she continued to make guest appearances on others' projects, as well as *I Believe in America*, a 2002 commemoration of the 9/11 attacks (characteristically, she wrote her own contribution, "Homesick Blues," even as other artists delivered covers of standards like "America the Beautiful," "Battle Hymn of the Republic," and Chuck Berry's "Back in the U.S.A."). But it wasn't until 2005 that she released *Let It Go!*—her next full-length CD under her own name, again on JSP.

With each studio outing, she sounded more comfortable and relaxed; by her own admission, she's always done her best work in front of an audience, and it took her a while to feel comfortable "stuck in a booth" with a headset and a microphone, missing the affirmation of a crowd's response. She'd always written a lot of her own material, but after breaking out on her own, she got the chance to fully showcase her songwriting. Many of the songs on *Let It Go!* approximated the familiar 12-bar form, but the horn arrangements sounded almost like backing tracks from some mythical, long-lost Stax Records session; harpist Matthew Skoller wailed and warbled with vintage Chicago fire alongside guitarist Billy Flynn's rich chording and serpentine, string-bending leads. The result was a roots-rich yet forward-looking melange—precisely the mix Deitra considers essential.

"*Let It Go!* captured me," she said at the time, "because it's *me*. I wrote everything. Billy can play soul just as well as he can play blues. And I brought that out of him. You're in for a big shock! Part of the reason why I wanted to do it, that's gonna be the bomb that I'm dropping. Because everybody sees Billy as a traditional player. Billy can play soul like you would not believe, and nobody knows that." (She had already achieved a similar transformation with the ostensibly traditionalist bassist Harlan Terson on the southern-soul–styled title song of *The Search Is Over*.)

In that same spirit, Deitra has also long made it a point to fill her live sets with as much original material as possible—surprisingly rare, even in Chicago, where many artists who feature their own songs on record continue to perform mostly covers in their shows. She's probably almost as well known, in fact, for her determination to avoid the dreaded "Set List from Hell" ("Sweet Home Chicago," "Woke Up This Morning," "Every Day I Have the Blues," and other overcooked chestnuts) as she is for the quality of her own music; it remains both her calling card and her manifesto. "Believe me," she asserts. "This is my pet peeve."

> I will not do it. I refuse. I'm not givin' in on that. If I have to do that, I will sit my fat black ass in this chair—and you can print that!—and I am not doing it. I'm Deitra, and I'm going to do Deitra.
>
> If [we] don't continue to create, the music is just going to die. I don't care what anybody says, it is going to die. This music has to go on, [and] it's only going to go on if people create. I preach this and preach this and preach this—I tell everybody. They gon' say that on my tombstone, that I preached doing original material. For this scene to survive, we gotta do some new stuff. It can't just stay like this—it can't. I see death. People been sayin' the blues is dyin'—well, yeah, it is. If you-all are gonna keep doin' these songs? Yeah! If you don't create, the music will die.

That's not to say Deitra avoids standards; she reveres the tradition she's inherited, and she honors it whenever she can. Nonetheless, "If I do a cover song, I'm changin' that sucker!" Her version of Little Walter's irony-toughened "Mean Old World," for example, is considerably slower than the original, and she alters the phrasing and melodic contours to emphasize the range and textural depth of her voice. It first appeared on Mississippi Heat's *Learned the Hard Way* album in 1993; an earlier rendition, recorded for Wolf in 1990 but unreleased, was included on *Chicago's Finest Blues Ladies* in 1998. She has continued to feature it in her live act—a brooding, deep blues ballad, girded by determination and faith.

Even that kind of respectful reimagining, though, is apostasy to some purists. She has encountered resistance, she says, for her updating of Walter's classic, and at times she's even had to butt heads with sidemen who've resisted adaptations as simple as altering a song's key. Part of the problem, she believes, is the folkloric mindset that still permeates a lot of the blues world. Blues was "rediscovered" in the 1960s and '70s by listeners and players who, for the most part, were far removed from the communities and the conditions that had incubated the music and so had never experienced it as a dynamic, ongoing facet of day-to-day cultural and social life. Thus, their notions of "authenticity" were largely defined by what they heard on old records or by what they read in books written by folklorists and musicologists: To be "authentic," an artist had to play or sing the music "correctly," and to do that, she had to copy. Today, a lot of those same people, or maybe younger acolytes who've followed in their wake, own nightclubs or play in bands, and in many cases their attitudes haven't changed much.

"I've gotten criticized," Deitra affirms, "for not singing songs in the key that the original artist did 'em in. Like, if Jimmy Reed did it in A, I was supposed to do it in A. And I would be tellin' 'em, 'Well, I'm not Jimmy Reed. I don't have his voice. I sing it in the key I'm comfortable singing it in.'"

> "Correctly"?! What the hell does that mean? That means note-for-note, that's what it means. If the original song was done in a certain way, that's the way you got to do it the rest of your life, and that's such bullshit I can't even believe people think that way. But that separates the artist from other people. The artist is not going to do it like that. Like Lady Day said, she never did a song the same way [as anyone else]. There is no way in the world I can sing a song the way it's written. I'm known for changing the whole damn line. I change my own damn songs sometimes, that I wrote! I might do 'em a different way. The audience is not as dumb and narrow-minded as these club owners think they are.

Yet and still, she insists, a blues artist who isn't rooted, or at least well-versed, in the music's heritage will also not be able to effectively carry that heritage into the future. The mentorship she received from the old masters remains her touchstone and lodestar, and she is concerned that the artists coming up today will not, for the most part, have that same opportunity. Although a few stalwarts from earlier eras continue to perform, they don't appear in town as often as they used to, and they certainly aren't a weekly or even monthly presence in the clubs the way Sunnyland Slim, the Myers brothers, Jimmy Rogers, Eddie Shaw, and others were when Deitra was coming up. The result, she says, is that younger musicians, even those who profess to adhere to "tradition," have little opportunity to actually experience that tradition firsthand and then develop their skills within that context. Thus she finds herself in the paradoxical position of decrying the loss of the living ancestral voice, even as she rails against the "moldy fig" mentality of purists.

"Picture yourself being eighteen years old," she suggests, "and you decide you want to play blues. Who are you gonna learn from? Our generation actually got a chance to hear real live people that we could learn from. They missed that whole thing. They didn't see Sunnyland and [pianists] Blind John Davis and Louis Myers, [drummer] Fred Below. I don't know what they're learning off of, because clearly they're not learning off their forefathers."

Deitra, like many of her contemporaries, is also concerned about what she perceives as the lack of interest in blues among younger black musicians. Although she's resolute in her color-blindness in terms of appreciating musical talent ("I lost my gig at [a Chicago club] because I had white musicians in my band—told me to get rid of Harlan Terson and hire Bob Stroger,[4] and I wouldn't do that"), she also believes that the blues is, at its heart, an African American music and that

Deitra Farr with violinist Anne Harris, benefit for 12-year-old Jameson Stokes, House of Blues Chicago, 2018.

something vital will be lost if this identity becomes erased. Unlike some, though, she sees the problem less as cultural theft than voluntary cultural abdication.

"We gave it away," she attests, echoing the late songwriter/producer Jimmy Lewis, whose "What's the Matter with the Blues," recorded by Billy Ray Charles on Lewis's Miss Butch label in 1998, addressed the issue in almost identical terms ("White folks didn't steal the blues / we gave them away").

"When I came around and decided to sing blues," she continues, "I was in my twenties. Valerie[5] was in her twenties, Sarah[6]—we all were young. Where's our young people comin' up now, singing the blues? Very, very few. We gave it away. They're not picking it up. They're listening to hip-hop and everything else."

There are, of course, still quite a few young black artists performing the blues in Chicago, especially if we stretch our definition of "young" to include people between the ages of thirty-five and fifty, but Deitra is reluctant to see even this as much of a silver lining. "I think," she maintains, "that a lot of people move in that [blues] direction, in this town 'cause that's where the work is. I'm not convinced that people suddenly like the blues when they're forty."

I think a lot of the guys coming on the scene now don't even buy the records. I remember Below had just died, and [a popular guitarist] said, "Who is Fred Below?"

This man, probably fifty-something—he didn't know! He's probably one of those people that fell into it because he could get work—"Okay, I can play twelve-bar blues." And I'm like, "See, y'all not learning this stuff. You're not buying the records, you're not reading the liner notes, seeing who's doing what, who's done what."

If musicians don't do their homework and get the root of the music—I'm not sayin' stay there, but at least learn the shit! It's very important. I knew who [drummer] Odie Payne was before I saw him. Why? Because I went out and bought records, I read books, I did everything these people comin' behind me are not doing.

Ironically, her point is not that different from the complaints soul-blues vocalist Lee Morris and his producer, Michael J. Mayberry, raised when I interviewed them for my earlier book *Chicago Blues: Portraits and Stories*. Morris and Mayberry, though, were coming at the problem from the opposite direction—their interest was in updating Morris's sound to be funkier and more contemporary (in other words, more likely to be played on black radio and picked up on by younger black listeners), and they felt shackled by the pressure to conform to what they saw as Chicago's provincial insistence on remaining "true to the blues," even if an artist didn't really want to. "A lot of clubs," Mayberry asserted, "you got to do more blues than soul or you won't get the gig." Lee concurred: "Can't make it over here, they fall back, lot of 'em, say, 'I got to play some blues.' 'Cause a blues band will beat an R&B band any day, 'cause that's what [club audiences] want to hear."

Although she admits that her outspokenness and spitfire ways have sometimes stigmatized her as a malcontent ("Most people keep their mouth closed about stuff, and I don't. That's one reason why I stay in trouble"), Deitra is adamant that despite the pitfalls and frustrations, she's deeply grateful for the opportunity she's had to forge a career doing something she believes in, and which she continues to love as much as she did when she first started. Some disappointments still rankle: *From the Soul*, recorded live in Sweden and released in 2016 on the Spinnup label, had the potential to finally capture this charismatic and versatile stylist at her in-person best (it also featured Johnny Rawls and vocalist Tad Robinson). She was dissatisfied, though, with the production—to the extent that she didn't even include the disk in the discography she compiled for her online bio.

Nonetheless, she's still able to look toward the future with, if not optimism, at least the kind of hope-girded fatalism that has characterized the blues since the beginning. These days she's fronting the band Chicago Wind, led by her longtime friend, harmonica player Matthew Skoller; if that group is a bit more wedded to the old "lump-de-lump" postwar sound than some she's worked with, she nonetheless continues to insist on featuring original material in her act, and she sees to it that her sidemen are ready to follow her on her journey into what she believes is the only possible future the music can have if it's going to stay alive.

"I have done remarkably well," she attests, "for someone that's never had anybody. I never had a manager, never had an agent, had to do everything myself. And I have done remarkably well, but my ship just hasn't come in. And you don't know when it's coming, and so you just keep on plugging away. That's all you can do."

Meanwhile, she also continues to write her "Artist to Artist" column for *Living Blues* magazine, in which she conducts succinct but often surprisingly revealing interviews with blues, soul, and southern soul artists both well-known and obscure; as a performing artist herself, she can establish rapport and coax things out of her subjects that another interviewer might not be able to summon. In 2017, citing Deitra's role in "preserving traditional blues heritage," the Jus' Blues Music Foundation chose her as that year's recipient of its "Koko Taylor Queen of the Blues Award" at its annual meeting in Tunica, Mississippi. Closer to home, she's an inductee in the Chicago Blues Hall of Fame, and she is also working on a combination CD/written memoir that she says will document her still-evolving life in the blues. The working title, as of this writing, is *Trouble Don't Last Always*, the name of the gospel standard that was "snatched" from her so many years ago when she was supposed to have made her singing debut at Holy Angels Church. After all this time, she says, "I'm gonna get it back."

Ronnie Baker Brooks

"The Blues Is a Healer"

1980—a hot August afternoon in Chicago. ChicagoFest, the city's annual two-week lakefront blowout, is in full wail. Navy Pier, which for years had been little more than a barren concrete slab jutting out into Lake Michigan,[1] is throbbing with music and packed with sweaty, gyrating bodies as bands both well-known and obscure perform on multiple stages, with the lake and the city skyline as their backdrop. On a blues stage sponsored by Olympia Beer and hosted by radio station WXRT, some of Chicago's most renowned blues legends—Muddy Waters, Willie Dixon, Son Seals, Mighty Joe Young, Koko Taylor, and more—will be paying tribute to the living legacy they helped create and have sustained over the years.

Also on the bill is another veteran, Louisiana-born Lonnie Brooks, who's been living and working in Chicago since 1959. Until recently, though, he's been something of a well-kept South and West Side secret. In 1978, he appeared on the Alligator Records anthology *Living Chicago Blues, Vol. 2*; the following year he released his debut under his own name for the label, *Bayou Lightning*. Largely on the strength of those disks, he has finally begun to garner the international recognition he's long deserved.

Among the onlookers at Navy Pier is Brooks's eldest son, thirteen-year-old Rodney Dion Baker.[2] Known to his family and friends as Ronnie, he's an aspiring guitarist who has seen his father perform, shared the stage with him at least once, and even appeared with him on a local TV commercial, but until this moment he's never really understood how special his dad is. As Brooks climaxes his set with a crowd-galvanizing "Sweet Home Chicago"—captured on the album *Blues Deluxe*, a live recording of the event released on Alligator in 1980—the force of that understanding hits Ronnie like a revelation.

"That's when I knew," he affirms today. "I saw all these people freaking out on my dad—all-white audience, college kids, even younger—I saw that, man, and I was like, 'Wow! This is my dad! This is the same guy I was just wrestling on the floor with!' And that's when I realized that it was something special."

· · ·

It can be difficult for the children of celebrities to rectify "My Parent, the Star" with the person who cooks their meals, plays catch with them in the backyard, and looks over their report card after school. And sometimes, if those children decide to pursue a performing career of their own, the pressure to both honor the family name and carve an independent niche for themselves can be overwhelming. Ronnie Baker Brooks, though, has felt little of this tension over the course of his career—a career that's taken him around the world and given him the opportunity to maintain an active touring schedule while releasing a series of highly acclaimed CDs, and which still finds him actively participating in his hometown's music scene, sitting in on various shows when he's not headlining his own. A good deal of his equanimity, he says, can be traced back to the home life his parents worked to provide him and his siblings, despite the vicissitudes that might sometimes have accompanied his father's chosen profession.

"Around the house, I knew him as 'Dad,'" he recollects. "My dad would always play with us. He and my mom were smart to do that, because we grew up in the ghetto on the South Side of Chicago—well, it was turning into the ghetto because we were in between the projects and [the university neighborhood] Hyde Park, we were right there. They kept us busy in the house with board games, cards, back then we used to play with jacks, or we'd be on the floor wrestling, and playing music. My dad and mom kept us in the house because of the stuff that was going on around us."

Even the everyday interaction with people whom he'd later come to recognize as internationally famous blues stars was accepted as a normal facet of life:

> I didn't realize that when [Howlin' Wolf's guitarist] Hubert Sumlin would come by the house, or Koko Taylor, or Son Seals or somebody like that, or even [Bobby "Blue" Bland's fretman] Wayne Bennett—Wayne Bennett taught me. The first time I learned how to play "Hide Away" was from Wayne Bennett. Eddy Clearwater used

to come by the house. I was around Buddy Guy; my mother and Buddy's first wife were best friends. I used to go to their house and see Buddy practicing: "Okay, he's like my dad"—just [another] guitar player to me. I didn't realize how important these people were. I knew the names, but I didn't know this wasn't normal until I got older.

When he wasn't meeting musicians face-to-face, young Ronnie was listening to them on records and on the radio. His father had played country music (as well as zydeco, swamp pop, and both traditional and modern blues) as a young man in Louisiana, and a lot of that eclecticism rubbed off: "It was always music, man, always music around the house. We would play blues, gospel—my dad loved country. He played Ernest Tubb, Hank Williams—we heard all different styles. Sam Cooke [was the person who] brought my dad to Chicago, so we had that R&B/gospel/soul music thing happening, as well. And if we weren't playing records, we were listening to WVON—a lot of different styles within that 'R&B.'"

Despite the thrill of discovering that his dad was a bona fide blues celebrity, though, it took Ronnie a few more years to commit himself to a musical career. Then, as now, young men growing up in the city cherished hoop dreams at least as much as they fantasized about spotlights and standing ovations, and Lonnie Brooks's son was no exception. He was tempted for a while, he says, to pursue basketball stardom—"I've always been competitive"—until an encounter with guitarist Bernard Allison, Luther Allison's son, got him back on track: Allison told him, quite simply, "We got enough Michael Jordans—we need some more B.B. Kings." After that, he remembers, "I started going on the road with Dad on weekends, while I was in high school. Then, once I graduated, I went on the road with him full-time. I became a full-time member around '89, and from then on I became my dad's bandleader."

Even then, though, his father was intent on grooming him to be more than just a prototypical blues "Son" or "Junior": "My dad was smart enough, and unselfish enough, to say, 'You create your own identity. They're already gonna say you're my son, but now you gotta embrace it and add onto the legacy. I don't want you to be just my son, playing a guitar.'"

Nonetheless, by Ronnie's own recollection, it took a bit of an extra push to get him out of the nest. In 1998, he released *Golddigger*, his debut as a frontman, on his own Watchdog imprint. "Dad played on the record," he remembers. "I cut it down in Memphis, and I brought it back and played it for Dad—sippin' on some wine in the basement, listening to the record—I'm thinking I'm going to stay with my dad, and we're going to do this together. He said, 'Son, I'm really proud of you, but in order to give this record the justification and make people look at you as a solo artist, you're going to have to go and support that record.' He wanted me to be accepted as an artist, not just as his son."

Further inspiration came from another of Lonnie's old friends. Ronnie admits that despite his dad's tutelage and encouragement, there were times when he wondered whether he'd be able to go out and do it on his own. It was Albert Collins, he says, who helped eradicate those last vestiges of self-doubt. "I was frustrated," he remembers, "caught under the umbrella of Lonnie Brooks, trying to find my own identity."

> I know what you're talking about when you talk about these other artists that go through that. But musically, Albert Collins saw my potential. It was the right time in my growth [that] Albert came along and told me the right thing—"Look, you can play, man. You're not gonna be like me; you're not gonna be like your dad. You gotta

Ronnie Baker Brooks, Buddy Guy's Legends, 2016.

be yourself"—and directed me out of my little hole I dug from being Lonnie Brooks's son, and these insecurities, and living up to expectations, and all that. I always say my dad started the fire, and Albert Collins threw the gasoline on it.

Listening to *Golddigger*, though, it's hard to imagine that Ronnie ever felt himself in a "hole" at all—the disk bristles with energy, inspiration, and self-confidence, with Ronnie's genre-spanning eclecticism on display. "Back then," he explains, "people were still listening to whole records. Then they started the alternative of making their own playlists, like, 'Okay, I want one song blues, I want one song rock, I want one reggae and one soul' I was thinking, okay, let me incorporate that, make my album a playlist as opposed to just one song with 'this' style, and riding that style all the way through."

In fact, *Golddigger* sounds less like a "playlist" than what we'd now call a "mash-up." The instrumentation—guitars, keyboards, bass, drums—is conventional for a blues set, but it's embellished by atmospheric studio effects along with Ronnie's own fuzz-tone/wah-wah enhanced guitar. Rhythmic patterns include postwar shuffles, 6/8 ballads, blues-rock explosions, and post-JB funk. Ronnie's vocals, urbane and tough, show the influence of blues-funksters like Johnny "Guitar" Watson as well as older-generation bluesmen like his father (who contributes a characteristically crisp guitar solo to the anthemic "Make These Blues Survive"). On one track, Ronnie and producer Jellybean Johnson briefly re-created the sound of an acoustically recorded, surface-scratched 78 before plunging into the boogie-rock drive of "Bald-Headed Woman"—a pointed appropriation and updating of a vintage blues theme.

True to his stated intention, on *Take Me Witcha*, his 2001 follow-up to *Golddigger*, Ronnie sounded intent on widening his aesthetic scope (and challenging his listeners) even more. The opening cut, "I Had My Chance," kicks off with a chiming guitar solo based on "Here Comes the Bride"—an obvious nod to Jimi Hendrix's legendary deconstruction of "The Star-Spangled Banner"—then plunges into a howling miasma of swirls, sonic explosions, and lightning-bolt fusillades before relaxing into verses prettified by sparkling acoustic guitar chording and disarmingly tender vocals. Overall, in fact, the CD sounds more oriented toward rock and blues-rock than the earlier outing had been, although there's still plenty of variety—exemplified by the jaunty blues shuffle "Give Me Your Heart," the gospel-flavored ballad "Time Will Tell," and, perhaps most memorably, the pop/folk "I Laugh to Keep from Cryin'," on which Lonnie Brooks steps in to deliver some of the most wracked, emotionally intense vocals of his career. Meanwhile, now fronting his own band on the road, Ronnie was cultivating a reputation as a performer whose shows were as varied—and, to some purists' dismay, uncompromisingly modernist—as his recordings. But he didn't release any new material for almost five years after *Take Me Witcha*. "I was financing it myself," he explains. "I was financing my own records. I was my record company, I was my publicist, my marketing, I was all that. And when you're on the road, it's when you don't have any help, man. You can only go so far by yourself."

Finally, in 2006, he came out with *The Torch*, a disk that proclaimed his musical agenda even more brazenly. For the title song, "The Torch of the Blues," he recruited his father again, along with veterans Jimmy Johnson, Eddy Clearwater, and Willie Kent, as guest vocalists. Although some listeners may have wished that these esteemed fretmen had gotten the opportunity to play as well as sing, the overall message—"We paved the way for you / now it's all up to you, to carry this torch of the blues"—resonated with a nearly prophetic power. Elsewhere, the sound was as uncompromising as *Golddigger's* had been, with blues rock, thunder-funk, and power-pop balladry sharing the spotlight with more standard-issue Chicago blues, as well as a few nods to vintage deep soul.

Perhaps most notable—and potentially controversial—was the presence of Memphis rapper Al Kapone on the topical "If It Don't Make Dollars Then It Don't Make Sense." The idea wasn't entirely unheard-of: A few younger blues artists, such as Louisiana's Chris Thomas King, had released blues/hip-hop fusion projects by then, and some southern soul singers were incorporating rap passages into their songs. Nonetheless, to blues traditionalists, it still seemed like apostasy. Ronnie maintains, though, that in the end it didn't turn out to be much of a problem. In fact, he says, reactions since then have indicated that even a lot of so-called "mainstream" blues lovers may have bigger ears than they're usually given credit for. "At first," he admits, "I was a little nervous about that. But once I played it live [he usually does his own rapping] and saw the response—Oh, okay. They can relate to it. They feel it. I think it comes down to your message, man, if it's rooted and it's true, and you're not saying it just to ride a wave. What comes from the heart, reaches the heart."

In 2008, Ronnie appeared along with Tommy Castro, Deanna Bogart, Magic Dick and others—billed as the "Legendary Rhythm & Blues Revue"—on *Command Performance* (Delta Groove), a "supergroup" concept masterminded by Legendary Rhythm & Blues Cruise founder Roger Nabor. But once again, fresh material was a long time coming: it wasn't until 2017's *Times Have Changed*, issued on Provogue, that he released another CD under his own name. This time out, he says, a conscious effort was made to strip down his sound. "I brought my big pedal board down to Memphis. We recorded at Royal Studios—Boo Mitchell [Willie Mitchell's son] engineered it—and I packed the bus up with all my big amps and pedal boards, and I brought most of my guitars down there, and a lot of 'em are Strats. And [producer] Steve Jordan said, 'We don't need no Strats, we don't need no pedal boards, all we need is that one amp. You plug straight into the amp.'"

Otherwise, though, *Times Have Changed* lives up to its name—Ronnie's professed determination to honor his legacy by expanding it into new directions remains paramount. Kapone has returned, but also on hand are such fabled veterans as Bobby "Blue" Bland and, on several tracks, Hi Rhythm Section guitarist Teenie Hodges (both of whom passed away before the album was released). Bland's contribution is especially poignant, sounding frail but resolute on the ballad "Old Love," possibly the last recording he ever made. Other guest vocalists range from pop chanteuse Angie Stone through festival/bistro celebrity and blues-roots revivalist "Big Head" Todd Mohr to Felix Cavaliere, who reprises 1966's "Come On Up," one of his early recordings as lead singer of the Young Rascals. Sidemen include Teenie Hodges's brothers and bandmates Leroy (bass) and Charles (organ); guitarists Steve Cropper and Lee Roy Parnell; and pianist Archie Turner.

"Ain't nothing wrong with going back to the basics," raps Kapone on the title song—but then he adds, "some thangs change for the better, too." In that spirit, the set list is split between standards (Joe Tex's "Show Me" and "Give the Baby Anything the Baby Wants;" Alvin Cash's Chicago dance classic, "Twine Time;" Curtis Mayfield's "Give Me Your Love [Love Song]," featuring Stone's sultry, multitracked vocals; and the aforementioned Young Rascals chestnut) and originals from Ronnie himself, as well as "Old Love," cowritten by Robert Cray and Eric Clapton (Clapton recorded it in 1989). Although the instrumentation is straight-ahead throughout, reflecting producer Jordan's professed back-to-basics aesthetic, the stylistic spectrum is again both wide and deep—and, of course, Kapone's rapping can be taken as a manifesto (and possibly a throwdown to purists), as well as a celebration of heritage evolving. Even Ronnie's behind-the-scenes team reflects his ongoing old-school/new-school fusion crusade: Boo Mitchell, of course, is a living link to the glory days of Memphis soul, but he has also masterminded such modern-day pop classics as Mark Ronson and Bruno Mars's 2014 smash "Uptown Funk;" multi-instrumentalist/songwriter/arranger Lester Snell, a legendary contemporary of Boo's father Willie Mitchell, contributed the string arrangement to Ronnie's southern soul ballad "When I Was We," the disk's closing cut.

Probably because it was his first release on an established label, *Times Have Changed* garnered somewhat more media attention than most of Ronnie's earlier outings, and his touring schedule has intensified in its wake. Meanwhile, when he's in town, he can still be seen sitting in at venues ranging from trendy North Side bistros (when Shemekia Copeland plays a venue like the City Winery, she makes it a point to invite Ronnie on stage to join her for a song or two) to neighborhood soul-blues strongholds like the Odyssey East on South Torrence, where bassist Joe Pratt and guitarist Sir Walter Scott co-lead the Source One Band, a versatile aggregation that includes veterans from the bands of Otis Clay, Tyrone Davis, Artie "Blues Boy" White, and others.

As if that weren't enough, in 2016 Ronnie also joined Todd Mohr in the latest incarnation of Mohr's ongoing roots-tribute project, the Big Head Blues Club. This time around, the Club featured Billy Branch, Muddy Waters's son Mud Morganfield, and Erica Brown as well as Ronnie, along with members of Mohr's regular working band, the Monsters, paying homage to the musical legacy of Willie Dixon. Their revuelike road show was enthusiastically received; their CD, *Way Down Inside*, issued on Mohr's Big imprint, featured thirteen Dixon covers.

Ronnie's work with the Big Head Blues Club, and—at least arguably—the eclectic but mostly straight-ahead blues and soul-blues sets he participates in at venues like the Odyssey, may seem in contrast to his sometimes-edgy performances and recordings, but in a way that's part of the point—academic debates about "authenticity" have obviously never meant much to him. And on a more practical level, of course, the wider the net an artist casts, the more likely his career is to thrive. As the economics of the music industry have tightened, gigs— like CD sales—have gotten harder to come by for all but the biggest names ("It's almost like we're losing the middle class," as Ronnie puts it). And even when the jobs are relatively plentiful, there's the sticky issue of trying to appeal to different audiences that embrace different styles and definitions of "blues."

"It's sad," Ronnie concurs. "Sad. That's a shame that we have that gap in America, man, where the labels come in and divide us."

You know, if you're a certain color you listen to this, and you're supposed to listen to that if you're this color. You know how many of my friends, now, that come to my show, didn't know that what I'm doing is "the blues"? "Man, that ain't what I thought the blues was. I thought it was cryin' in your drink, 'My baby left me—' [but] you have *fun* up there!" Yeah!

Over here at the Odyssey and these [other] black clubs that I go to, when I hit the slow blues—I always get surprised at how much they accept me. Because they're so used to hearing the dance R&B style—Tyrone Davis, Johnnie Taylor, that kind of thing—[but] then when I hit that slow B.B. thing or Albert King thing, they embrace it. They're connected to it. I grew up in them clubs, man, as far as being a total musician—being able to play to all people, not just one audience. Having some versatility, to be able to touch all people.

The road, meanwhile, throws up its own challenges. Most blues clubs and festivals these days are far removed—geographically, socially, culturally—from the neighborhood taverns and show lounges where even major figures like Muddy Waters and Howlin' Wolf did most of their performing before the '60s-era white blues "revival" catapulted them into international fame. An artist like Ronnie, who for all his genre-jumping iconoclasm is still associated in the popular imagination with the postwar Chicago tradition, thus finds himself performing primarily for white audiences, at least when he's not sitting in at a club like the Odyssey. In and of itself, this isn't a problem. The fans are enthusiastic, they love the music, and they're usually willing to go wherever he takes them—after all, they seem to have accepted his rapping (and Kapone's rapping on his CDs), along with his neo-Hendrix guitar pyrotechnics, as part of the package, apparently with few qualms. For his part, Ronnie insists that, at least at the beginning, it was something he was barely even aware of.

"I didn't think about that, to be honest," he maintains. "It didn't faze me that they were white or black. I just looked at it as people listening to music, because I guess I came up different, by my father being black, my mom being white—so when I saw at, ChicagoFest, I saw all these white people listening to my dad, I was just thrilled by the abundance of people, like, 'Whoa!' I knew that was special."

Still, there have been instances when the underlying, usually unspoken, tensions that lurk within the allegedly "color-blind" modern-day blues circuit have made themselves manifest. One, in fact, occurred during Ronnie's very first tour with his father: "[Our] first gig was opening for George Thorogood," he told journalist Rosalind Cummings-Yeates. "A week or two into the tour, we were booed off the stage. They came to see George. I was angry, but my dad said, 'Don't get mad; you learn from this. [Thorogood] was introducing us to another audience. . . . It's a process.'"[3]

That's not to say, though, that Lonnie Brooks always took such insults lying down. When they came from upstart musicians, his reaction could be quite different:

A white group—I ain't even going to say who it was—this popular white group, they didn't want my dad. We had done a show, like in Texas somewhere, and they were like, "Get everybody off the stage! Including Lonnie!" And my dad was kind of hurt about that. Like, "Wait a minute, man—y'all gonna kick me off the stage?" So we got down to Mississippi where we used to do the Greenville Blues Festival down there. Bobby Rush was on the show, Betty Wright, my dad, and this same white group is at this festival, they're headlining it, and it's all blacks [in the audience], opposed to the other one, [which] was all white.

And we did our show, and they embraced us, and of course Bobby came up and did his thing, and then this group came up. And [the audience] were looking at them like, "Who are you guys? This ain't the blues. Who is these white guys up here?" And they start leaving. And [by] the third song—"We gonna get Lonnie Brooks up here! C'mon Lonnie! Get up here!" And my dad, "Na-a-h-h, you got it, man. Remember y'all kicked me off the stage? So y'all got it!" I think he did go up and jam with them anyway, but that's the first time I recognized that, okay, there's a difference here. There is a difference.

Those incidents, of course, occurred before Ronnie left his father's band and went out on his own; it's conceivable that things have mellowed since then, maybe even in the South. A more pressing issue, in Ronnie's view, is how to create music that not only bridges various aesthetic/cultural divides, but might also make "the blues"—not just as a musical genre or even several genres, but as an idea worthy of honor and respect—viable again among mainstream African American listeners:

That's a heavy question. I think it will never die, first of all, because there's always someone that we probably don't even know of that's doing it; they're just not out there yet, and it's going to come a time that they're going to get that platform and deliver the truth—the authentic, the real. There's always going to be somebody that likes the blues if you play it at the right time. Any time you're speaking the truth, the truth gon' find the truth.

But it's hard for an African American that's growing up in the ghetto to adapt to the blues and take it on as a career; you've got to be adapted to it and love it enough to want to do that. But the inspiration to want to do that is going to be gone, because you're trying—your whole thoughts and everything is to get out of the ghetto. Now! Right now! I can't wait! Whereas if you consider doing blues for a living, it's a long-traveled road you got to go through to even get close to being successful. If you don't give an artist a chance, they lose it. The determination breaks down, like, "Forget it, man, I have to take care of my family." That's why it goes back to the hip-hop artists. They're getting their money now, they're getting out of the ghetto. That's what they want.

Ronnie praises labels like Alligator, which played such an important role in kickstarting his father's latter-day career, for helping keep the music commercially

Ronnie Baker Brooks (R) with Donald Kinsey, benefit for 12-year-old Jameson Stokes, House of Blues Chicago, 2018.

viable while allowing at least some younger black artists to break out of local anonymity and garner "mainstream" (usually meaning "white") acceptance. "[Owner] Bruce Iglauer is a soldier," he attests. "He's a soldier, man. For him to be around forty-five years [Iglauer founded Alligator in 1971]—that says a lot, right there, because at one time it wasn't nothing else happening in the blues but Alligator Records. He just signed Toronzo Cannon, he just signed Jarekus Singleton, he signed Selwyn Birchwood. Then of course, Delmark [which boasts a largely African American blues roster marketed—yet again—to an almost entirely white audience] got Mike Wheeler and Omar Coleman, Sharon Lewis . . . so that helps keep the ball rolling."

At the same time, it's profoundly ironic that in today's blues world, "cross-over" can often mean expanding one's listenership from a *white* audience to a *black* one—the opposite of what it used to mean. With that in mind, Ronnie finds encouragement in the work of some of Chicago's younger black blues artists. He cites vocalist/guitarist Melody Angel, who is still in her twenties ("Good songs, good message. She's got all those [stylistic] elements in there, and I think that's what captures the younger people's ears that's fed up with what they've been hearing. It's definitely a bridge there, and she's probably helping to build it") and the even younger Jamiah Rogers ("Someone needs to sign this dude, man—he's incredible, how he can touch them kids his age, that look like him") as two who have especially impressed him.

Meanwhile, embracing both synchrony and contradiction, Ronnie continues to honor his father's memory on the contemporary circuit, pushing his music into new directions even as he welcomes the opportunity to work with earnest white revivalists like Todd Mohr along with carriers of the blues legacy like Mud Morganfield and Billy Branch. Most importantly, his optimism remains girded by a refusal to succumb to bitterness or cynicism. In songs like "Times Have Changed," "Doing Too Much," and "Bring Back the Love," he'll serve up denunciations of social inequality, urban blight, and the soul-killing ennui of twenty-first-century life; at the same time, though, he'll declare his determination to "Turn a Bad into a Positive" and, in the juker's anthem "Long Story Short," stare down despair by having "a drink or two" and going out to "hear the band play that groove that I choose," leaving no doubt that the twin bulwarks of faith and music—especially the timeless, affirming power of the blues—can provide a key to redemption, or at least survival.

"I can't stop," he affirms. "I got to keep going. When you get bitter, it gives the thing strength. It's like a cancer; it takes over you; that's detrimental. I've learned, and I'm learning—I'll just be fifty—I'm learning that in order to forgive, and this goes with race, this goes with love, across the board, you have to learn to forgive in order to heal. And the blues is a healer."

PART IV

Heirs Apparent

This section could just as easily have been titled "Clubbing around Chicago." Casting as wide a stylistic net as possible, I have tried to give a good overview of what the contemporary Chicago scene looks and sounds like on any given night (as the city's Convention & Tourism Bureau likes to boast, Chicago hosts a blues festival 365 days a year—and for once, the hype is pretty much justified).

I have tried, first and foremost, to include working musicians who are direct family members of older-generation blues artists—"Inheritors," in other words, of a legacy that is more than merely musical. However, many of the artists included here aren't from blues families; they came into the music the way almost anyone else might—through being inspired by, and emulating, what they heard on radio or in recordings; meeting and being taught by elders intent on passing it on; realizing that this music was their passion and their calling. (In the interest of avoiding redundancy and conserving space, I have chosen not to include anyone I profiled in my previous books; Lurrie Bell, as nominative leader of the Bell Dynasty, is the sole—and partial—exception.) Once again, the listing is far from comprehensive; like the lover in song who promises that "just a little bit" will have you coming back for more, I intend this as a taste, which I hope will motivate readers to explore the music further in all its evolving richness and depth.

Lurrie Bell & the Bell Dynasty

The late harmonica maestro Carey Bell learned his craft from elders such as Big Walter Horton and then passed it on to younger acolytes such as Billy Branch and his own son Steve. But it's another son, guitarist Lurrie, profiled in my previous book, *Chicago Blues: Portraits and Stories*, who has thus far been the dominant Bell voice. When Lurrie was a young boy, his father organized a Bell family band, waggishly dubbed the Ding Dongs, which consisted of Lurrie on guitar and Steve on harmonica, along with bassist Tyson and drummer James. Unfortunately, though, Lurrie isn't the only Bell whose career has been sidelined at times by personal crises, and it's been only recently that the four have been able to re-coalesce into a working unit. Their 2018 debut, *Tribute to Carey Bell* (Delmark), thus represents a triumph both musical and personal. The disk also features contributions from guitarist Eddie Taylor Jr., Billy Branch, pianist Sumito "Ariyo" Ariyoshi (a veteran of Branch's Sons of Blues), and harpist Charlie Musselwhite.

Whether the Bell Dynasty members will be able to sustain themselves long enough to become a regular working unit is unclear; their appearance at the 2018 Chicago Blues Festival was encouraging, but there haven't been a lot of gigs since then, and no tours have been announced. Nonetheless, even if they end up being little more than a "one-disk wonder," the Bells can take comfort in knowing that that disk comes close to being a modern-day Chicago blues masterpiece.

Wayne Baker Brooks

Like his brother Ronnie, Wayne Baker Brooks updates the blues tradition he gleaned from their father, Lonnie Brooks, with elements drawn from rock, R&B, and hip-hop. His output under his own name thus far has consisted of two CDs on his own Blues Island imprint: 2004's *Mystery*, and the 2012 EP *Tricks up My Sleeves*.

Wayne favors atmospheric, studio-enhanced aural settings that often sound as if he's invoking the old trope of the Louisiana blues man possessed by spirits (a feeling intensified by offerings like "Changeling" and "I Can Read Your Mind"—both from *Tricks*—and the title tune of *Mystery*), even as virtually everything else about him defies tradition. He favors crunching on-the-one drum patterns; his melodic lines owe more to power-pop and heavy metal than 12-bar blues; and his leads erupt with an explosive, molten-lava tone. As if to remove all doubt, the presence on his recordings of guests like turntablist D.J. Ajax and hip-hoppers Twista and GLC—along with roots/future fusionist Sugar Blue on harmonica—makes clear Wayne's determination to proclaim his modernist pedigree, challenging everything preservationists hold sacred, relishing his role as disrupter of boundaries and stereotypes.

Toronzo Cannon

Born in Chicago in 1968, Toronzo Cannon cultivated a love for music early on, but he didn't actually come into the blues until he was in his twenties, and even then it was by a circuitous route. Inspired by John Cougar's power-pop balladry, he began playing acoustic guitar, and from there he went on to immerse himself in the work of rootsier artists like Bob Marley, as well as classic blues-rockers such as Jimi Hendrix.

As he began to participate in local jam sessions, the blues became more paramount in his music ("When I had a jam to go to," he has remembered, "it would be a blues jam"); honing both his chops and his blues focus, he began working steadily as both leader and sideman, and in 2007 he self-released his debut CD, *My Woman*. Since then, he's recorded for both Delmark (*Leaving Mood* in 2007; *John the Conquer Root* in 2013) and Alligator (2016's *The Chicago Way*), and in the process he's shown remarkable development, harnessing his neo-Hendrix bombast with increasing mastery. He has also widened his emotional range: The ballad "When Will You Tell Him about Me," the centerpiece of his Alligator release, found him summoning a soulful suavity reminiscent of Johnnie Taylor or Bobby "Blue" Bland.

Omar Coleman

Omar Coleman, one of Chicago's few younger-generation blues harpists, cites influences as diverse as John Lee Williamson (the original, prewar "Sonny Boy"), Little Walter, Junior Wells, Bobby Rush, and modernist innovator Sugar Blue. He recorded his first CD under his own name, *West Side Wiggle*, on the Honeybee label in 2011; he's cut several more since then, including a live recording issued on Delmark in 2016.

Although not the iconoclast Sugar Blue is, Omar can be a formidable improviser: He'll lock into a 12-bar shuffle, then switch gears and scoot through a series of boogity-foot rhythmic variations, as his improvised melodic lines both challenge and complement the song's melodic structure. As a singer, he summons both machismo and vulnerability, and his songwriting ranges from fresh takes on themes like wrong-doing women caught in the act to more sophisticated meditations on love and loss (such as the urban-contemporary styled "I Was a Fool" from 2015's *Born & Raised*, on Delmark).

Omar Coleman's music is an un–self-conscious mix of enthusiasm, passion, and worldliness, and it bodes well for both the future of the harmonica and the ongoing evolution of the blues itself.

Tomiko Dixon

As monumental a figure as Willie Dixon was, his progeny have garnered only modest success on their own—his son Freddie currently plays bass for the Original Chicago Blues All Stars; another son, keyboardist Butch (née Arthur), was killed in an auto crash in 2004 while working as a bodyguard for Chicago

Tomiko Dixon, Muddy Waters tribute, Harold Washington Cultural Center, Chicago, 2018.

rapper Twista. In recent years, Dixon's granddaughter Tomiko has arisen as the latest aspirant to the throne. She has recorded several albums in digital format including *My Inheritance*, *Blues around the World*, and the EP-length *Living in the Blues*.

Tomiko's voice, at least on record, tends toward delicacy—somewhat anomalous for a blues singer—although she brings an encouragingly sassy grit to the funkified "You Don't Want to Mess with the IRS," which she added to her online catalogue in 2017. Even more impressive was her earlier "Living in the Hood" from *My Inheritance*, a straight-ahead rap outing that highlighted her rhythmic dexterity and unforced emotional intensity. It may be, in fact, that despite her fealty to the Dixon blues lineage, her strongest potential lies in hip-hop—like her grandfather, she's a skilled wordsmith with a powerful social conscience, and that genre could be the perfect vehicle for her to showcase these gifts to their best advantage.

Honeydew

Vocalist Honeydew came by her stage moniker and her vocation almost as birthrights: Her given name is Melon Greene (after her mother's favorite fruit), and she grew up in Chicago surrounded by music. Her father, Albert Greene, was a musician, and he began taking her to concerts, African festivals, and other cultural events when she was a young girl. Her first public performance came at age seven, when she sang the National Anthem for her school assembly, and by the time she'd finished grammar school, she'd already set her sights on a musical career.

Honeydew's style combines Aretha Franklin's churchy muscularity ("Rock Steady" is one of her show-stoppers) with a dexterous, bright-timbred pop sensibility all her own, with a dollop of jazz-honed phrasing and harmonic adventurousness thrown in. In performance, she's both fervid (her reading of Jill Scott's "The Way" masterfully melds soap-opera bathos with slice-of-life storytelling) and flamboyant, as she punctuates her delivery with sassy hip-shakes, full-body rolls, and quick-step dance moves, apparently as delighted and entertained by her music (and herself) as her audience. She unerringly chooses tightly disciplined, versatile musicians to accompany her, and her shows—often costarring vocalist Theo Huff, a soul-blues wunderkind I profiled briefly in my previous book, *Southern Soul-Blues*—are some of the local scene's most entertaining and well-crafted.

Syleena Johnson

Mainstream blues and soul fans probably know Syleena Johnson's name primarily because her father is Chicago soul/R&B/blues legend Syl Johnson; her 1995 recording debut was alongside him on *This Time Together by Father and Daughter* (Twinight). In subsequent years, though, she's been a force in mainstream R&B, landing several chart hits and working alongside such luminaries as R. Kelly, Busta Rhymes, and Kanye West.

Nonetheless, she's never abandoned her roots: Her voice, supple yet grainy, shows her deep-soul inheritance, and throughout her career her songs have been distinguished by a courageous willingness to express vulnerability—emotional and otherwise—in a genre where postmodernist ironic detachment and blunt aggression have increasingly become state of the art.

Rebirth of Soul, produced by Syl and released in 2017 on Shanachie, returns Syleena to her deep-soul birthright. Backed by old-school production and arrangements, she covers a set of classic-era soul and R&B hits, breathing new and urgent life into such standards as Etta James's "I'd Rather Go Blind," Betty Everett's "There'll Come a Time," and Aretha Franklin's "Chain of Fools." Her father's anthemic "Is It Because I'm Black?" becomes an even more ominous mediation in her hands—reminding us that the anger and frustration borne of racial injustice still seethes, and the eruption of what James Baldwin called "the fire next time" may be closer than we think.

Vance Kelly

Guitarist Vance Kelly's recorded catalogue on the Wolf label provides a decent taste of what he's capable of, but to really appreciate him you need to capture him live. At any given moment, he's likely to segue from a blues standard into a '60s-era Chicago dance classic like "Twine Time," then explode into a high-energy rendition of Stephen Stills's "Love the One You're With" or Santana's "Black Magic Woman," fire off an original 12-bar blues or two from one of his CDs, and then veer back into a funk-charged James Brown medley or a tribute to Marvin Gaye. He might also detour down South for a couple of Johnnie Taylor or Z. Z. Hill soul-blues chestnuts, and then top everything off with an extended, psychedelia-infused workout on "Purple Rain"—and that's just the first set.

His Back Street Band, meanwhile, is skintight and responsive, able to shift gears and take off in whatever direction he chooses, often apparently without warning. They're all first-rate soloists, too, adding yet another implement to Vance's already daunting musical toolkit. For my money, he and his crew are the finest club band on the circuit (Source One, profiled later, is at least their match musically, but they usually back up guest vocalists—these guys are a self-contained unit), and they seem only to get better with time.

Masheen Company

Keyboardist Ronnie Hicks and his Masheen Co. are one of Chicago's most highly esteemed blues/soul/R&B backup aggregations, having recorded and/or performed with artists as varied as the late Artie "Blues Boy" White, Cicero Blake, Nellie "Tiger" Travis, and bar-band blues-rocker Jimmy Nick. This means, of course, that versatility is their stock in trade, and on their own shows they play it like an instrument. They'll segue from a 12-bar Chicago blues standard through a series of deep-soul houserockers and hard-funk workouts into a pop-glitzed cover of a Culture Club chestnut, all without missing a beat. But however antic their imagination or irreverent their rule-breaking and genre-jumping, they never lose sight of the commitment and musical excellence that remain their most distinctive asset and calling card.

Melody Angel

At her best, young singer-guitarist Melody Angel comes on like a one-woman Black Rock Coalition. Updating ideas drawn from blues and old-school rock & roll with a hard-rock ferocity that never crosses into overkill, she also incorporates generous helpings of R&B, hip-hop, and Tracy Chapman–esque balladry into her style.

Melody's emotional range is both wide and deep, intensified by her socially conscious lyric sensibility. She inhabits her politically charged vignettes of struggle and survival as one who's lived them, compelling her listeners to experience them the same way, with no room for liberal bromides or ironic detachment ("I dare you judge me / in your glass house," she snarls in "Cease Fire," on her 2016 CD *In This America*). But she won't give in to cynicism or despair: As she sings in "Rebel," from the same disk: "I got the looks, I got the clothes, I got the sex appeal. . . . I'm a rebel with a cause and it feels so good!"

Recently, Melody (that's her real name) has expanded her artistic scope to include both theater and film. In 2018, she appeared in a Chicago production of

Melody Angel playing the
National Anthem, Chicago
Blues Festival, 2017.

Suzan-Lori Parks's *Father Comes Home from the Wars* at the Goodman Theatre, and
she was also selected to play one of the leads in the Court Theatre's 2019 production of Ntozake Shange's award-winning *For Colored Girls Who Have Considered
Suicide / When the Rainbow Is Enuf*. Also in 2018, she starred in the independently
produced film *Knockout*, the story of a young African American woman who faces
down her family's disapproval of her passion for boxing. The film, directed by
Erik Scanlon, concluded with a searing rendition of Melody's blues-rock anthem
"Always on Me." It was named Best Picture at the 14th Annual 48 Hour Chicago
Film Project, and Melody's performance earned her Best Lead Actress recognition at the 2018 Filmapalooza competition in Orlando. In May of 2019, *Knockout*
was screened at the world-renowned Cannes Film Festival in France.

If the blues is to survive and grow as a contemporary African American art
form, it will take artists like Melody Angel to make it happen.[1]

Big James Montgomery and the Chicago Playboys

The title of their 1998 debut, *Funkin' Blues*, could stand as a manifesto for trombonist Big James Montgomery and his Chicago Playboys. Originally inspired by Fred Wesley and other James Brown/P-Funk horn men, Montgomery was also an avid jazz listener when he was young, idolizing such masters of tone, articulation, and dexterity as J. J. Johnson. Like his idols in the JBs, he eventually fused his jazz chops with his love for funk and soul.

The original Playboys played behind vocalist Johnny Christian, a West Side mainstay until his death in 1993. After that, they struck out on their own, ramped up the funk, and eventually became one of the most exciting and intense (both musically and emotionally) on the Chicago circuit. Montgomery's arrangements are intricately textured, yet they never forsake the band's trademark danceability and forward-thrusting drive (even when they take on a hard-rock warhorse like Deep Purple's "Smoke on the Water," an unexpected highlight of 2012's live *The Big Payback* on Blind Pig).

In a guitars-and-harmonicas obsessed blues town like Chicago, a horn band like the Playboys often doesn't get its due, but in fact they rank among the city's finest—and funkiest—blues-based aggregations.

Mud Morganfield

Mud Morganfield's vocal delivery is so reminiscent of his father, Muddy Waters, that it often sounds as if he's channeling the man directly. Born Lawrence Williams in Chicago in 1954, he grew up surrounded by music, but he didn't consider making it a career until he saw a 1997 PBS broadcast of a Kennedy Center tribute to Muddy, which included his brother Big Bill along with a host of blues and rock celebrities. At that moment, he has said, he realized he should have been on that stage, too. With the encouragement of veterans like vocalist Mary Lane and guitarist Bobby "Slim" James, he soon began to perform at various locations on the West Side, not far from where he lived.

In 2008, Mud released a self-produced CD titled *Fall Waters Fall*; he followed that up in 2012 with *Son of the Seventh Son* on the Severn label. His latest solo outing, 2018's *They Call Me Mud*, finds him dipping into some tantalizing pop/R&B and soul-blues grooves, but his calling card is still "that" voice—invoking, almost eerily, the spirit of one of the blues' most fabled creative geniuses.

Mud Morganfield, Chicago Blues
Festival, 2017.

Jo Jo Murray

Jo Jo Murray complements his gritty-sweet baritone with a guitar style that's
sharp-toned and supple, full of shimmering bends and nimble-fingered runs. His
repertoire, both borrowed and original, ranges from Chicago "soft soul" through
blues and soul-blues to Brook Benton/Lou Rawls–influenced pop-soul balladry. He's been recording since the early 1970s; nonetheless—perhaps because
in performance he sometimes over-relies on his trick of covering standards in
spot-on imitations of the masters' voices—he's been mostly consigned to "local
legend" status.

That may be changing: A few years ago, he signed with Coday Records,
the Memphis-based label headed by Anna Coday, wife of the late vocalist Bill
Coday. His initial release for Coday, 2015's *From the Inside*, found him hewing to

Jo Jo Murray and bassist Joe Pratt (Source One Band), Odyssey East, Chicago, 2018.

a contemporary southern soul-blues sound; his themes ranged from the usual dispatches from the front lines of the erotic battlefield to thoughtful meditations on contemporary life as exemplified by the title tune, written and sung as a young man's letter from prison to his wife and family. Since its release, he's been touring more (and farther) than he has in years—an encouraging sign that he may finally garner the wider recognition he has long deserved.

The Kinsey Report

In the old days, guitarist Donald Kinsey, along with his brothers Kenneth (on bass) and Ralph (on drums), would lock himself patiently into a grinding postwar Chicago shuffle as their father, Lester "Big Daddy" Kinsey, kicked off the show with his gravel-voiced renditions of standard-issue blues themes, patterned after Muddy Waters and other vintage-era blues pioneers. When Big Daddy exited the stage, though, it was throwdown time—even as traditionalist-minded aficionados clutched their ears in horror, the younger Kinseys and guitarist Ron Prince, their partner in crime, would explode into an onslaught of hard-edged funk, screaming blues-rock fusillades, and proto-gangsta back-alley swagger.

Big Daddy passed away in 2001, and since then the boys have taken their music even further (Prince eventually left to join James Cotton for a few years, and he has since formed his own band). Their recorded legacy is somewhat sparse—2013's downloadable EP, *Standing (I'll Be)* was their first since the late '90s—and through the years they've encountered various roadblocks due to health problems and other personal issues, but at their best they remain among the most incendiary acts in blues. It may take big ears and an open mind (to say nothing of galvanized feet and a strong backbone) to meet them on their own terms, but doing so can be rewarding and deeply satisfying.

Mzz Reese

The neighborhood clubs of Chicago's South and West Sides are no longer the incubators of blues talent that they used to be, but there are still some artists on that circuit who have the potential to break out into wider recognition. One

Mzz Reese, Motor Row Brewing, Chicago, 2018.

is vocalist Mzz Reese, a sultry-toned alto who cites the late Denise LaSalle as her primary inspiration. Reese's song "Cookies," a sexual throwdown in the LaSalle mode ("If you don't treat my cookies right / I'll be dippin' someone else's milk") is the title tune of her self-released 2015 debut CD, and it's already become her signature.

Nonetheless, audiences in the clubs she usually works tend to prefer covers of well-known standards, so that's what Reese gives them. To her credit, though, she does her best to choose songs—the Pointer Sisters' "Fire," Gwen McCrae's "Rockin' Chair"—that haven't been overdone, along with guaranteed crowd pleasers like "I Can't Stand the Rain" or any of the several offerings from LaSalle's songbook that she includes in most of her shows. She's a straightforward stylist, preferring nuance and subtlety to pyrotechnics, but—no doubt drawing on her gospel background—she infuses everything she sings with fervor. She has recently assembled a new band, her strongest and most versatile yet, which she has dubbed Reese's Pieces, and together they've already become a semiregular opening attraction at Buddy Guy's Legends—an encouraging sign for the future.

Original Chicago Blues All Stars

In 2016, three members of Willie Dixon's last working band—drummer Jimmy Tillman, bassist Freddie Dixon (Willie's son), and guitarist John Watkins—reunited with the purpose of honoring the great man's legacy and helping to cultivate a new generation of blues enthusiasts. Tillman and Dixon continue to form the group's nucleus; as of this writing, Michael Damani plays lead guitar, Watkins having returned to Detroit to pursue his own career. Their musical fare remains heavy on postwar standards with a few originals and soul/soul-blues offerings thrown in, all played solidly in the old style, although Damani's fretwork adds a bracing modernist tinge.

The All Stars wrestle with the same paradox that confronts other blues roots-revivalists: Dedicated to carrying on and preserving this inextricable facet of African American cultural history, they play mostly to white audiences in primarily white venues. It becomes even more bedeviling in light of their 2018 single "Black Bags," Tillman's anguished jeremiad against the genocidal toll taken by gun violence in poor and black neighborhoods. Augmented by Merwin "Harmonica" Hinds, saxophonist Maurice John Vaughn (better known as a guitar player but excellent here), and violinist Phyllis Calderon, it exemplifies Tillman's (and his

Freddie Dixon with the Original Chicago Blues All Stars, Chicago Blues Hall of Fame induction ceremony, Buddy Guy's Legends, Chicago, 2017.

bandmates') commitment to cultural and community awareness, even if too few in the intended community will probably ever hear it.

Chick Rodgers

It takes a pretty audacious diva-in-waiting to silence Patti LaBelle with a rendition of LaBelle's own best-known song, but that's exactly what Melvia "Chick" Rodgers did one night in Memphis in 1988. Chick, a Memphis native who had already made her mark as a gospel vocalist and earned acclaim around town as lead singer in the group Clockwise, was sitting quietly in the audience at LaBelle's show when Patti decided to spice things up by asking if there was anyone there brave enough to come up and sing. After a friend literally picked her up and thrust her onto the stage, Chick grabbed the mic and tore into a version of LaBelle's classic "Lady Marmalade" that wrecked the house and left Patti wide-eyed in amazement. The next day, photos of the diminutive young aspirant and the astounded-looking superstar were all over the Memphis media.

Chick moved to Chicago not long after that, and although she has recently returned to Memphis, Chicagoans still consider her an adopted homegirl. Blessed with a vocal prowess as apparently effortless as it is spellbinding—her burnished, church-honed timbre, her multioctave range, and her ability to segue from whispered intimacy to soul-bearing testimonials are immediately recognizable and utterly distinctive—she prides herself on her versatility. On 2014's five-song EP *This Kind of Love*, for instance, backed by musicians ranging from a string quartet to free-jazz saxophone master Ernest Khabeer Dawkins, she transformed herself into a full-fledged art-music chanteuse. But she always ends up returning to the fervid blend of gospel-infused deep soul and blues that's been her trademark since the beginning. Given the breadth of her talent, it's almost unbelievable that a major label hasn't picked up on her—by rights, she should be an internationally acclaimed blues (or soul-blues) star by now.

Jamiah Rogers

If anyone today personifies the old saying "born to the blues," it's Jamiah Rogers. Mentored by his father, drummer/guitarist Tony Rogers, Jamiah was playing drums by the time he was three years old. He recorded his first CD, 2002's *In the Pocket*, when he was seven; as the years progressed, he began to focus more on the guitar, and at sixteen he formed the blues power trio, Jamiah on Fire & the Red Machine, which he has fronted ever since.

He has also recorded several more CDs; the most recent, 2017's *Blues Superman*, shows him melding his primary influences—Hendrix, Albert King, Stevie Ray Vaughan, et al.—into a style that's not yet entirely personalized but generally avoids both imitation and overkill (rare in a Hendrix acolyte, especially one so young). He's a promising lyricist, his voice becomes more mature and nuanced every time out, and now that he's of age he can command stages at grown-up venues like Buddy Guy's Legends without his father looking out at him from behind the trap set. It's too early to saddle Jamiah with an unnecessarily burdensome appellation like "future of the blues," but his presence on the scene—and his ongoing upward trajectory as an artist—is certainly cause for optimism.

Source One Band

If there's such a thing as a sidemen's supergroup, Source One comes close to being it. Between bassist/bandleader Joe Pratt, lead guitarist Sir Walter Scott, and keyboardist Stan Banks, along with any of several first-call drummers they regularly employ, the list of major artists they've performed and/or recorded with is virtually endless—start with Koko Taylor, the Chi-Lites, the Jackson 5, Tyrone Davis, Otis Clay, Denise LaSalle, Johnnie Taylor, Artie "Blues Boy" White, Willie Clayton, Latimore, and go on from there. It's not surprising, then, that they're able to make almost any vocalist sound as if he or she has been their personal headliner for years.

These days they're based at the Odyssey East on South Torrence Ave., where they back up hard soul-blues belter New Orleans Beau, along with a seemingly endless parade of guests both famous and less known. Pratt, quite literally leading from behind, sets the tone with his affable stage presence—it's almost impossible for even the most unexpected (or inebriated) onstage intruder to ruffle his composure—and the overall impression they give is that of a vintage-era show band, dedicated and professional yet loose enough to imbue their music with the kind of swaggering ebullience that can still feel like the epitome of hipness when the groove gets good and the solos start to lock in.

Tre'

"One name, one game—nothing but the blues." That's how vocalist/guitarist Tre' introduces himself in performance, and it's an image he cultivates further on his recordings. He debuted in 1996 with *Delivered for Glory—Reclaiming the Blues* (Wolf), which he followed up with *Blues Knock'n Baby* on JSP the next year. (The title of 2011's *I'm through with the Blues*, again on Wolf, was intended to be ironic—his grudge is against the way bluesmen, especially black bluesmen, are exploited and mistreated, not the music itself.)

The son of the late singer/guitarist L. V. Banks, Tre' was born in Grenada, Mississippi, and raised on Chicago's South Side. For all his protestations of rootedness, though, his first musical experience was with a garage rock band. It wasn't until after being reunited with his father in the mid-'70s and working alongside him at various South Side locations that he recast himself as a bluesman and honed his distinctively percussive lead technique—each note is hammered out fiercely, defining itself in space. The results can be a bit choppy, but he's in command of sufficient melodic acumen to construct solos that bristle with both logic and ferocity. His singing, laced with the same insouciant machismo he radiates on stage and off, adds an additional element of eros-charged intensity.

Willie White

Willie White has played keyboards and/or sung background for several notable blues and southern soul artists over the years—he was Bobby Rush's musical director for a time—but as a frontline vocalist he remains virtually unknown outside the circuit of Chicago clubs, primarily on the South and West Sides, where he usually performs. Recently, though, he signed with Coday Records in Memphis, and along with fellow Chicagoan Jo Jo Murray he's already been featured on several of the label's package show tours (primarily regional excursions in the South), so his territory shows tantalizing signs of expanding.

Willie's voice is thick and muscular, resonant with passion, augmented with a tightly controlled vibrato and an armamentarium of shadings. As a balladeer, he conveys deep feeling with his choked gasps and gruff, blues-inflected murmurs before finally ascending into soaring testimonials of desire and release. On more up-tempo fare, meanwhile, such as his trademark, "Taking Me for Granted," and the title tune of his debut (and so far, only) full-length CD, 2008's self-released *Party Hardy*, his crisp enunciation and rhythmic sureness create an aura of good-natured machismo along with a street-toughened determination to stare down sorrow and hard times. A physically compact man with an impish smile, he's a sexy entertainer who often concludes his shows surrounded by women jockeying for position to dance as close to him as possible—a bit of unexpurgated chitlin' circuit funk transplanted to the hard-bitten urban setting of Chicago.

Postscript

"Our Spirit Makes Us the Blues"

'm guessing some readers will have been surprised, and maybe a little non-plussed, by at least a few of the names included here and in previous sections, and probably by some of the opinions expressed by the artists themselves over the course of this book. As the musicians' own stories should make clear, blues is one of those genres in which lively—often contentious—debates about legitimacy, appropriateness, and "authenticity" often seem to rage louder than the music itself.

But that, in fact, is part of the point. I have intentionally tried to recognize and encompass as wide an array of styles, genres, and opinions as possible, emphasizing once again the primary thesis of this book: the living blues tradition is a continuation of a cultural and historical legacy that remains vital, even as it changes and adapts in the face of changing mores and tastes. The multigenerational, multisubgenre perspective I've tried to employ here emphasizes this living tradition as a dynamic and flexible one, capable of maintaining both its cultural specificity and its universal humanistic appeal as it continues to widen its scope and its range among musicians and audiences, both locally and on the national and international levels. As vocalist Sharon Lewis, profiled in my earlier book, *Chicago Blues: Portraits and Stories*, has said: "It's all blues if it comes from the heart."

Open your heart, free your mind—Seek out, listen, and enjoy.

Notes

In several cases, I have included information here on musicians who were mentioned by some of the people profiled in this book. I have chosen to do this mostly for artists who (1) may not be well known to a general audience, and/or (2) are mentioned only in passing, but are significant to the story being told. More familiar names, or people who figure more prominently in the narrators' stories, are not annotated.

Introduction

The title quote is from the song "Dat Dere." Original melody by Bobby Timmons, lyrics by Oscar Brown Jr. © Nov. 15, 1960, Upam Music Co., a division of Gopam Enterprises, Inc.

1. This is not a new phenomenon. Robert Johnson, to cite only one well-known example, is known to have adapted his style and borrowed song ideas from such popular recording artists as Lonnie Johnson and Leroy Carr, as well as ragtime pianists and vaudeville entertainers. He most likely learned Skip James's "Devil Got My Woman," on which he based his famous "Hell Hound on My Trail," from a record. In 1960, when Jim Dickinson met jug band veteran Gus Cannon in Memphis, he was surprised to hear Cannon say that he'd learned his material "from the radio." While this wasn't literally the entire truth—the first commercial radio broadcast was in 1920, and a lot of Cannon's repertoire predated that—it indicated that even a "folk" musician like Cannon grew up attuned to popular culture and tastes, and had fashioned his own music accordingly (Gordon, *It Came from Memphis*, 78–79; Hay, ed., *Goin' Back to Sweet Memphis*.

2. Interview with the author, March 7, 2003. The quote originally appeared in Whiteis, *Chicago Blues: Portraits and Stories*, 189.

3. Lomax, *The Land Where the Blues Began*, 414.

4. Buddy Guy, interview with the author, January 2006. If further proof were needed, a song list from Memphis Minnie's 1940s-era performance repertoire, apparently in Minnie's own handwriting, includes such fare as "How High the Moon," "That's My Desire," "I Love You for Sentimental Reasons," "On the Sunny Side of the Street," and "Woody Woodpecker" (Garon and Garon, *Woman with Guitar*, 65–66; illustration no. 42).

5. Denise LaSalle, interview with the author, April 2017.

6. This issue has been addressed numerous times in the scholarly literature, as well as by many artists themselves. See, for instance, Barlow, *Looking Up at Down*; Bolden, *Afro-Blue*; Davis, *Blues Legacies and Black Feminism*; Finn, *The Bluesman*; Floyd, *The Power of Black Music*; Garon, *Blues and the Poetic Spirit*; Hay, "Introduction," in Hay, ed., *Goin' Back to Sweet Memphis*; Jones, *Blues People*; Murray, *Stomping the Blues*; Neal, *What the Music Said*; Oliver, *Blues Fell This Morning* and *The Story of the Blues*; Otis, *Upside Your Head!*; Emily Edward's chapter on singer/guitarist Chick Willis in Edwards, *Bars. Blues, and Booze*, 71–99; and Willis's own writings, "A Real Blues Artist and Inventor." Billy Branch, Sharon Lewis, Corey Harris, Chris Thomas King, Tré, the late Willie Dixon, and many other artists have expounded at length on this topic.

7. Chicago blues researcher and activist Janice Monti is conducting an ongoing survey of U.S. blues festivals, awards ceremonies, and Blues Society events. Data show that the percent of African American artists represented at these functions has steadily declined since 2012, with some festivals now featuring all-white lineups.

Part I. Bequeathers

The lyric quoted is from "Memo Blues" by Andrew "Big Voice" Odom, Leric Music, BMI. *Feel So Good!* Evidence ECD-6027-2, 1992.

James Cotton

I interviewed James Cotton in March of 2013 and followed that up with several email inquiries via Jacklyn Cotton for a profile that appeared as "James Cotton: I'm All Right with the Blues," 8–17. This chapter is derived from that article. Unless otherwise specified, all quotes here are from my interview with Cotton. I thank Marc Lipkin of Alligator Records, along with Jacklyn Cotton, for helping to arrange the interview.

Discographical information is from Whitburn, *Billboard Hot R&B Songs, 1942–2010 (6th Edition)*; I thank Bill Dahl, Scott Dirks, and Tom Morris (aka Illinois Slim) for further discographical assistance. Additional information on Cotton's recordings for Sun was taken from the website *706 Union Avenue Sessions*, http://www.706unionavenue.nl/. I also thank Jacklyn Cotton for her kindness and support.

1. PBS. *American Roots Music*.

2. Connor and Neff, *Blues*, 22.

3. Ibid., 117.

4. Ibid., 23.

5. PBS. *American Roots Music*.

6. Connor and Neff, 38.

7. PBS. *American Roots Music*.

Eddie Shaw

I interviewed Eddie Shaw at his home in Chicago on April 9, 2016, and followed that up with several phone calls over the next few weeks. Unless otherwise specified, all quotes here are from those discussions. I thank Bill Dahl for assistance with Eddie Shaw's early discography. I also consulted the website 45cat (http://www.45cat.com/artist/eddie-shaw) for documentation of his early recording activity. Howlin' Wolf discographical information is from Segrest and Hoffman, *Moanin' at Midnight.*

1. Oliver Sain became one of the twin pillars, along with Ike Turner, of the torrid 1950s/'60s-era St. Louis R&B scene. Willie Dotson played on sessions for the Trumpet label; he eventually switched to bass and participated in some important dates in St. Louis with Ike Turner, Little Milton, and Fontella Bass, among others. Otis Green went on to record with Willie Love and Sonny Boy Williamson; C. W. Tate did some work at Sun, most notably with Little Milton.

2. This phrase, which Shaw apparently remembered as a song title, is actually a verse that occurs in Booker's "No Riding Blues," recorded in 1952 and released on the California-based Blues & Rhythm label. There's no sax on that record. The session Eddie Shaw participated in appears to have been lost. He has remembered the other band members as bassist T. J. Green and drummer Junior Blackmon, along with Booker.

3. There were two clubs in that vicinity, close to each other: Frazier's K.O. Lounge (6229 S. Cottage Grove) and Joe's Los Angeles Show Bar (6223 S. Cottage Grove). The Pershing Hotel, which also housed several performance venues, was located nearby, at 64th and Cottage Grove. I thank one of the manuscript's reviewers for this clarifying information.

4. Bonner, "Eddie Shaw," 29.

5. Eddie doesn't remember the precise year he joined Wolf, but he does recall that Pat Hare was Muddy's guitarist when he quit Muddy's band. Hare left Muddy in the early '60s and moved to Minneapolis; he went to prison after killing his girlfriend, as well as the police officer who was called to the scene, in late 1963. Thus, it would have been before then that Eddie jumped from Muddy to Wolf.

6. Dahl, email to the author, June 30, 2017.

7. He remembers, for instance, that Denise LaSalle was singing with Otis Rush when he played sax in Rush's band; but she didn't begin singing professionally until 1964 or so, and for several years after that she worked mostly with her mentor, Billy "The Kid" Emerson.

8. Widely reported. Verified by Wolf's stepdaughter, Bettye Kelly, via email, July 10, 2017.

9. Jimmy "Fast Fingers" Dawkins, Delmark, 1969.

10. Some of these can be heard on Eddie's 1985 LP *King of the Road* on the Rooster Blues label.

11. At least one source—Wirz, "Magic Sam Discography" magisfrm.htm—cites three other songs recorded that day with Eddie at the helm, including one with the unlikely title "I'm Eddie Shaw from Chicago's West Side," but nothing is known about these tracks, if in fact they ever existed.

12. Most of the material Eddie recorded with Magic Sam has been made available over the years. Previously unissued tracks from the sessions for *Black Magic* (along with *West*

Side Soul, Sam's other now-classic Delmark LP, on which Eddie did not participate), as well as "Lookin' Good" and "I Feel So Good" from Eddie and Sam's first in-studio pairing in 1966, appear on 1989's *The Magic Sam Legacy* (Delmark). "Lookin' Good" and "Blues for the West Side," are included on Eddie's 1985 Rooster Blues LP, *King of the Road*. Two more songs from the 1966 session, "Bad Luck Blues" and "That's Why I'm Crying," along with (yet again) the two Colt sides, appear on the unimaginatively titled *Sweet Home Chicago*, a 1969 Delmark anthology. In 2016, Delmark reissued *Black Magic* on a "Deluxe" CD that featured alternate takes and two previously unreleased tracks from the original *Black Magic* session.

13. Email to the author, August 28, 2017.

14. Bonner, "Eddie Shaw."

15. Segrest and Hoffman (*Moanin' at Midnight*) give the date as June 1975; other sources have suggested a few years earlier. Guitarist/bassist Benny Turner relates in his autobiography that Eddie was already running the 1815 club when Little Walter was still alive. Walter died in 1968, so this would push the club's history back several more years. However, it's likely that the club Turner remembers was actually the original Eddie's Place on Madison.

16. In late 1963 and early 1964 Delmark recorded Magic Sam at the 1400 W. Roosevelt Road location; some of these tracks were included, along with recordings made at the 1969 Ann Arbor Blues Festival, on the 1981 Delmark LP *Magic Sam Live*.

17. This would include, at the very least, their tracks on the anthology *Living Chicago Blues, Vol. 1* (Alligator, 1978); their full-length LPs *King of the Road* and *In the Land of the Crossroads* (Rooster Blues, 1985 and 1992); and *Can't Stop Now* (Delmark, 1997). *Still Riding High*, Eddie's 2012 project with a rotating assembly of no fewer than fifteen musicians and singers—all locked tightly into his groove—deserves mention (and a listen) as well.

18. "Stan Shaw." *Gargoyle Bob*.

Jimmy Johnson

I interviewed Jimmy Johnson at his home in Chicago on June 21, 2016. Unless otherwise specified, all quotes are from that interview. Discographical information on Syl Johnson is from Whitburn, *Billboard Hot R&B Songs*; I thank Bill Dahl and Bob Pruter for further discographical assistance. Additional information on the Thompson family in Holly Springs is from Eagle and LeBlanc, *Blues*.

1. "Thompson" is the family name. In 1959, when Jimmy's brother Syl released his first 45 on the Federal label, he discovered that he'd been billed as "Syl Johnson" on the record, and he adopted the new surname as his professional moniker. Jimmy soon followed suit, and he's been using the name ever since.

2. Dahl and O'Neal, "Jimmy Johnson," 15.

3. Ibid.

4. Ibid.

5. One of these early aggregations included his brother Mac on bass. Mac is best known today for his tenure with Magic Sam; in fact it was he who suggested Magic Sam's stage name to him, as a variation on Sam's birth name, Samuel Maghett.

6. Dahl and O'Neal, "Jimmy Johnson," 17.

7. In my previous book, *Southern Soul-Blues*, Bobby Rush remembered working some of those "curtain" gigs, and he also remembered being ordered to stay in the dressing room with his band.

8. The Festivals, which toured Europe annually between 1962 and 1970, in 1972, and then again in the early- and mid-1980s, brought such artists overseas as Dixon himself, Howlin' Wolf, T-Bone Walker, Muddy Waters, Memphis Slim, Sonny Boy Williamson, Victoria Spivey, and Big Mama Thornton, among many others. Attendees included Mick Jagger, Brian Jones, and other young Europeans who would soon initiate the blues-fueled rock & roll "British Invasion."

9. Some discographies, including Whitburn's, credit Jimmy with "Don't Answer the Door," a 1965 release on the Magnum label by "Jimmy Johnson and His Band Featuring Hank Alexander." That Jimmy Johnson, however, was actually a Los Angeles–based artist performing his original version of the song that's mostly known today for B.B. King's version, released on ABC the following year.

10. The alternate spellings "Jerrio" and "JerryO" were used at different times.

11. In Syl's defense, the Deacons' "Sock It to Me" was basically an instrumental version of his earlier hit (it could almost pass as a backing track), and he probably didn't want to give his signature tune away to another artist, even his own brother. Jimmy did not sing on the record, and his guitar leads are buried in the mix.

12. Dahl and O'Neal, "Jimmy Johnson," 18.

13. Ibid., 19.

14. Ibid., 20.

15. Ibid.

16. Renshaw, "2 Blues Band Members Die in Indiana Crash."

17. Actually, Jimmy was sixty years old when the accident occurred.

18. Essential reading: *Lost Highway: Journeys and Arrivals of American Musicians* (New York, Harper and Row, 1979). The most recent reprint is July 1999, by Back Bay Books.

19. The precise reason for the name change is unclear, but Bobby Rush's comment to me during an October 30, 2010, interview should not be discounted: "If it had been the Elvis Presley Awards, they'd never have changed it—never."

20. *Rock & Roll* was originally the name for the high-energy, small-group rhythm & blues, also called "jump blues," that arose as a popular African American youth music during the late 1940s and early '50s. White disc jockey Alan Freed, who is usually credited with popularizing the term, booked all-black "rock & roll" revues during the years before Elvis and his compatriots forged a new, country-infused version of the genre. This, of course, actually substantiates Jimmy's point: Not just the music, but the term *rock & roll* itself, was appropriated by whites in Elvis's wake.

Eddy Clearwater

I interviewed Eddy Clearwater at his home in Skokie, Illinois, on June 29, 2015, for a profile that appeared in *Living Blues* 238 (August 2015), 10–17. This chapter is derived from that article. Unless otherwise specified, all quotes here are from that interview and/or from several follow-up calls I made to Eddy and his wife, Renée. For additional information on Eddy Clearwater's career, I consulted Stiles, "Interview with . . . Eddy 'The Chief' Clearwater," and Cianci, "Eddy 'The Chief' Clearwater." I thank Jim O'Neal and Bill Dahl for assistance with discographical data and other historical details.

1. Moon, "Eddy Clearwater," 16.
2. Ibid., 21–22.
3. Dahl, "Eddy Clearwater."
4. Ibid.

Jimmy Burns

I interviewed Jimmy Burns at his home in Chicago on July 22, 2018; we followed that up with telephone conversations over the course of the next several weeks. Unless otherwise specified, all quotes are from these conversations. I also thank Bill Dahl and Bob Pruter for discographical assistance and for furthering my knowledge and understanding of the Chicago soul and doowop scenes in the 1950s and '60s.

1. "The Ritz We Ain't."
2. "It's Cotton-Pickin' Fun at the Shack Up Inn."
3. The history becomes a bit confusing at this point because the group changed their name several times over the course of the next few years. Jimmy remembers that by the time of the "Two Months out of School" sessions, they'd begun to call themselves the Regals (not to be confused with the Cleveland-based group who recorded for Aladdin and Atlantic in the mid-'50s).
4. Wright even released a couple of folk albums in the late 1950s and early '60s, featuring such offerings as "Come Back Liza," "Sinner Man," "Joshua Fought the Battle of Jericho," "Wagon Wheels," "Cotton Eyed Joe," and "Mah Lindy Lou."
5. Clearwater worked for a time in the early '60s with a Tex-Mex aggregation called Mando and the Chili Peppers.
6. Bassist Charles Colbert Jr. was originally a member of The Daylighters, who also recorded on Cobert Sr.'s Nike and Tip Top labels. He was later the only black member of Gary and the Knight Lites (fronted by guitarist/vocalist Gary Loizzo), who evolved into The American Breed. The American Breed, in turn, were the nucleus of the band that eventually became Rufus.
7. Sumsuch, "Rasputin Stash Founder Talks Reissue of Cult Classic Album." According to Coleman's remembrances, he was the Epics' drummer until he got drafted, and then he rejoined them after being discharged. Lamont Turner was apparently their percussionist in the interim.
8. The group was billed variously as Rasputin's Stash, r-Stash, and Rasputin Stash.
9. Jimmy participated in the 2018 project *Chicago Plays the Stones* (Raisin' Music), along with such blues stalwarts as John Primer, Billy Boy Arnold, Omar Coleman, and Carlos Johnson, among others. He contributed his version of "Dead Flowers" and appeared in a duet with Keith Richards on "Beast of Burden."

Part II. "Council of Elders"

1. An earlier version of the section on Billy Boy Arnold appeared in "The *Reader*'s Guide to the Chicago Blues Festival."

2. Interview with the author, January 13, 2010. The quote originally appeared in Whiteis, *Southern Soul-Blues*.

3. Christie. "Holly Is Reincarnation of Billie, Ella, et al."

4. An earlier version of the section on Otis Rush appeared in "The *Reader*'s Guide to the Chicago Blues Festival."

5. Byther Smith's birthplace has been variously listed as Jayess, Mississippi, and Monticello, Mississippi. Eagle and LeBlanc's research confirms his year of birth as 1932 instead of 1933, as has often been reported (Eagle and LeBlanc, *Blues)*.

Lil' Ed

I interviewed Lil' Ed at his home in Riverwoods, Illinois, on December 12, 2016. Unless otherwise specified, all quotes here are from that interview. Discographical information was gleaned from the websites of Alligator Records (https://www.alligator.com/artists /Lil-Ed-and-The-Blues-Imperials/) and Earwig records (https://www.earwigmusic .com/earwig-artists/lil-ed-williams). I thank Marc Lipkin and Bruce Iglauer of Alligator, along with Michael Frank from Earwig, for additional assistance with discographical details and other factual clarifications. I also thank both Marc Lipkin and Pamela Price Williams for helping to arrange the interview with Ed.

1. Koda, "J.B. Hutto Artist Biography."

2. "J.B. Hutto," *All about Blues Music.*

Big Bill Morganfield

I interviewed Big Bill Morganfield by phone on August 11, 2016. I followed that up with several additional phone calls to check facts and add details. These discussions formed the basis for a profile, "Big Bill Morganfield." This chapter is derived from that article. Unless otherwise specified, all quotes come from those discussions.

1. Gordon, *Can't Be Satisfied*, 178.

2. Ibid.

3. Ibid., 244.

4. Seigal, "A Little Muddy."

5. Gordon, *Can't Be Satisfied*, 244.

6. Ibid., 203.

7. Ibid., 260.

8. Seigal, "A Little Muddy."

9. Gordon, *Can't Be Satisfied*, 277.

Kenny Smith

I interviewed Kenny Smith on March 3, 2011, for a profile that appeared as "Kenny Smith: You Gotta Embrace It." This chapter is derived from that article. All quotes are from our interview. Historical information on Willie "Big Eyes" Smith and his work with Muddy Waters is from Gordon, *Can't Be Satisfied*.

The Taylor Family

"Remembering Eddie Taylor" is adapted from my liner notes to *The Eddie Taylor Blues Band*. Discographical information on Eddie Taylor's career is from "Eddie Taylor—Discography," and Wirz, "Jimmy Reed Discography." I thank Bill Dahl for further discographical assistance. Additional details of Eddie Taylor's experiences working with Jimmy Reed were gleaned from Romano, *Big Boss Man*. Information on Jimmy Reed's chart hits is from Whitburn, *Hot R&B Songs*.

Portions of "Demetria Taylor: Let Everybody Know What I Can Do" are adapted from my liner notes to the CD *Demetria Taylor: Bad Girl*. I interviewed Demetria on March 30, 2011, and again in February of 2018, at the club Blue Chicago. Unless otherwise specified, all quotes are from those interviews. Additional information on Demetria's recording session with Delmark was provided by Steve Wagner. I interviewed Eddie Taylor Jr. at his home in Maywood, Illinois, on January 30, 2018, and I followed that up with a telephone interview on February 3. Unless otherwise specified, all quotes are from those conversations. Discographical information was confirmed by consulting the website of Wolf Records, http://www.wolfrec.com/index.php?g=cd_shop&h=Taylor.

I interviewed Larry Taylor at his home in Chicago on February 2, 2018. Unless otherwise specified, all quotes are from that interview. Additional biographical detail is from his autobiography, *Stepson of the Blues*.

I interviewed Tim Taylor at his home in Chicago on February 1, 2018. All quotes here, unless otherwise specified, are from that interview.

1. Eddie Taylor's childhood reminiscences are from Rowe, *Chicago Blues*, 155, 156, 157.

2. Guitarist/bassist Floyd Jones, born in Marianna, Arkansas in 1917, moved to Chicago in the mid-1940s and recorded for Marvel, Vee-Jay, and Chess, among other labels; he was known for his introspective, brooding lyrics and vocals on such now-classic sides as "Stockyard Blues," "School Days On My Mind," and "Dark Road." The rock group Canned Heat scored a hit in 1968 with his song "On the Road Again," which he had recorded for JOB in 1953. In later years, he appeared with other veterans such as Eddie Taylor, Big Walter Horton, Sunnyland Slim, and Honeyboy Edwards on aficionados' labels like Testament, Magnolia, and Earwig; he died in 1989.

3. In 2018 she recorded a new track, "Riverboat," which appeared on the Delmark CD *Tribute* (a compilation of tributes to earlier Delmark artists, released in celebration of the label's 65th anniversary). As of Spring, 2019, she was back in the Delmark studio, finally working on her long-awaited follow-up to *Bad Girl*.

4. As of February, 2018.

5. LaSalle, "Prodigal Son."

6. Larry Taylor's first appearance on an official release was on the 1987 compilation, *Chicago's Best West- and Southside Blues Singers* (Wolf); he sang lead vocals on three songs. Those same three songs appeared on a subsequent Wolf anthology, which also included

his brother Eddie Taylor Jr.'s recorded debut. Over the next sixteen years, Larry appeared as a drummer and/or backup vocalist on thirteen more albums, including four featuring his brother Eddie Taylor Jr. and one featuring both Eddie Taylor Sr. and Vera Taylor, as well as Vera Taylor's sole solo release (*You Better Be Careful*, Wolf, 2000). His two releases under his own name, as of February, 2018, are *They Were in This House* (AV, 2004, reissued on Wolf in 2011 with a slightly altered set list) and *The New Chicago Sounds of Larry Taylor and the Soul Blues Healers: Real Music for All People* (AV, 2017). I thank Bonni McKeown for discographical information.

7. Robert Johnson, for instance, never had an actual hit (his biggest record, "Terraplane Blues," was a moderate regional success, selling an estimated 5,000 copies), nor did Son House, Tommy Johnson, Skip James, Big Bill Broonzy, J.B. Hutto, pre- '60s "crossover" James Cotton, Eddy Clearwater, or Magic Sam, to name just a few others. Before they were discovered by the white audience, Otis Rush and Buddy Guy had a total of one chart appearance each (1956's "I Can't Quit You Baby" and 1962's "Stone Crazy," respectively).

8. Guitarist "Left-Hand" Frank Craig was active on the West Side from the mid-1950s until the late 1970s. He appeared on Alligator's 1978 anthology, *Living Chicago Blues, Vol. 1* and posthumously on *Live at the Knickerbocker Café* (New Rose, 1994).

9. Brewer Phillips, best known as Hound Dog Taylor's second guitarist from the late 1960s until Taylor's death in 1975, worked in the Memphis area with the likes of Roosevelt Sykes and R&B saxophonist/bandleader Bill Harvey before moving to Chicago in the late 1950s. Aside from his work with Hound Dog Taylor [no relation to the Taylor family profiled here), he also appeared under his own name on several labels, including Delmark, JSP, Wolf, and Black Rose.

10. Harpist Little Arthur Duncan was a longtime West Side mainstay. He recorded albums with the labels Random Chance and Delmark, and he also owned several West Side clubs over the years. He died in 2008.

11. James Scott is remembered in Chicago as a sideman who worked the local circuit until his death in the early 1980s. But he's known by record label historians as coleader, with vocalist L. B. Lawson, of the Blues Rockers, who recorded at Sam Phillips's Memphis Recording Service (the precursor to Sun) in the early 1950s. The sides were unreleased at the time, but they have since appeared on anthologies.

12. Pianist John "Big Moose" Walker performed and recorded prolifically as a sideman from the 1940s through at least the late '80s, working alongside such legends as Elmore James, Earl Hooker, Otis Rush, Son Seals, and Jimmy Dawkins (to name just a few). He recorded a handful of singles and albums under his own name, but he was primarily a "musician's musician," highly respected and sought after by the cream of the blues world, when he was in his prime. In the early '90s he suffered several strokes, and he died in 1999.

13. Guitarist Otis "Big Smokey" Smothers was a Chicago-based journeyman whose musical associates through the years included Muddy Waters, Howlin' Wolf, Bo Diddley, Freddie King, and Big Walter Horton. His 1962 album for King, *Smokey Smothers Sings the Backporch Blues*, is treasured by collectors. He also recorded albums on International Polydor in 1966 and Red Beans in 1986.

14. Guitarist Albert Abraham "Little Smokey" Smothers (who usually went by his middle name), like his brother Otis, appeared at various times alongside the cream of the postwar blues generation, including Magic Sam, Otis Rush, Buddy Guy, James Cotton, and Howlin' Wolf. He was a mentor to Paul Butterfield (and a founding member of the Butterfield Blues Band) and Elvin Bishop. He recorded albums for Black Magic, Crosscut, and Alligator.

15. Guitarist Hip Linkchain, born Willie Richard in Jackson, Mississippi, in 1936, was active in Chicago from the 1950s onward (his band, the Chicago Twisters, backed up Tyrone Davis during Davis's scuffling days in the late 1950s). He was highly respected as a solid, no-frills fretboard stylist; his discography includes a handful of singles on obscure local labels, along with later LPs on P-Vine, Storyville, Evidence, and Teardrop.

16. Willie James Lyons was an active West Side–based guitarist from the 1950s until his death in 1980. His recorded legacy is sparse, but he is fondly remembered, both for his own performances and his work in the bands of such leading lights as Luther Allison, Jimmy Dawkins, and Bobby Rush (when the future funk-folklorist was working in Chicago as a straight-ahead bluesman).

17. On September 26, 1937, Bessie Smith died at the G. T. Thomas Afro-American Hospital in Clarksdale following an automobile accident on Highway 61, just outside of town. In 1944, the building was reopened as the Riverside Hotel; through the years, its guests included many well-known blues, R&B, and gospel musicians. Today, it is an internationally renowned tourist attraction.

18. Carey Bell, born in Macon, Mississippi, in 1936, moved to Chicago in 1956 with his godfather, pianist Lovie Lee. He became active on the local circuit (as both a harmonica player and a bassist), but it wasn't until his 1969 album for Delmark, *Carey Bell's Blues Harp*, that he began to cultivate an international reputation as a harmonica master. His style, with its sharply punctuated tongue stops and patented "whooping" vocal effects, has been highly influential. A member of the same Harrington clan as Eddy Clearwater, he also sired a musical family that includes guitarist Lurrie (profiled in my earlier book, *Chicago Blues*), harpist Steve, bassist Tyson, and drummer James. They are featured on the 2018 Delmark CD *Lurrie Bell & the Bell Dynasty: Tribute to Carey Bell*. Carey Bell passed away in 2007.

19. John Wrencher was a harmonica player known mostly for his many years busking in Chicago's Maxwell Street Market. He appeared on albums on the Testament, Big Bear, and Barrelhouse labels.

20. Harpist/drummer "Mad Dog" Lester Davenport was a respected Chicago veteran who accompanied Bo Diddley on some of Bo's early Chess sides but didn't get the chance to record under his own name until 1992, when he cut *When the Blues Hit You* for Earwig. In 2002, he recorded *I Smell a Rat* on Delmark; he died five years later.

21. Guitarist Ben Murphy, known as Big Bad Ben, was a West Side mainstay for years, even though few people from outside the neighborhood knew of him. His son, guitarist David Lindsey, enjoyed a modestly successful local career before his death in the mid-1990s.

22. This was in 2018.

John Primer

I interviewed John Primer by phone on November 4, 2009, for a profile that appeared as "John Primer: I Can Tell the World—I Was Born with It" in *Living Blues*. This section is adapted from that article. I also thank Lisa Becker Primer for assisting me with further details and clarifications.

1. His manager, Lisa Becker, explains how he came to be called "John": "John's real name is Alfonzo Primer. His father's name was John. When his father died, Alfonzo was about 4 years old. . . . Whenever people saw John's son, Alfonzo, they would say 'Hi, Johnny's Boy.' [This became] the nickname 'Johnny-Boy,' so everyone down south now calls him that. Up north it just got shortened to John. Only his mother called him Al or Alfonzo. He was named after his grandfather Alfonzo (his mother's dad's name)." Email to the author, July 26, 2017.

2. Stiles, "Interview with John Primer."

3. Ulry, "John Primer."

4. Actually, Randy's Record *Shop*. This confusion comes up in quite a few accounts, probably because another record outlet, Ernie's Record Mart, was also a well-known sponsor on WLAC.

5. Ulry, "John Primer," 26.

6. Stiles, "Interview with John Primer."

7. Limnios, "John Primer."

8. Stiles, "Interview with John Primer."

9. Examples of what John Primer sounded like warming up the stage for Magic Slim can be found on *Easy Baby*, recorded live at Lincoln, Nebraska's Zoo Baer sometime in the '80s and released on Wolf in 1999; or *You Can Make It if You Try!*—also on Wolf—recorded in Europe the following decade and released in 2014. Both are billed as by "John Primer & the Teardrops."

10. Owens, "AllMusic Review."

11. John Primer's official discography, which includes appearances on anthologies and others' projects, credits him with upwards of sixty-eight albums and CDs. "John Primer: 68 Albums, 2 Grammy Nominations." *John Primer* (website), 2017, accessed 7/26/2017, https://www.johnprimerblues.com/ music.

12. Deitra Farr, interview with the author, January 15, 2005.

Shemekia Copeland

I interviewed Shemekia Copeland at her home in Beverly, Illinois, on December 17, 2015. Unless otherwise specified, all quotes are from that interview. I thank John Hahn for answering numerous follow-up queries and facilitating further communication with Shemekia. I also thank Marc Lipkkin and Bruce Iglauer of Alligator Records for assisting me with chronological and discographical details and clarifications.

1. Dahl, "Shemekia Copeland: *Turn the Heat Up*."

2. Personal conversation with the author: Hartford, Connecticut, ca June 17, 1994.

3. Reich, "Shemekia Copeland's New Life."

4. Ibid.

5. Ibid.

6. Ibid.

7. Ibid.

8. Earlier interview with the author, June 18, 2005.

9. *Bluzapalooza 2008* was a twelve-day tour that featured Shemekia, along with Michael Burks, Deanna Bogart, Zac Harmon, and others performing for U.S. troops in Iraq and Kuwait.

10. "I hope when I'm gone on, the blues will still be alive with Shemekia Copeland," she told me. As my editors at *Down Beat* had instructed, I then asked her whether she thought Shemekia might someday be the next Queen of the Blues. Koko answered (sweetly but firmly): "When I'm gone."

11. Confirmed via email by Alligator president Bruce Iglauer and publicist Marc Lipkin, October, 2017.

12. Reich, "Shemekia Copeland's New Life."

13. Ibid.

14. On February 21, 2012, as if to complete the circle she had begun at that mess hall in Kuwait on election night in 2008, she performed John Hahn's "Beat Up Old Guitar" at the White House for an audience that included Barack and Michelle Obama, for the PBS special "Red, White and Blues," part of that network's *In Performance at the White House* series, http://www.rollingstone.com/music/pictures/in-performance-at-the-white-house-red-white-and-blues-20120222/b-b-king-0510527.

15. In 2018, Shemekia released *America's Child* on Alligator. It's her boldest foray yet into social commentary and, with guests like John Prine, Rhiannon Giddens, Steve Cropper, and Emmylou Harris, easily her most star-studded. Among the highlights are the self-explanatory "Ain't Got Time for Hate" (which promptly ascended to the Top 20 on *Americana Radio*, the online survey of radio charts specializing in "Americana" roots music [chart@americanamusic.org]); the melting-pot manifesto, "Americans"; "I'm Not Like Everybody Else," a libertarian-tinged declaration of independence; "One I Love," in which a woman in an (unspecified) unconventional relationship goes toe-to-toe with the haters; and, as if to remind some of those "white faces" in her audience where her music comes from and what it really means, "In The Blood of the Blues," a celebratory but unabashedly militant proclamation of the music's living Africanist heritage.

Sugar Blue

I interviewed Sugar Blue in Forest Park, Illinois, on August 12, 2016. Unless otherwise specified, all quotes are from that interview. Discographical information was drawn from the Alligator Records website (https://www.alligator.com/store/index.cfm/CID/-1/ArtistID/28/Sugar-Blue/), Sugar Blue's website (http://www.sugar-blue.com/12music.htm), and Allmusic.com (https://www.allmusic.com/artist/sugar-blue-mn0000482856/discography).

Details about Sugar Blue's sessions for Victoria Spivey's Spivey label were gleaned from Wirz, "Spivey Records Discography."

1. Peterson, *A Century of Musicals in Black and White.*

2. Radenhausen, "Harmonicist Sugar Blue Reminisces."

3. The precise chronology of Sugar Blue's '70s-era activities is somewhat unclear. His bio on his website says he recorded with Victoria Spivey in 1976 (the year she passed away); most discographies, however, cite 1970 as the release date for *Spivey's Blues Parade.* On the other hand, Blue recorded "Catfish" with Bob Dylan, a song originally slated for Dylan's 1976 *Desire* LP, in 1975—and *Desire* was ostensibly the album that Spivey herself had identified as Dylan's "next" one when she introduced him to Blue. By the same token, it's difficult to discern whether his '70s-era sessions with Brownie McGhee and Roosevelt Sykes occurred after, or possibly just before, he met Spivey.

4. Alex "Easy Baby" Randle was a harp blower who was active in Chicago for years, but his first released recording was on Barrelhouse in 1977; he recorded another CD on Wolf in 2002, and he appears on a Chicago blues harp anthology on the Random Chance label. Despite his meager recorded legacy, he was held in high esteem for the sparse eloquence of his harmonica style and taut, high-pitched singing voice.

5. Cott, "Mick Jagger."

6. Wilcock: "Featured Interview—Sugar Blue."

7. Or possibly 1998. The Centre's online mission statement reads: "Since 1997, we have been committed to providing treatment of the highest quality that is affordable to all." However, on another page of the same website, Clapton himself writes that "Crossroads opened its doors to the world in 1998" (https://crossroadsantigua.org/a-letter-from-eric-clapton/ N.D., accessed August 17, 2017).

8. "Sugar Blues's Wedding," *Sugar Blue,* 2012. Accessed August 17, 2017, http://sugar-blue.com/wp/?page_id=167.

9. Dylan Roof is the young white supremacist who murdered nine African American parishioners in the Emanuel African American Episcopal Church in Charleston, South Carolina, on June 17, 2017. He had been attending a Bible study meeting at the church when he pulled out a gun from his fanny pack and began his killing spree.

Nellie "Tiger" Travis

I interviewed Nellie Travis in Chicago on January 4, 2017. I followed that up with several brief telephone interviews. Unless specified otherwise, all quotes here are from those conversations. Discographical information is from the website *Southern Soul Rhythm & Blues* (http://www.soulbluesmusic.com/nellietigertravis.htm).

1. Mound Bayou was founded as an independent black community in 1887 by a former slave named Isaiah Montgomery (its population is still over 98 percent African American). It was once known as "the Jewel of the Delta" for its "rich history of black self-enterprise, economic development and empowerment." James, "The Jewel of the Delta."

2. Thompson, "Featured Interview—Nellie 'Tiger' Travis."

3. Historical details about Ed Townsend and his work in Mound Bayou are from Martin, "Natural Resources."

4. Thompson "Featured Interview—Nellie 'Tiger' Travis."

5. Interview with Ray and Leola Grey, May 10, 2002.

6. Thompson, "Featured Interview—Nellie 'Tiger' Travis."

7. Ibid.

8. Related to me by Koko Taylor's daughter, Joyce "Cookie" Threatt.

9. Porter, "Nellie Travis, the Tiger Queen."

10. Ibid.

11. The first part of this quote originally appeared in "Introducing . . . Nellie Tiger Travis." The second part is from Nellie Travis's interview with the author, January 4, 2017.

12. By Aretha Franklin's own account, Spann was the one who originally gave her the title Queen of Soul when he anointed her with a "beautiful bejeweled crown" during a show at Chicago's Regal Theater. Franklin and Ritz, *Aretha: From These Roots*, 111.

13. Mississippi Delta Blues Association, "Denise LaSalle to Be Crowned."

14. Thompson, "Featured Interview—Nellie 'Tiger' Travis."

15. Farr, "Artist to Artist: Nellie 'Tiger' Travis."

Floyd Taylor

I interviewed Floyd Taylor in Chicago on March 9, 2010. I conducted a follow-up interview with him by phone on April 1, 2010, and I spoke to him again in March of 2011 during the week of his March 4 appearance at the Star Plaza Theatre in Merrillville, Indiana, as part of the annual "The Blues Is Alright" tour. Unless otherwise specified, all quotes from Floyd Taylor are from these conversations. Biographical information on Johnnie Taylor is drawn from Guralnick, *Dream Boogie*, and Bowman, *Soulsville U.S.A.* Johnnie Taylor discographical information is from Whitburn, *Top R&B Singles, 1942–1999*.

1. Floyd was reluctant to give me his precise date of birth, but in an article published in 2002, Heikki Suosalo quoted him as saying he was born on January 25, 1954 (Suosalo, "Floyd Taylor").

2. Johnnie Taylor usually gave his year of birth as 1938. His gravestone inscription reads "Johnnie H. Taylor, May 1937–May 2000." However, his Social Security file documents that he was born Johnnie Harrison Taylor, May 3, 1934 (Eagle and LeBlanc, *Blues*; Rogers, "Johnnie Harrison Taylor [1934–2000]").

3. Sam would have still been spelling his name "Cook" in those days; he changed it legally to "Cooke" in 1957, after he crossed over into secular music.

4. The Highway QCs actually had six members when Cooke sang with them. The term *quartet* generally referred to the four-part harmony the groups usually specialized in, rather than the number of singers in the groups.

5. Guralnick, *Dream Boogie*, 340.

6. Suosalo, "Floyd Taylor."

7. Ibid.

8. Ibid. There's a deeper "father/son" irony to this story: Johnnie Taylor himself had originally signed with Malaco in 1984 after Malaco's Tommy Couch Sr. heard him singing at Z. Z. Hill's funeral.

9. "Floyd Taylor," *Malaco Music Group*.

10. Stephenson, Liner notes to *Legacy*.

11. Suosalo, "Floyd Taylor."

Deitra Farr

I interviewed Deitra Farr at her home in Chicago on January 15, 2005, for a profile that appeared as "Deitra Farr: Don't Stay In the Root—Build From the Root!" This chapter is adapted from that article; unless otherwise specified, all quotes are from our interview.

1. Pianist Erwin Helfer, now in his eighties, is probably the only living Chicagoan still dedicated to carrying on the city's rich boogie-woogie and stride piano tradition. Mentored by some of Chicago's most storied pianists, he has been a fixture on the city's club scene for decades, and his recorded catalog—on Flying Fish, The Sirens, Steeplechase, and other labels—is an all-too-necessary reminder that Chicago's blues tradition consists of much more than wailing harmonicas and screaming slide guitars.

2. Estelle "Mama" Yancey was the wife of boogie-woogie pianist Jimmy Yancey. She sometimes sang alongside him; after his death in 1951, she continued on as a solo artist, eventually becoming one of the most beloved blues figures in Chicago. She died in 1986.

3. Thomas A. Dorsey, known as "the father of gospel music," was the composer of "Precious Lord, Take My Hand" and other gospel standards. He had earlier been known as the blues singer Georgia Tom, famous for his long-running collaboration with guitarist Tampa Red. Although for a while in the 1930s he balanced his secular and sacred musical interests, he eventually gave up blues for the church.

4. Robert Stroger is one of Chicago's most highly esteemed bass players. Born in Hayti, Missouri in 1939, he moved to the city in 1955. By the end of the decade, he'd joined the band of guitarist Eddie King, with whom he played, off and on, for about fifteen years. Others he's worked with include Otis Rush, Bo Diddley, Sunnyland Slim, Willie "Big Eyes" Smith, Carey Bell, Eddy Clearwater, and Pinetop Perkins. He continues to be a first-call bassist in Chicago.

5. Valerie Wellington was a classically trained vocalist and pianist who began singing blues professionally in the early 1980s. She also worked in theater, portraying "classic" women blues singers such as Bessie Smith and Ma Rainey. She released *Million Dollar Secret* on the Rooster Blues label in 1984); she appeared on *The New Bluebloods*, an Alligator Records anthology in 1987, and she recorded the album *Life In the Big City* for the Japanese GBW label in 1991. She died two years later at the age of 33.

6. Vocalist Big Time Sarah, born Sarah Streeter in Coldwater, Mississippi, in 1953, was mentored by piano great Sunnyland Slim. She recorded a single on his Airways label, then went on to become a fixture in Chicago's blues clubs and, eventually, out of town and overseas. She recorded for Delmark and B.L.U.E.S. R&B; she also appeared on several compilations. Sarah died in 2015.

Ronnie Baker Brooks

I interviewed Ronnie Baker Brooks at his home in Dolton, Illinois, on September 9, 2016, for a profile in *Living Blues 248* (April 2017), 20–25, titled "Ronnie Baker Brooks: What

Comes From the Heart, Reaches the Heart." This chapter is adapted from that article. Unless otherwise specified, all quotes are from our interview.

1. "History of the Centennial Vision"; "History / Navy Pier."

2. "Baker" is the actual family name. Ronnie's father, born Lee Baker Jr. in Dubuisson, Louisiana, in 1933, changed his stage name from "Guitar Jr." to "Lonnie Brooks" in the '60s after he'd moved to Chicago.

3. Related to me by Ms. Cummings Yeates in a discussion on December 19, 2016. On March 2, 2017, she emailed me a transcript of Ronnie's precise quotations.

Part IV: Heirs Apparent

1. An earlier version of the section on Melody Angel appeared in "The *Reader*'s Guide to the Chicago Blues Festival."

Postscript

The phrase "Our Spirit Makes Us the Blues" is from the poem "Funk Lore" by Amiri Baraka in Baraka, *S O S: Poems 1961–2013*.

Works Cited

45Cat—Discographies, Discussions, Discoveries. http://www.45cat.com.

706 Union Avenue Sessions: Memphis Recording Service—Sun Records—Flip Records—Phillips International—More. http://www.706unionavenue.nl/, 2019.

"A Letter from Eric Clapton." Crossroads Centre Antigua. https://crossroadsantigua .org/a-letter-from-eric-clapton/, N.D.

"All Merchandise for Sugar Blue." *Alligator Records.* https://www.alligator.com/store/index .cfm/CID/-1 /ArtistID/28 /Sugar-Blue/, 2019.

Ankeny, Jason. "Sugar Blue." *Allmusic.com.* https://www.allmusic.com/artist/sugar-blue -mn0000482856/discography.

Baraka, Amiri. "Funk Lore." In Amiri Baraka, *S.O.S.: Poems 1961–2013.* New York: Grove Press, 2014.

Barlow, William. *Looking Up at Down: The Emergence of Blues Culture.* Philadelphia: Temple University Press, 1989.

Bolden, Tony. *Afro-Blue: Improvisations in African American Poetry and Culture.* Urbana: University of Illinois Press, 2003.

Bonner, Brett. "Eddie Shaw." *Living Blues* 124 (November–December 1995), 26–39.

Bowman, Rob. *Soulsville U.S.A: The Story of Stax Records.* New York: Schirmer, 1997.

Christie, Roy. "Holly Is Reincarnation of Billie, Ella, et al." *The Star*, December 5, 1978. qtd. in *KJAZZ Radio, UK*: "Weekly Ezine for 16th August 2015." http://www.kjazzradiouk .com /2015/08/11 /weekly-ezine-for-16th-aug-2015/.

Cianci, Bob. "Eddy 'the Chief' Clearwater: They Say Good Things Come to Those Who Wait." *Vintage Guitar Magazine.* http://www.vintageguitar.com/2883/eddy-the-chief -clearwater/, 2002.

L

Connor, Anthony, and Robert Neff. *Blues*. Boston: David R Godine, 1975.

Cott, Jonathan. "Mick Jagger: The Rolling Stone Interview." *Rolling Stone*, June 29, 1978. http://www.rollingstone.com/music/features/the-rolling-stone-interview-mick-jagger-1978-19780629.

Dahl, Bill. "Eddy Clearwater." *billdahl.com*, 2014. http://billdahl.com/pages/eddy_clearwater.html.

———. "Shemekia Copeland: *Turn the Heat Up*" (CD review). *Living Blues* 140 (July/August 1998), 65.

Dahl, Bill, and Jim O'Neal. "Jimmy Johnson." *Living Blues* 47 (Summer 1980), 15–22.

"Dat Dere." Original melody by Bobby Timmons, lyrics by Oscar Brown Jr. © Nov. 15, 1960. Upam Music Co., a division of Gopam Enterprises, Inc.

Davis, Angela Y. *Blues Legacies and Black Feminism*. New York: Pantheon, 1998.

Eagle, Bob, and Eric S. LeBlanc. *Blues: A Regional Experience*. Westport, Conn.: Praeger, 2015.

"Eddie Taylor—Discography." *45cat*, 2018. http:/www.45cat.com/artist/eddie-taylor/us.

"Eddie Taylor—78 RPM—Discography." *45worlds*. http://www.45worlds.com/78rpm/artist/eddie-taylor, 2019.

Edwards, Emily D. *Bars, Blues, and Booze: Stories from the Drink House*. Jackson: University Press of Mississippi, 2016.

Farr, Deitra. "Artist to Artist: Nellie 'Tiger' Travis." *Living Blues* 245 (October 2016), 7.

Finn, Julio. *The Bluesman: The Musical Heritage of Black Men and Women in the Americas*. London: Quartet, 1987.

Floyd, Samuel. *The Power of Black Music*. Cary, N.C.: Oxford University Press, 1996.

"Floyd Taylor." *Malaco Music Group: "The Last Soul Company."* https://www.malaco.com/artists/blues-r-b/floyd-taylor/, 2019.

Franklin, Aretha, and David Ritz. *Aretha: From These Roots*. New York: Villard, 1999.

Garon, Paul. *Blues and the Poetic Spirit*. San Francisco: City Lights, 2001.

Garon, Paul, and Beth Garon. *Woman with Guitar*. San Francisco: City Lights, 1992.

Gordon, Robert. *Can't Be Satisfied: The Life and Times of Muddy Waters*. Boston: Little, Brown, 2002.

———. *It Came from Memphis*. Boston: Faber and Faber, 1995.

Guralnick, Peter. *Dream Boogie: The Triumph of Sam Cooke*. New York: Back Bay, 2005.

———. *Lost Highway: Journeys and Arrivals of American Musicians*. New York, Harper and Row, 1979.

Hay, Fred J., ed. *Goin' Back to Sweet Memphis: Conversations with the Blues*. Athens: University of Georgia Press, 2001.

"History / Navy Pier." *100 Years of Navy Pier*. https://navypier.com/blog/history-navy-pier/.

"History of the Centennial Vision." *100 Years of Navy Pier*. https://navypier.com/history-centennial-vision/.

"Introducing . . . Nellie Tiger Travis." *Soul Express*, March 2005. http://www.soulexpress.net/nellietravis.htm.

"It's Cotton-Pickin' Fun at the Shack Up Inn." *HotelScoop*. https://www.hotel-scoop.com/its-cotton-pickin-fun-at-the-shack-up-inn, March 20, 2015.

James, Susan [aka "Suzasippi"]. "The Jewel of the Delta: Mound Bayou, Mississippi." *Preservation in Mississippi: It Ain't All Moonlight and Magnolias.* https://misspreservation .com/2011/07/12/the-jewel-of-the-delta-mound-bayou-mississippi/, July 12, 2011.

"J.B. Hutto." *All about Blues Music.* https://www.allaboutbluesmusic.com/j-b-hutto/.

"John Primer: 68 Albums, 2 Grammy Nominations." *John Primer.* https://www.john primerblues.com/ music, 2017.

Jones, LeRoi (Amiri Baraka). *Blues People: Negro Music in White America.* New York: Harper Perennial, 1999.

Keyes, Johnny. *Du-Wop.* Chicago: John M. Keyes, 1987.

Koda, Cub. "J.B. Hutto Artist Biography." *Allmusic.com.* https://www.allmusic.com/artist /jb-hutto-mn0000777780, 2019.

LaSalle, Denise. "America's Prodigal Son." © 1989, Denise LaSalle. The poem also appeared in Whiteis, David, *Southern Soul-Blues.* Urbana: University of Illinois Press, 2013.

"Lil' Ed and the Blues Imperials." *Alligator Records.* https://www.alligator.com/artists /Lil-Ed- and-The-Blues-Imperials/, 2019.

"Lil' Ed Williams." *Earwig Music.* https://www.earwigmusic. com /earwig-artists/lil-ed -williams, 2019.

Limnios, Michael. "John Primer: The Original Bluesman." *Blues.GR.* blues.gr/profiles /blogs/an-interview-with-bluesman-john-primer-a-powerful-force-in, 2012.

Lomax, Alan. *The Land Where the Blues Began.* New York: Delta Books, 1995.

Martin, J. M. "Natural Resources." *Oxford American.* http://www.oxfordamerican.org /magazine/item/944-natural-resources, August 15, 2016.

"Memo Blues." Andrew "Big Voice" Odom, Leric Music, BMI. *Feel So Good!* Evidence ECD-6027-2, 1992.

Mississippi Delta Blues Association. "Denise LaSalle to Be Crowned Undisputed Queen of the Blues Saturday, October 24, 2009." Press release, October 21, 2009.

Moon, D. Thomas. "Eddy Clearwater: It's a Hard Way to Make an Easy Living." *Living Blues* 127 (May/June 1996), 14–27.

Murray, Albert. *Stomping the Blues.* Chicago: McGraw-Hill, 1976.

Neal, Mark Anthony. *What the Music Said.* New York: Routledge, 1999.

"Nellie 'Tiger' Travis." *Soul Blues Music.* http://www.soulbluesmusic.com/nellietiger travis.htm.

Oliver, Paul. *Blues Fell This Morning.* London: Cassell and Company, 1960.

———. *The Story of the Blues.* London: The Cresset Press, 1969.

Otis, Johnny. *Upside Your Head!: Rhythm and Blues on Central Avenue.* Middletown, Conn.: Wesleyan University Press, 1993.

Owens, Thom. "AllMusic Review: John Primer, Poor Man Blues: Chicago Blues Sessions, Vol. 6." *AllMusic.com.* http://www.allmusic.com/album/poor-man-blues-chicago -blues-session-vol-6-mw0000274584, July 25, 2017.

PBS. *American Roots Music.* "Oral Histories: James Cotton." http://www.pbs.org /americanrootsmusic/pbs_arm_oralh_jamescotton.html, 2001.

Peterson, Bernard L. Jr. *A Century of Musicals in Black and White*. Westport, Conn.: Greenwood, 1993.

Porter, Aaron. "Nellie Travis, the Tiger Queen: Lookin' Good, Singin' Good." *Blues and Music News*. http://bg.buddyguy.com/nellie-travis-the-tiger-queen/, May 9, 2014.

Radenhausen, Jim. Harmonicist Sugar Blue Reminisces in Advance of Jim Thorpe Concert." *Pocono Record*. https://www.poconorecord.com/entertainmentlife/20150813 /harmonicist-sugar-blue-reminisces-in-advance-of-jim-thorpe-concert, August 13, 2015.

Reich, Howard. "Shemekia Copeland's New Life Includes a Baby and the Blues." *Chicago Tribune*, June 6, 2017. http://www.chicagotribune.com/entertainment/music/reich/ct -shemekia-copeland—ae.

Renshaw, Elizabeth, "2 Blues Band Members Die in Indiana Crash." *Chicago Tribune*, December 4, 1998. http://articles.chicagotribune.com/1988 12 04/news/8802210773 _1_chicago-blues-van-james-johnson.

Rogers, Bryan. "Johnnie Harrison Taylor (1934–2000)." *The Encyclopedia of Arkansas History and Culture*. http://www.encyclopediaofarkansas.net/encyclopedia/entry-detail .aspx?entryID.

Rolling Stone. "In Performance at the White House: Red, White, and Blues." http://www .rollingstone.com/music/pictures/in-performance-at-the-white-house-red-white -and-blues-20120222/b-b-king-0510527.

Romano, Will. *Big Boss Man: The Life and Music of Bluesman Jimmy Reed*. San Francisco: Backbeat, 2006.

Rowe, Mike. *Chicago Blues: The City and the Music*. New York: Da Capo, 1982.

Segrest, James, and Mark Hoffman. *Moanin' at Midnight: The Life and Times of Howlin' Wolf*. New York: Pantheon, 2004.

Seigal, Buddy. "A Little Muddy." *OC Weekly*. https://ocweekly.com/music/a-littlemuddy, August 12, 1999.

"Stan Shaw." *Gargoyle Bob*. http://gargoylebob.com/?page_id=124.

Stephenson, Wolf. Liner notes to *Floyd Taylor: Legacy* (Malaco MCD 7511, 2002).

Stiles, Ray. "Interview with . . . Eddy 'The Chief' Clearwater, Duluth, August 14, 1998, and by phone August 29, 1998." *Blues on Stage*. http://www.mnblues.com/review /clearwater-intv.html, 1998.

———. "Interview with John Primer." *Blues on Stage* 2000. http://www.mnblues.com /review/primer-intv4-00.html.

Sugar Blue Music. . . . . . . Got Sugar? http://www.sugar-blue.com/12music.htm, 2018.

Sumsuch, Will. "Rasputin Stash Founder Talks Reissue of Cult Classic Album." *WaxPoetics*. http://www.waxpoetics.com/blog/features/articles/rasputin-stash-founder-talks -reissue-cult-classic-album, February 9, 2016.

Suosalo, Heikkie. "Floyd Taylor." *Soul Express*, February 2002. www.soulexpress .net/floydtaylor.htm.

Taylor, Larry, *Stepson of the Blues: A Chicago Song of Survival*. Tapon Springs, W.Va.: Peaceful Patriot, 2010.

"The Ritz We Ain't." *Shack Up Inn*. https://www.shackupinn.com/ourstory.

Thompson, Mark. "Featured Interview—Nellie 'Tiger' Travis." *Blues Blast*. http://www
.bluesblastmagazine.com/featured-interview-nellie-tiger-travis/, August 14, 2017.

Turner, Benny, and Bill Dahl. *Survivor: The Benny Turner Story*. Bradenton, Fla.: Nola Blue,
2017.

Ulry, Lois. "John Primer." *Magic Blues* 2 (1991), 22–29.

Whitburn, Joel. *Billboard Hot R&B Songs, 1942–2010 (6th Edition)*, Menomonee Falls, Wisconsin: Record Research, Inc., 2010.

——. *Top R&B Singles, 1942–1999 (5th Edition)*. Menomonee Falls, Wisconsin: Record
Research, Inc., 1999.

Whiteis, David. "Big Bill Morganfield: It's about Touching Lives." *Living Blues* 238 (August
2015), 10–17.

——. *Chicago Blues: Portraits and Stories*. Urbana: University of Illinois Press, 2006.

——. "Deitra Farr: Don't Stay In the Root . . . Build From the Root!" *Living Blues* 177
(March/April 2005), 18–23.

——. "Eddy Clearwater: A Little Bit of Blues, a Little Bit of Roll 'n' Roll." *Living Blues* 238
(August 2015), 10–17.

——. "James Cotton: I'm All Right with the Blues." *Living Blues* 224 (April 2013).

——. "John Primer: I Can Tell the World—I Was Born with It." *Living Blues* 205 (February 2010), 10–19.

——. "Kenny Smith: You Gotta Embrace It." *Living Blues* 213 (June 2011), 18–21.

——. Liner notes to *Demetria Taylor: Bad Girl* (Delmark DE-814, 2011).

——. Liner notes to *The Eddie Taylor Blues Band: My Heart Is Bleeding,* Evidence ECD 26054-
2, 1994.

——. "Ronnie Baker Brooks: What Comes From the Heart, Reaches the Heart." *Living
Blues* 248 (April 2017), 20–25.

——. *Southern Soul-Blues*. Urbana: University of Illinois Press, 2013.

——. "The *Reader*'s Guide to the Chicago Blues Festival." Chicago *Reader*, June 7, 2016.

Wilcock, Don. "Featured Interview—Sugar Blue." *Blues Blast*. http://www.bluesblast
magazine.com/featured-interview-sugar-blue/, June 2, 2016.

Willis, Robert L. (Chick). "Classic Soul: A Real Blues Artist and Inventor." *Soul Patrol*.
http://www.soul-patrol.com/soul/chickwillis.htm.

Wirz, Stephan. "Jimmy Reed Discography." *American Music*. https://www.wirz.de/music
/reedjfrm.htm, 2018.

——. "Magic Sam Discography." *American Music*. https://www.wirz.de/music/magisfrm
.htm, 2017.

——. "Spivey Records Discography." *American Music*. https://www.wirz.de /music
/spiveyfrm.htm, 2018.

Wolf Records. http://www.wolfrec.com/index.php?g=cd_shop&h=Taylorhttp://www.pbs
.org/americanrootsmusic/.

Index

DAVID WHITEIS is a journalist, writer, and educator living in Chicago. He is a past winner of the Blues Foundation's Keeping the Blues Alive Award for Achievement in Journalism. He is the author of *Southern Soul-Blues* and *Chicago Blues: Portraits and Stories*.

PETER M. HURLEY is a photographer, muralist, graphic designer, and songwriter, and an active contributing photographer to *Living Blues* magazine.

MUSIC IN AMERICAN LIFE

"Happy in the Service of the Lord": Afro-American Gospel Quartets
    in Memphis   *Kip Lornell*
Paul Hindemith in the United States   *Luther Noss*
"My Song Is My Weapon": People's Songs, American Communism,
    and the Politics of Culture, 1930–50   *Robbie Lieberman*
Chosen Voices: The Story of the American Cantorate   *Mark Slobin*
Theodore Thomas: America's Conductor and Builder of Orchestras,
    1835–1905   *Ezra Schabas*
"The Whorehouse Bells Were Ringing" and Other Songs Cowboys Sing
    Collected and Edited by Guy Logsdon
Crazeology: The Autobiography of a Chicago Jazzman
    Bud Freeman, as Told to Robert Wolf
Discoursing Sweet Music: Brass Bands and Community Life
    in Turn-of-the-Century Pennsylvania   *Kenneth Kreitner*
Mormonism and Music: A History   *Michael Hicks*
Voices of the Jazz Age: Profiles of Eight Vintage Jazzmen   *Chip Deffaa*
Pickin' on Peachtree: A History of Country Music in Atlanta, Georgia   *Wayne W. Daniel*
Bitter Music: Collected Journals, Essays, Introductions, and Librettos
    Harry Partch; edited by Thomas McGeary
Ethnic Music on Records: A Discography of Ethnic Recordings Produced
    in the United States, 1893 to 1942   *Richard K. Spottswood*
Downhome Blues Lyrics: An Anthology from the Post–World War II Era   *Jeff Todd Titon*
Ellington: The Early Years   *Mark Tucker*
Chicago Soul   *Robert Pruter*
That Half-Barbaric Twang: The Banjo in American Popular Culture   *Karen Linn*
Hot Man: The Life of Art Hodes   *Art Hodes and Chadwick Hansen*
The Erotic Muse: American Bawdy Songs (2d ed.)   *Ed Cray*
Barrio Rhythm: Mexican American Music in Los Angeles   *Steven Loza*
The Creation of Jazz: Music, Race, and Culture in Urban America   *Burton W. Peretti*
Charles Martin Loeffler: A Life Apart in Music   *Ellen Knight*
Club Date Musicians: Playing the New York Party Circuit   *Bruce A. MacLeod*
Opera on the Road: Traveling Opera Troupes in the United States,
    1825–60   *Katherine K. Preston*
The Stonemans: An Appalachian Family and the Music
    That Shaped Their Lives   *Ivan M. Tribe*
Transforming Tradition: Folk Music Revivals Examined   *Edited by Neil V. Rosenberg*
The Crooked Stovepipe: Athapaskan Fiddle Music and Square Dancing
    in Northeast Alaska and Northwest Canada   *Craig Mishler*
Traveling the High Way Home: Ralph Stanley and the World
    of Traditional Bluegrass Music   *John Wright*
Carl Ruggles: Composer, Painter, and Storyteller   *Marilyn Ziffrin*
Never without a Song: The Years and Songs of Jennie Devlin,
    1865–1952   *Katharine D. Newman*
The Hank Snow Story   *Hank Snow, with Jack Ownbey and Bob Burris*
Milton Brown and the Founding of Western Swing   *Cary Ginell,
    with special assistance from Roy Lee Brown*

The University of Illinois Press
is a founding member of the
Association of University Presses.

———————————————————————

Composed in 10.25/13 Marat Pro
with Trade Gothic LT Std display
by Kirsten Dennison
at the University of Illinois Press
Cover designed by Dustin J. Hubbart
Cover illustration: Photo of Melody Angel by Peter M. Hurley.
Chicago skyline Shutterstock/Ray_of_Light.
Manufactured by Sheridan Books, Inc.

University of Illinois Press
1325 South Oak Street
Champaign, IL 61820-6903
www.press.uillinois.edu